D1521364

PERCEPTUAL KNOWLEDGE

PHILOSOPHICAL STUDIES SERIES IN PHILOSOPHY

VOLUME 22

GEORGES DICKER

State University of New York College at Brockport

PERCEPTUAL KNOWLEDGE

An Analytical and Historical Study

D. REIDEL PUBLISHING COMPANY

DORDRECHT : HOLLAND / BOSTON : U.S.A.

LONDON : ENGLAND

Library of Congress Cataloging in Publication Data

Dicker, Georges, 1942–
    Perceptual knowledge.

    (Philosophical studies series in philosophy ; v. 22)
    Bibliography: p.
       1.   Perception (Philosophy)   2.   Knowledge, Theory of
I.   Title.
B828.45.D52   121'.3   80–20288
ISBN 90–277–1130–5

Published by D. Reidel Publishing Company,
P.O. Box 17, 3300 AA Dordrecht, Holland.

Sold and distributed in the U.S.A. and Canada
by Kluwer Boston Inc.,
190 Old Derby Street, Hingham, MA 02043, U.S.A.

In all other countries, sold and distributed
by Kluwer Academic Publishers Group,
P.O. Box 322, 3300 AH Dordrecht, Holland.

D. Reidel Publishing Company is a member of the Kluwer Group.

For Keith Christopher Dicker

TABLE OF CONTENTS

PREFACE

This book grew out of the lectures that I prepared for my students in epistemology at SUNY College at Brockport beginning in 1974. The conception of the problem of perception and the interpretation of the sense-datum theory and its supporting arguments that are developed in Chapters One through Four originated in these lectures. The rest of the manuscript was first written during the 1975–1976 academic year, while I held an NEH Fellowship in Residence for College Teachers at Brown University, and during the ensuing summer, under a SUNY Faculty Research Fellowship. I wish to express my sincere gratitude to the National Endowment for the Humanities and to the Research Foundation of the State University of New York for their support of my research.

I am grateful to many former students, colleagues, and friends for their stimulating, constructive comments and criticisms. Among the former students whose reactions and objections were most helpful are Richard Motroni, Donald Callen, Hilary Porter, and Glenn Shaikun. Among my colleagues at Brockport, I wish to thank Kevin Donaghy and Jack Glickman for their comments and encouragement. I am indebted to Eli Hirsch for reading and commenting most helpfully on the entire manuscript, to Peter M. Brown for a useful correspondence concerning key arguments in Chapters Five and Seven, to Keith Lehrer for a criticism of one of my arguments that led me to make some important revisions, and to Roderick M. Chisholm for his comments and encouragement during the year that I spent at Brown. Needless to say, I alone am responsible for whatever shortcomings this book contains.

An embryonic version of Chapter Seven was presented under the title, 'Phenomenalism and the Causal Theory of Perception', at the Eastern Division meeting of the American Philosophical Association in December, 1973. The commentator, Marshall Swain, made some astute criticisms, which I have tried to take into account. Chapter One and parts of the Introduction have appeared in article form in 'Is There A Problem About Perception and Knowledge?', *American Philosophical Quarterly* **15** (1978). I wish to thank the Editor of *APQ* for permission to reprint this material.

January 1980   GEORGES DICKER

ix

INTRODUCTION

This book is a systematic study of the problem of perception and knowledge. I intend to analyze the problem, to expound and criticize the most important attempts that have been made to solve it, and to propose an original solution to it. The problem of perception has fascinated philosophers for many centuries. Contemporary discussions of it grow out of a dialogue whose participants include virtually every major figure in the history of Western philosophy. Accordingly, in the course of analyzing the problem and evaluating possible solutions to it, many classical and contemporary works dealing with perception will be discussed. The choice and treatment of these works, however, is governed by an overall conception of the problem of perception, rather than by a desire to cover all the important figures or to expound any philosopher's views in their entirety. In this sense, this book attempts to combine the 'problem' and the 'historical' approaches to its subject. It is hoped that this method will make the book useful both to students who wish to acquire an understanding of perceptual epistemology rooted in a knowledge of its history, and to professional philosophers who feel the need for a re-examination of the issues that is sympathetic to classical treatments but informed by the important strides in the philosophy of perception that have been made within the last two or three decades.

The primary aim of the first four chapters is to present and analyze the problem of perception. There are two reasons for devoting a significant portion of the book to this task. The first is simply that before evaluating possible solutions to a problem, one should be clear as to the nature of the problem. The second is that the present state of the literature calls for a fresh examination of the question: Is there a philosophical problem about perception and knowledge?

Concerning this question, much of the current literature falls into one or the other of two camps. In one camp, which includes several recent works by American epistemologists, it is more or less taken for granted that there is a genuine problem concerning the relation between perception and knowledge. So the problem itself is presented rather summarily, and the bulk of the authors' efforts is devoted to expounding and defending a solution. For example, in both Harman's *Thought* and Pollock's *Knowledge and Justification*, the

1

problem of perception is introduced by appealing directly to the most radical
sceptical argument of all; namely, the suggestion that possibly all of our sense-
experiences are caused by some superscientist stimulating our brains by
means of electrodes.[1] No doubt, some persons who have already become
'corrupted' by the study of philosophy will immediately appreciate the force
of this Cartesian consideration. But from the point of view to be adopted in
the early chapters of this book — that of an uninitiated person who wishes to
understand why perception should be thought to pose a fundamental philosophical problem, or even of an anti-sceptical philosopher who concedes, but
remains unmoved by, the logical possibility of a deceiving superscientist —
what needs to be seen is whether any genuine puzzles concerning perception
and knowledge arise from less far-fetched considerations. Even R. M.
Chisholm's elegant way of presenting the problem of perception is, from this
point of view, rather unconvincing. Roughly put, Chisholm argues that if a
person S were asked to justify a perceptual claim such as 'I see a book on the
table', it would be reasonable for S to appeal to a more cautious claim such as
'I see what looks like a book on the table', and then to justify that claim by
appealing to a still more cautious one, and so on, until in the end S came to
a maximally cautious claim such as 'I seem to see what I take to be a book on
a table' or 'I am appeared to book-on-the-table-ly'.[2] The problem is then to
formulate the principles of justification or 'rules of evidence' in virtue of
which such 'self-justified' or 'directly evident' claims can justify the original
perceptual claim. However, the fact that it is always possible to make a series
of increasingly cautious claims like the one just indicated doesn't of itself
show that such a procedure is reasonable or appropriate for justifying perceptual claims; unless one is already convinced on *other* grounds that such claims
stand in need of (this kind of) justification. And beyond a bare reference to
the fallibility of the senses, Chisholm does not tell us what these grounds are.[3]

The somewhat cursory and, in a way, scholastic treatment of the *problem*
of perception that one finds in some recent works is particularly unfortunate
in light of the other main current approach to philosophy of perception,
namely, the Oxford 'Ordinary-Language' approach. Although ordinary-
language analysis is no longer as dominant a mode of philosophizing as it was
only a few years ago, the general position on the topic of perception epi-
tomized in J. L. Austin's *Sense and Sensibilia* continues to have considerable
influence and appeal. According to this position, the puzzles about perception and knowledge that have perplexed philosophers for centuries are largely
pseudo-problems generated by confusions and errors in the language that
has been used in philosophizing about perception. Therefore, the so-called

problem of perception does not call for the elaborate theories of perception (e.g. representationalism, phenomenalism) that have been proposed to solve it. Rather, it can be dissolved by careful attention to ordinary, non-philosophical ways of talking about perception.

The specific target of the ordinary-language philosophers was, of course, the sense-datum theory. Before these philosophers' onslaught against this theory, the majority of philosophers maintained that we never immediately perceive physical objects. Instead, we immediately perceive only certain special entities variously called 'sensations', 'ideas', 'sense-impressions', 'sensa', 'sense-data'. So long as this view was widely accepted, there seemed to be a genuine epistemological problem concerning perception: how can it yield knowledge of the physical world if physical things are never immediately perceived? The ordinary-language philosophers, however, argued persuasively that the traditional arguments for introducing sense-data were unsound ones turning on various linguistic confusions and factual errors. They professed themselves unable even to find any clear meaning in the thesis that sense-data rather than physical things are 'immediately perceived'. The epistemological difficulties generated by the sense-datum theory, they concluded, must be spurious. Once the sense-datum theory was laid to rest, the problem of perception was supposed to disappear.

If the position to be taken in this book is correct, then this general diagnosis of the problem of perception is fundamentally mistaken. The mistake is to suppose that the problem arises *from* or *after* the introduction of sense-data. If this were true, then to refute the arguments for introducing sense-data would indeed be to solve, or dissolve, the problem. But the truth of the matter, as I shall argue, is that the epistemological problems concerning perception arise quite indepently of the sense-datum theory. One problem arises when we consider directly Plato's question: is perception (a species of) knowledge? On the one hand, it is obvious that perception is indeed our basic way of acquiring knowledge of the world we live in. But on the other hand, when we try to formulate the conditions under which perception yields knowledge, we run into difficulty. For one of the conditions we are forced to introduce, as will be shown in Chapter One (where this problem is presented more fully), is that the perceiver knows that the conditions of observation are normal. But the only way the perceiver can know this is by other perceptions that themselves constitute knowledge only if he knows that they are occuring under normal conditions of observation, which he can know to be the case only by still other perceptions, etc. The sense-datum theory is an attempt to avoid this vicious regress, by calling attention to objects of a special kind, which can be perceptually known regardless of the conditions of observation. In other words, far from being what generates the problem, the sense-datum theory is an attempt to *solve* it, by calling attention to objects for which Plato's question can be answered affirmatively.

A somewhat different problem arises, as will be shown in Chapter Three, from elementary reflection on the causal facts of perception. We know that perception requires a very complex causal chain from the object perceived to the perceiver's brain. Thus, as Descartes pointed out in his *Meditations*, any given perceptual experience obtained by perceiving a physical object could be exactly duplicated though no physical object were stimulating the person's sense-receptors; simply by producing in some other manner one of the intermediate links in the causal chain which is sufficient to produce the kind of perceptual experience in question (e.g. by directly stimulating the optic nerves or the visual areas of the brain). It follows that a person cannot know, solely on the basis of a given perceptual experience, that he is really perceiving a physical object. Other perceptions − e.g. those that occurred shortly before and after the experience in question − must be brought in for corroboration. But the considerations just adumbrated apply to the corroborating perceptions no less than the original one. So a person cannot know, solely on the basis of the perceptual experience obtained in any of the corroborating perceptions, that he is really perceiving a physical object. Yet a corroborating perception must yield knowledge of some sort; otherwise it is a mere surd that cannot serve to corroborate anything. Thus a second vicious regress arises: a case of perception P can yield knowledge only if it is corroborated by another case P_1, but P_1 can corroborate P only if P_1 is itself corroborated by another case of perception P_2, but P_2 can corroborate P_1 only if P_2 is in turn corroborated by still another case of perception P_3, and so on *ad infinitum*. The purpose of the sense-datum theory is to avoid this regress, too, by calling attention to a kind of object that can be perceptually known solely on the basis of a present perceptual experience, and so independently of any corroboration from other cases of perception.

This interpretation of the sense-datum theory is borne out by analyzing the traditional arguments for introducing sense-data. These arguments are commonly viewed, roughly on the model of proofs for the existence of God, as straightforward attempts to demonstrate that there are sense-data. Interpreted in this manner, however, the arguments are all unsuccessful. Contemporary philosophers, and ordinary-language philosophers in particular, performed a valuable service to philosophy by exhibiting the weakness of these arguments, viewed as proofs that there are sense-data. But their claim that this weakness stems primarily from linguistic confusion does not go to the bottom of the issue. The weakness of the traditional arguments stems, fundamentally, from a different source. It stems from the fact that each of them tacitly assumes, in its premises, a proposition which on examination turns out to be virtually identical with the affirmation that there are sense-data. This is the proposition that in every case of perception, there is an object whose existence and nature can be known solely on the basis of one's present perceptual experience. Now sense-data, as can be seen by analyzing the arguments for their introduction, may be *defined* as objects whose existence and nature can be known solely on the basis of a given perceptual experience. (This definition of course does not imply that there *are* any sense-data!) But physical objects, as is shown by those same arguments, are demonstrably *not* objects whose existence and nature can be known solely on the basis of a given perceptual experience. Therefore, to assume in the arguments' permisses that there are such objects is really to assume that there are sense-data. Yet, as will be shown by analyzing each of the traditional arguments — the argument from perceptual relativity (Chapter Two), the supposedly 'scientific' causal argument (Chapter Three), and the argument from hallucination (Chapter Four) — they all turn on this assumption (or, in the case of the argument from perceptual relativity, on a closely related assumption).[4] In the latter two arguments, the assumption is packed into the supposition that perception has 'immediate' or 'direct' objects. Analysis of the arguments reveals that 'x is immediately (directly) perceived' has, as its fundamental meaning, 'x is perceived in such a way that its existence and nature can be known solely on the basis of a given perceptual experience'. Since this is true of sense-data by definition but demonstrably not true of other kinds of objects, the claim that perception *has* immediate or direct objects amounts to the claim that there *are* sense-data. The upshot is that if the traditional arguments are regarded, in the usual way, as attempts to prove that there are sense-data, they are simply question-begging. They should be seen, instead, as illustrating in various ways the epistemological problem that the sense-datum theory is designed to solve, and as showing that it is *possible* to describe perceptual experience as the immediate perception (sensing) of sense-data. Thus, as previously noted, the relation between the problem of perception and the sense-datum theory is *not* that there are certain arguments which logically compel us to introduce sense-data, and that after introducing these we are faced with an epistemological problem. Rather, there is a problem about perception and knowledge which arises independently of the sense-datum theory, and the classical arguments simultaneously illustrate this problem and suggest a solution, by trying to call our attention to objects for which the problem does not arise.

Interpreting the sense-datum theory as an attempt to solve the problem of perception provides a criterion for evaluating the theory: does it succeed in solving the problem? Recall the general contours of the problem.[5] On the one hand, it is obvious that perception is our fundamental way of acquiring knowledge about the world we live in. But on the other hand, when we attempt to specify the conditions under which perception yields knowledge, so as to grasp intellectually the relation between perception and knowledge, we run into difficulties. These difficulties may even drive us to deny the original datum − perception is a source of knowledge − thereby embracing scepticism. Thus, like many other philosophical problems, the problem of perception is basically an antinomy. One pole of the antinomy (*of course* perception yields knowledge) explains the inclination to dismiss the problem as unreal or artificial. The other pole (*how* can perception possibly yield knowledge?) explains why perceptual epistemology nevertheless continues to engage even some of the wisest philosophers. The sense-datum theory is an attempt to resolve the antinomy, by calling attention to a kind of object to which the difficulties that arise when we reflect on the relation between perception and knowledge do not apply. However, even if it is true that these difficulties do not arise with respect to knowledge about sense-data, this by itself hardly solves the problem of perception. For that problem, after all, concerns the kind of knowledge we all think we obtain by means of our senses; namely, knowledge about the physical things in our environment. Therefore, to solve the problem of perception by means of the sense-datum theory, it would have to be shown that this kind of knowledge can be based upon or legitimately derived from knowledge about sense-data. Historically, two main theories have been proposed to show this: the causal theory of perception, which will be discussed in Chapter Five, and phenomenalism, which will be discussed in Chapter Six. These theories will be viewed as alternative hypotheses as to how the problem of perception can best be solved, within the framework of a sense-datum epistemology. And in evaluating the theories, we shall at the same time be evaluating the sense-datum theory. Only if it is shown that neither theory nor any other sense-datum-based epistemology is successful will the sense-datum theory have been definitively refuted − a result which, far from showing that the problem of perception had been dissolved, would only show that the sense-datum theory provides no adequate solution to it.

Our interpretation of the sense-datum theory has certain implications concerning how the causal theory of perception should be understood. This theory is commonly thought to imply that sense-data are perceived *instead* of physical things, which themselves are in principle unperceivable. But the idea that the causal theory implies such a paradox is a misconception. If something's being immediately perceived is merely its being perceived in such a way that its existence and nature can be known solely on the basis of a given perceptual experience, then in holding that only sense-data are *immediately* perceived, the causal theory does not imply that the physical things causing our sense-data are unperceivable. It only implies that they are not perceived in the same *way* as sense-data, i.e. are not immediately perceived – which is hardly a paradox, given the meaning of 'immediately perceived'. The idea that the causal theory implies the unperceivability of physical things, it will be shown, stems largely from a confusion of the epistemological sense of 'immediately perceived' already mentioned with a psychological sense in which the term means 'perceived without any inference or reasoning'. In any case, since the causal theory does not imply the unperceivability of physical things, certain standard, textbook objections to the theory – e.g. that we cannot know whether physical things exist if they are unperceivable, that we cannot tell whether sense-data resemble physical things if we can never compare the two, etc. – are simply irrelevant.

Although the causal theory does not imply the paradox commonly thought to follow from it, the theory still does not succeed. The basic reason is that, in the classical formulations that it has taken from Locke to Russell, the causal theory maintains both (*a*) that the only way in principle of *knowing* that any physical thing is perceived is by immediately perceiving certain sense-data, and (*b*) that there is only a *contingent* relation between immediately perceiving any sequence of sense-data and perceiving any physical thing(s). But holding both (*a*) and (*b*), as will be shown in Chapter Five, makes it impossible to defend successfully the causal theory's 'Justification Thesis', according to which the claim to perceive a physical thing can be justified by some form of causal reasoning, such as Locke's prototypical inference to the best explanation in the *Essay Concerning Human Understanding*.

Phenomenalism, on the other hand, is a theory which acknowledges (*a*) but denies (*b*). In the earlier, ontological version of phenomenalism devised by Berkeley and modified by J. S. Mill, the denial of (*b*) is achieved by maintaining that a physical object *is* nothing but the family of sense-data which are or could be obtained by perceiving that object. It follows that the relation between immediately perceiving the family of sense-data and perceiving the

appropriate physical object is not contingent but necessary. An important
corollary is that the difference between perceiving a certain physical thing
and having an illusion, hallucination, or dream in which one only seems to
perceive that thing – the difference between 'appearance' and 'reality' – can
be made out perceptually. Thus from a purely epistemological point of view,
ontological phenomenalism is on much stronger ground than the causal
theory of perception. Unfortunately, however, this form of phenomenalism
is incompatible with the element of the causal theory which is indisputably
true: its 'Analytic Thesis', according to which a person S perceives a physical
thing X if and only if X, in a manner to be indicated by examples, partly
causes S's perceptual experience. (This formulation, which is essentially
H. P. Grice's, is explained in Chapter Five.) For, as is demonstrated in Chapter
Six, combining ontological phenomenalism with the Analytic Thesis of the
causal theory entails the absurdity that the sense-data obtained by perceiving
a physical thing are effects which are identical with constituents of their
own part-causes. Critics of phenomenalism have argued that it leads to other
paradoxes as well, e.g. that unperceived objects are mere possibilities, and
that actual effects can be caused by these mere possibilities. However, these
paradoxes depend on a metaphysical assumption about sense-data which is
not strictly warranted by the various methods for introducing sense-data,
namely, that sense-data are 'mental' entities whose *esse* is *percipi*. Nevertheless, it will be shown that even on our narrowly epistemological construal of
sense-data as objects of immediate perception, the paradoxes still follow from
ontological phenomenalism, albeit in a somewhat altered form. The upshot is
that ontological phenomenalism's cure for scepticism is worse than the disease.

   The analytical phenomenalism introduced by A. J. Ayer in 1940 was an
attempt to preserve the epistemological advantages of ontological phenomenalism without incurring its metaphysical liabilities. Ayer sought to accomplish
this by a radical reinterpretation of the sense-datum theory, according to
which the introduction of sense-data is merely the introduction of a special
terminology, rather than of special objects. Thus, phenomenalism became the
view that statements referring to physical things can be reformulated in the
sense-datum terminology. Phenomenalism could no longer even be put as
the view that physical things are literally composed of sense-data. Since the
paradoxes of phenomenalism all presuppose such an ontological construal,
Ayer's theory was supposed to avoid them neatly. However, Ayer's 'linguistic'
version of the sense-datum theory provided no positive view of the nature of
perceptual experience (of what Chisholm has called 'the status of appearances')
to replace the traditional sense-datum theory. Indeed, by continuing to talk

of 'sensing sense-data' and the like, Ayer invited us to continue thinking of perceptual experience as consisting in the immediate perception of special objects. Consequently, phenomenalism continued to be associated with J. S. Mill's paradoxical view of the physical world as being composed mainly of 'permanent possibilities of sensation'. Moreover, analytical phenomenalists (with the possible exception of C. I. Lewis) were prevented from seeing that their position is compatible with the Analytic Thesis of the causal theory and the realistic metaphysic it entails.

In Chapter Seven, entitled 'Phenomenalism and the Causal Theory of Perception: A Combined Theory', I shall argue that a strictly epistemological version of phenomenalism can be combined with a causal analysis of perceiving to yield a unified and plausible theory, provided that the ways physical things appear to perceivers are not reified into sense-data. Thus, the sense-datum theory will ultimately be rejected in favor of an 'adverbial' analysis of perceptual experience, of the type pioneered by Reid and Ducasse, and formulated very clearly in our own day by Chisholm. The adverbial theory makes it possible to preserve the epistemological function of sense-data, without countenancing any objects of perception other than the physical things that do the appearing. Furthermore, it makes it possible to combine the central insights of the causal theory and phenomenalism: respectively, that perceptual knowledge is knowledge of certain causes of the ways we are appeared to (i.e. of our perceptual experiences conceived 'adverbially'), and that our knowledge of physical things is exhaustively knowledge of the ways they do and would appear to us under various conditions ('Epistemological Phenomenalism'). Finally, it will be shown that contemporary objections to the phenomenalist element of the combined theory — notably the objection that statements referring to physical things are not logically equivalent to complex statements describing ways of appearing — can be refuted.

NOTES

[1] Gilbert Harman, *Thought* (Princeton University Press, Princeton, 1973), p. 5. John L. Pollock, *Knowledge and Justification* (Princeton University Press, 1974), pp. 3–4.
[2] Roderick M. Chisholm, *Theory of Knowledge*, Second Edition (Prentice-Hall, Englewood Cliffs, N. J., 1977), pp. 17–34. See also R. M. Chisholm, *Perceiving: A Philosophical Study* (Cornell University Press, Ithaca, 1957), pp. 55–62.
[3] R. M. Chisholm, *Theory of Knowledge*, Second Edition, pp. 77–78.
[4] The only argument for sense-data which does not turn on such an assumption is the 'Time-Gap' or 'Time-Lag' argument, which is discussed briefly in Chapter Three, Section 1.

[5] As should be apparent from the foregoing discussion, there are really two different 'problems of perception', which will be discussed in Chapters One and Three respectively, and both of which involve vicious regresses. Nevertheless, it is often useful to speak in general terms of 'the problem of perception', and I shall continue to do so in contexts where this does not distort the issues.

CHAPTER ONE

A PHILOSOPHICAL PROBLEM CONCERNING PERCEPTION AND KNOWLEDGE

It is obvious that there is a fundamental relationship between perception and knowledge. This is not to say that the two are identical. At any given time, we each know many things that we do not perceive. I know at this moment that there is ice at the North Pole, but I am not perceiving this to be the case. Further, at any given time we each know many things that we are not even thinking about. At this moment I know certain facts of history and geography, for example, which are in no sense present to my mind; and I shall continue to know these facts even while sound asleep. For these and other reasons, perception cannot be simply identified with knowledge.

The relationship between perception and knowledge, rather, is that perception is our basic way of *acquiring* factual knowledge about things that can exist outside the surfaces of our own bodies. (The qualification 'factual' is intended to exclude knowledge of conceptual relations; the phrase '*can* exist outside the surfaces of our own bodies' is intended both to exclude matters knowable only by introspection and to include physical objects that no longer exist or do not yet exist.) Such knowledge is always acquired, directly or indirectly, by sense-perception. For example, I know that De Gaulle was a tall man, though I am not now perceiving this to be so. But how could I know it unless I, or someone who informed me of it, or someone else who informed that person, etc., had originally come to know it by perception or inferred it from some other fact known by perception?

One way to impress upon oneself the fundamental role of perception in acquiring knowledge is to compare it with memory. Although memory is a way of knowing, it is not a way of acquiring knowledge. Suppose you ask someone if he knows your telephone number. The person concentrates for a few moments and then gives the correct number. If the person had no previous knowledge of the number, it would *follow* that this was not a case of remembering. In other words, if the person had somehow just come to know the number, then we could not correctly say that he had just remembered the number. This shows that unlike perception, memory is not a way of acquiring knowledge (which is not to deny, however, that memory is in some sense involved in acquiring knowledge by perception and, indeed, in any use of concepts).

11

This example also shows something about the status of the proposition that all factual knowledge about things that can exist outside the surfaces of our own bodies is ultimately acquired by sense perception. It shows that this proposition is not a necessary or a logical truth. For there is nothing logically absurd about the idea of someone's coming to have such knowledge in ways other than sense-perception — say by intuition, clairvoyance, telepathy, or whatnot. So the proposition that all such knowledge is ultimately derived from sense-perception is a very general contingent proposition, not a logical truth.

The basic relationship between perception and knowledge, then, is that perception happens to be ultimately our only way of acquiring factual knowledge about things that can exist outside the surfaces of our own bodies. (Anyone who believes in telepathy, clairvoyance or the like may substitute 'main' for 'only'.) The epistemological problem to be presented in this chapter arises when we attempt to understand this relationship. More specifically, it arises when we ask: under what conditions does perception yield knowledge? To formulate this question more clearly, let us put it in the formal mode, as follows: Under what conditions does 'S perceives x to be F' imply 'S knows that x is F?' (where 'S' stands for a person, 'x' for some object or event, and 'F' for some property or relation).

1. WHY PERCEPTION DOES NOT AMOUNT TO KNOWLEDGE

We cannot claim that every case of perceiving x to be F is also a case of knowing that x is F, i.e. that the following conditional is true for any S, x, and F:

(A)   If S perceives x to be F, then S knows that x is F.

This statement is false because there are cases where its antecedent is true but its consequent is false. To see this, one need only think of a case where S perceives x to be F but x is not F. In such a case, S does not *know* that x is F, for the elementary reason that x *isn't F*. Obviously, I am here assuming the correctness of the truth-condition for knowledge, i.e. of the general principle that one can know something to be the case only if it is the case. (If S knows that p, then p.) Given this fundamental requirement for knowledge and the existence of cases where S perceives x to be F but x is not F, it follows that (A) is false.

This may be illustrated as follows. Suppose that S has just come indoors after a walk on a cold winter's day. During the walk, S was not wearing gloves and his hands were exposed to the cold air. Upon coming indoors, S accidentally drops his watch into a sink full of lukewarm water, and plunges a hand into the water in order to retrieve the watch. Ordinary language provides several ways to describe the painful experience that results for S. We can say, of course, that

The water feels (seems) hot to S.

We can also say, without deviating from ordinary usage, that

S perceives the water as hot.

Finally we can say, also without stretching the language, that

S perceives the water to be hot.

This last statement is especially relevant here, since it is an instance of our general schema, 'S perceives x to be F'. Yet in this case x is not F: by hypothesis, the water is not hot but only lukewarm. It follows, given the truth-condition for knowledge, that S does not know that the water is hot. S does, however, perceive it to be hot. Therefore, one can perceive x to be F without knowing that x is F; the conditional statement (A) is accordingly false.

This shows that if we want to understand the relation between 'S perceives x to be F' and 'S knows that x is F', we need to qualify (A) in some way. Surely it must be possible to formulate a suitable qualification, since perception obviously does yield knowledge in many cases.

Before considering how to amend (A), however, let us make two observations. First, the example of the water is by no means a special or isolated case. Other cases of perceiving x to be F though x is not F can easily be given, not only for the sense of touch but also for vision, taste, smell, and hearing. In his *Meditations*, Descartes gives the example of perceiving a distant tower to be round though in fact it is square, and of perceiving a statue on top of a nearby tower to be quite small though in fact it is colossal. A sweet wine can be perceived to be sour if one has been eating candy, or to be almost tasteless if one has a bad cold. The deafening roar of a large waterfall can be perceived to be just a faint whooshing sound if one is a few hundred feet away. The strong, putrid smell of a meat-packing plant is perceived to be rather aromatic and appetizing if one is not too close to its source. In general, it is clear that simply by varying the external conditions of observation or the physiological state of the perceiver, a perceiver can be made to perceive things quite otherwise than they really are.

The second observation is that these are all examples of perception in a central, full-blooded sense of the term 'perceives'. This is because in all of them, the person perceives something *to be* such-and-such. When we say that someone perceives something, we usually mean that he perceives it to be a certain kind of thing, that he takes it to have some characteristic(s) — if only basic ones like shapes, size and color. We do not usually mean only that the person's sense-receptors are functioning and are being stimulated by some object, which the person may not even notice. If the person does not notice the object, we hesitate to say that he perceives it at all. Such a case seems to be a peripheral or borderline case of perception. Cases of perceiving something to be such-and-such, on the other hand, are cases of perception in a central sense of the term 'perceives'. Now it is interesting to find that in cases captured by this central sense of the term — cases of perceiving x to be F — perception does not amount to knowledge. The reason is simply that one can perceive a thing to be such-and-such even though the thing isn't such-and-such.[1]

Accordingly, it might be suggested that the condition under which 'S perceives x to be F' implies 'S knows that x is F' is, simply, that it be *true* that x is F. The following equivalence would then constitute the correctly amended version of (A):

(B)   (If S perceives x to be F, then S knows that x is F) if and only if (x is F).

But this will not do. For suppose that x is red and that S perceives x to be red. However, x is illuminated by extremely powerful red lamps, under which any object would look red to S no matter what color it was. Or, alternatively, suppose that S's color vision is defective, in such a way that all objects always look red to him no matter what color they are. It is clear that in these cases, S may not know that x is red; even though x is red and S perceives it to be red. Therefore, (B) is incorrect.

2. DOES PERCEPTION UNDER NORMAL CONDITIONS OF OBSERVATION AMOUNT TO KNOWLEDGE?

It may well seem that the cases considered so far do not present any serious difficulty regarding the relation between perception and knowledge. For in the cases where x is perceived to be F but is not really F, it is the conditions of observation which are to blame for this fact. The lukewarm water is perceived to be hot because the perceiver's hand is chilled; Descartes's square tower is seen to be round because it is too distant for accurate observation;

the sweet wine tastes sour because one has been eating something very sweet, and so on. In each case, it is the present conditions of observation that prevent the perceiver from perceiving the object to be what it really is. And in the cases where perceiving x to be F does not amount to knowledge that x is F even though x is F, it is again the conditions of observation which are at fault. Perceiving the red object to be red doesn't constitute knowing that it is red, just because under the prevailing conditions of observation any object would be perceived to be red, even if it were yellow or grey or blue or some other color.

This suggests that in order to specify the conditions under which perception yields knowledge, we need only introduce a clause to rule out abnormal conditions of observation. Consider, then, the following attempt to formulate the conditions under which 'S perceives x to be F' implies 'S knows that x is F':

> If S perceives x to be F, then S knows that x is F
> if and only if

(1)   The conditions of observation are normal
        and

(2)   Under normal conditions of observation, S would not perceive x to be F unless x were F.

This may be regarded as an intended analysis of perceptual knowledge, inasmuch as it purports to provide both necessary and sufficient conditions for it to be true that a case of perceiving x to be F is a case of knowing that x is F.

Before considering whether the analysis is adequate, some clarificatory remarks need to be made.

(*i*) As previously noted, S cannot know that x is F if it is false that x is F. Nevertheless, it is not necessary to add 'x is F' as an additional condition to the proposed analysis. For (1) and (2), in conjunction with 'S perceives x to be F', entail that x is F.

(*ii*) The *analysandum* must not be interpreted as a material conditional. For then the analysis could be trivially falsified by making 'S perceives x to be F' and condition (1) both false. Since the notion of a material conditional is a technical one which does not capture the full meaning of the vast majority of conditional statements in natural languages, this constitutes no serious objection to the analysis.

(*iii*) It is widely (though not universally) agreed by philosophers that knowledge entails belief (if S knows that p, then S believes that p). However, it might be argued, 'S perceives x to be F' does *not* entail 'S believes that x is F'; since if it did, 'S perceives x to be F but S does not believe that x is F' would be inconsistent, which it plainly is not. Therefore, the condition that 'S believes that x is F' must be added to the analysis.

I think it is true that 'S perceives x to be F but S does not believe (or even: S disbelieves) that x is F' need not be inconsistent. Nevertheless, I also think it unnecessary to add 'S believes that x is F' to the analysis. This is not because I would deny that knowledge entails belief; for present purposes I shall remain neutral on that question. Rather, it is because on *one* natural construal, the notion of perceiving x to be F does involve (so much as) taking or believing x to be F. This can be seen by noting that on one natural interpretation, 'S perceives x to be F and S believes (accepts, judges, thinks, takes it) that x is F' is *redundant*. Thus, in one sense of 'S perceives x to be F', this statement does not entail that S believes that x is F; but in another sense of 'S perceives x to be F', the statement does entail this. So if knowledge entails belief, then 'S perceives x to be F' should be taken in the latter sense; while if there can be knowledge without belief, 'S perceives x to be F' may be taken in the former sense. In either case, it is unnecessary to add 'S believes that x is F' to the proposed analysis.

(*iv*) It might be suggested that condition (2) should be regarded as a definition or analysis of 'normal conditions', i.e. as a logical equivalence (whose right-hand side is a subjunctive conditional). But this would not be correct because, as I shall show presently, the fact that S would not perceive x to be F unless x were F is not by itself *sufficient* for the conditions of observation to be normal. At most, then, (2) might be held to provide a logically necessary condition for it to be true that the conditions are normal, i.e. a partial analysis of 'normal conditions'. Can we affirm, then, that in order for the conditions of observation to be normal, it is necessary that S would not perceive x to be F unless x were F; e.g. that S would not perceive the water to be hot unless it were hot, or perceive the wine to be sour unless it were sour, or perceive the tower to be round unless it were round, etc.?

Even this weaker suggestion would have to be qualified in order to be correct. For suppose that S is inattentive to his experience, or confused about the (criteria for applying the) concept 'F'. In that case S might perceive x to be F though x were not F, even if the conditions of observation were completely normal. Surely a person can misperceive things as a result of inattentiveness or of some confusion about the relevant concepts. In order for (2) to specify a necessary condition for 'normal conditions', it must accordingly be amended to read:

(2′)   Under normal conditions of observation, if S is attentive to his
            experience and is not confused about the concept 'F', then S
            would not perceive x to be F unless x were F.

Notice that (2′) allows for considerable variation, depending upon the
circumstances, in what counts as normal conditions. This is as it should be.
Normal conditions for visual perception are not the same as normal conditions for gustatory perception. Normal conditions for visual perception of a
thing's size are not the same as those for perception of its color. Normal
conditions for visual perception of a ship's length are not the same as those
for a shoe's length. This looseness, which in effect highlights the analytic connection between normality of conditions and correct perception, is a feature
of the ordinary conception of normal conditions of observation. Thus, suppose that a person misperceives a table's shape (e.g., takes it to be oblong
though it is round), although he is attentive to his experience and knows
how to apply the relevant concepts. Does it not then *follow* that the conditions of observation are not normal (for observation of the table's shape)? If
they were normal, then − since the person is being attentive to his experience
and knows how to apply the relevant concepts − he would not be misperceiving the table's shape.
    It may be objected that the ordinary conception of normal conditions of
observation is not as tightly connected with correctness of perception as I am
suggesting. For isn't there a sense in which, for example, a person looking
at Descartes's square tower from a great distance, and perceiving it to be
round, is perceiving it under perfectly normal conditions of observation,
provided that there is no unusual impediment to visual perception? Although
it could be replied that the person's great distance from the tower in itself
prevents the conditions for visual perception of its shape from being normal,
let me concede the force of this objection. Anyone who feels that the objection has enough force to show that I am misusing the term 'normal conditions
of observation' may substitute 'favorable conditions' for 'normal conditions'
in (2) and (2′). With one minor exception which will be noted at the appropriate place, this substitution would not affect the course of my argument.
    The above considerations show that strictly speaking, the proposed analy-
sis should be modified by substituting (2′) for (2). A third condition should
also be added to the analysis, namely:

            S is attentive to his experience and is not confused about the
            concept 'F'.

However, for the sake of simplicity I shall leave these refinements understood rather than including them explicitly in the analysis. Since the problem concerning perception and knowledge that I shall present does not turn on the inattentiveness of perceivers or on their failure to master concepts, this simplification should not lead us astray and should help to focus our attention on the central issues.

Do conditions (1) and (2) really provide the necessary and sufficient conditions for perception to yield knowledge? If they do, then it is difficult to see why there should be any problem about the relation between perception and knowledge. For after all, conditions usually are normal. So, perceiving x to be F will usually be a way of knowing that x is F. Furthermore, cases where conditions are not normal are precisely those in which we cannot know that x is F merely by perceiving it to be F. So it is a point in favor of the proposed analysis that it does rule out such cases. Of course, even in cases where conditions are not normal we can still know that x is F, provided we compensate for the abnormality by appealing to independent information. For example, if I am perceiving a white object to be yellow because I am viewing it under strong yellow lights, I can still know that it is white by reasoning that in this light it wouldn't look yellow unless it were white; or, if that seems too risky an inference, by carrying it into a better light and looking at it again. In such a case, perception has to be supplemented by some sort of inference or experiment before it can yield knowledge. All this is faithfully reflected by conditions (1) and (2). For they are supposed to specify the conditions under which perception yields knowledge even though it is not supplemented by any inference or experiment. The proposed analysis, then, does have a good deal of plausibility, and this suggests that the relation between perception and knowledge isn't nearly as problematic as many philosophers have supposed.

I shall now give an example purporting to show that conditions (1) and (2) are not sufficient for perception to yield knowledge, i.e. an example purporting to describe circumstances in which S perceives x to be F, conditions (1) and (2) are satisfied, but S does not know that x is F. Although I do not think that this example really refutes the proposed analysis, I want to present it anyway because it suggests a line of argument (to be presented in Section 3) which does refute the analysis.

The example is as follows. Suppose that S is a person whose sensitivity to heat and cold fluctuates frequently and irregularly. Sometimes when things feel hot to S they really are hot, but just as often when things feel hot to S they are not really hot. S is like a thermometer that works only intermittently:

sometimes it tells the right temperature, at other times it is way off. Suppose that at a given time, call it time t, S's sensitivity to temperature happens to match that of an average person at most times; at time t S is like the thermometer when it happens to be working properly. And suppose that at time t, S plunges his hands into a tub of hot water and perceives the water to be hot. It is clear (assuming S has no independent information about the water's temperature or his present sensitivity to it) that S does not know that the water is hot, despite the fact that it is hot. For it is merely a lucky coincidence that S is perceiving the water as it really is. In other words, it is purely accidental, coincidental, or lucky that at time t S's sensitivity to heat is an accurate index of the water's temperature. Had S plunged his hands into the water a moment earlier or a moment later, he would have perceived it to be cold, or lukewarm, or whatever. Think once more of the eccentric thermometer with which S can be compared. If you had such a thermometer, you obviously could not rely on it for knowledge of the temperature *even when it happened to be working properly*; unless you had some independent way of knowing that it was working properly at that particular time. Likewise, S, whose sensitivity to heat and cold fluctuates widely and irregularly, cannot rely on his senses for knowledge of the water's temperature even at t when his sensitivity to temperature happens to be normal; unless of course he has some way of knowing that at t his sensitivity to temperature is normal.

This example illustrates an important general principle. This is that one cannot know something if one is right about it merely by coincidence, luck, or accident. Otherwise, why should not every lucky guess be an instance of knowledge? Yet, that would be absurd: a correct guess does not amount to *knowledge, because* its being correct rather than incorrect is a matter of chance or luck. One contemporary philosopher, Peter Unger, has even attempted to analyze knowledge in terms of this principle. Unger proposed that:

> S knows that p (at a time t) if and only if (at t)
> it is not at all accidental that S is right about
> its being the case that p.[2]

Whether or not this provides an adequate analysis of knowledge, it certainly does provide a necessary condition.[3] If it is even somewhat accidental that S is right about its being the case that p, then S does not know that p.

Does the example refute the proposed analysis? The argument for thinking that it does would go as follows. At time t, S perceives x to be F (perceives the water to be hot) but does not know that x is F; so the *analysandum* is false. But the *analysans* is true. For condition (1) is satisfied: at time t, the conditions of observation are normal. This is because at t, S's sensitivity to temperature exactly matches that of an average perceiver at most times, so that at t the water wouldn't feel hot to S unless it really were not. Moreover, condition (2), being an analytic truth, is also satisfied. Therefore, the example constitutes a counterexample to the proposed analysis.

However, this argument is unsound. For although in the example the *analysandum* is certainly false, the *analysans* is false as well. This is because it is not really the case that the conditions of observation are normal, and so condition (1) isn't really satisfied. For by hypothesis, S is a radically abnormal perceiver, whose sensitivity to temperature fluctuates widely and irregularly. Threfore, even at t, when S's sensitivity to temperature happens to match that of an average perceiver at most times, the conditions of observation are not normal. Surely if the *external* conditions of observation began to vary wildly — e.g. if the light by which objects are seen began to vary irregularly in color and intensity — then we would not consider them normal *even when* they happened not to be misleading. For these conditions to be normal, they must have a certain stability. (This is why I claimed under [*iv*], above, that the fact that S wouldn't perceive x to be F unless x were F is not by itself *sufficient* for the conditions of observation to be normal.) But conditions of observation, after all, include not only factors external to the perceiver's body, but also the perceiver's physiological condition. So for the conditions of observation to be normal at t, S's sensitivity to temperature would have to be roughly as stable as an average perceiver's. Therefore, the example is not a genuine counterexample to the analysis.

(It is here that my argument would have to be modified if 'favorable conditions' were substituted for 'normal conditions' throughout. In that case, the example would be a counterexample to the analysis, because at t the conditions of observation do happen to be *favorable*; since they are such that S wouldn't perceive the water to be hot unless it were hot. But then the analysis could be amended so as to avoid the counterexample, simply by adding a condition requiring that the perceiver be normal, i.e. not have any radical perceptual handicap akin to S's fluctuating sensitivity to temperature — a manuever that corresponds exactly to the defense just given of the analysis cast in terms of 'normal conditions').

3. THE REQUIREMENT THAT THE CONDITIONS BE KNOWN TO BE NORMAL

I shall now advance an argument to show that the proposed analysis of perceptual knowledge is incorrect. Specifically, I shall try to show that conditions (1) and (2) fail to provide *sufficient* conditions for perception to yield knowledge. I am going to argue, in other words, that even when S perceives x to be F and conditions (1) and (2) are satisfied, S may not know that x is F. If my argument is sound, then there is a philosophical problem about the relation between perception and knowledge.

Consider the entire class of perceivers who do not have the radical sort of perceptual disability that we have imagined. For convenience, let us refer to this class as the class of 'normal perceivers'; though its members include, for example, blind or deaf persons whose other senses function normally. Now consider the entire class of cases where these normal perceivers perceive anything to be F. Among this class of cases, there will be a large number of cases where the conditions of observation are normal and where, therefore (assuming that the perceiver is attentive to his experience and not confused about the concept 'F'), x really is F. But there will also be a smaller number of cases where the conditions of observation are not normal. Thus, the class of cases in which normal perceivers perceive x to be F includes both cases where the conditions of observation are normal and cases where they are not normal. Therefore, it is always somewhat lucky, coincidental, or accidental that a particular case, selected randomly from this class of cases, is one in which the conditions of observation are normal (just as it is always somewhat lucky, coincidental, or accidental that a marble picked at random from a bag of white and black marbles is a white one). Therefore, it is also somewhat lucky, accidental or coincidental that this case of perceiving x *to be F* is one where x really is F. So, it is also somewhat lucky, coincidental or accidental that it is a case where the perceiver is right about x's being F. Therefore, even in a case of perceiving x to be F under normal conditions of observation, it is somewhat lucky, coincidental or accidental that the perceiver is right about x's being F. (Notice that I am not saying that *given* that the conditions of observation are normal, it is still somewhat lucky that the perceiver is right about x's being F. On the contrary, given that the conditions of observation are normal, it *follows* that the perceiver is right about x's being F; assuming that he is attentive to his experience and not confused about the concept 'F'. Rather, the point is that since it is always somewhat lucky that the conditions of observation *are* normal, it is *also* somewhat lucky that the perceiver is right about x's being F.) It follows that perceiving x to be F under normal conditions of observation is not sufficient for knowing that x is F.

If you doubt that this conclusion follows, think again of the person with abnormally fluctuating sensitivity to temperature. Why would we refuse to say that he knows that the water is hot by perceiving it to be hot, even when his sensitivity to temperature happens to match that of an average perceiver at most times? Because it is a matter of luck or chance that his perceiving the water to be hot coincides with its being the case that the water is hot. But even if we consider only normal perceivers, it is still partly a matter of luck or chance that any particular case of perceiving x to be F is one where x really is F. For even normal perceivers sometimes suffer temporary malfunctions of the senses, and sometimes get themselves into situations where the external conditions of observation are abnormal, resulting in various illusions and perceptual errors. The difference between the person with abnormally fluctuating sensitivity to temperature and normal perceivers is a matter of degree. Accordingly, if you agree that the person with abnormally fluctuating sensitivity to temperature does not know that the water is hot by perceiving it to be hot even when his sensitivity to temperature happens to match that of an average perceiver at most times, then for the same reason you should agree that a perceiver may not know that x is F by perceiving x to be F even when the conditions of observation happen to be normal.

I contend, then, that the proposed analysis of perceptual knowledge is inadequate: perceiving x to be F, even under normal conditions of observation, does not constitute knowing that x is F. If we lived in a world where the conditions of observation were always normal — where neither external factors such as the light or medium nor internal factors such as malfunctions of the senses or nervous system ever produced illusions or perceptual errors — then perhaps the analysis would be acceptable as it stands. For in such a world it would never be the least bit lucky, coincidental, or accidental that when one perceived x to be F, x really was F. Perception would be an infallible guide to reality. But obviously we do not live in that kind of world. Perception, in our world, is sometimes deceptive; occasionally grossly so. It is deceptive when the conditions of observation — either external or internal — are abnormal. Therefore, a further condition must be added to the analysis. This is the condition that

(3)   S knows that the conditions of observation are normal.

In other words, in order for S to perceptually know that x is F, S must know that this is not one of those unlucky cases where, because the conditions of observation are abnormal, he perceives x to be F but x is not really F.

As soon as we introduce condition (3), however, we are faced with a question. How does S know that the conditions of observation are normal? The only way available seems to be: by perceiving them to be normal. For how else could S know that the present conditions of observation are normal?[4] But now, it is obvious that we have run into a difficulty. For the chance that some abnormality in the condition of observation is producing a perceptual error or illusion attaches to S's perceiving the conditions of observation to be normal no less than to S's perceiving x to be F. So even if the conditions of observation under which S perceives the original conditions of observation to be normal are normal, it is somewhat lucky or accidental that they are and so that S perceives the original conditions of observation correctly. Therefore, S can know that the original conditions of observation are normal by perceiving them to be normal only if S *knows* that the conditions of observation under which he perceives the original conditions of observation to be normal are themselves normal. But S can know this only by still other perceptions, that themselves constitute knowledge only if S knows that they are occuring under normal conditions of observation, which S can know to be the case only by still other perceptions . . . etc. *ad infinitum*. This regress, which has every appearance of being a vicious one, can also be seen to arise from the analysis (as newly amended), as follows. By the analysis,

> S perceives the conditions of observation to be normal

implies that

> S knows that the conditions of observation are normal

only if

> S knows that the conditions of observation under which he perceives the (original) conditions of observation to be normal are normal

which S can know, it would seem, only by perception. But again, by the analysis,

> S perceives the conditions of observation under which he perceives the (original) conditions of observation to be normal, to be normal

implies that S has the corresponding knowledge only if

> S knows that the conditions of observation, under which he perceives the conditions of observation under which he perceives the (original) conditions of observation to be normal, to be normal, are normal[5]

which S can know, it would seem, only by perception. Thus, the introduction of conditions (3) launches us into a vicious regress.

Let me emphasize that I have no wish to assert that one can never know that the conditions of observation are normal, and so that condition (3) can never be satisfied. It seems to me, for example, that at this moment I do know that the conditions under which I am perceiving the objects around me are normal. I am not denying that we can have perceptual knowledge, but presenting a problem that arises when we try to specify the conditions under which we can have it. The problem of perception and knowledge, as I conceive it, is not *whether* perception yields knowledge (it is obvious that it does) but *how* it can do so: it is an intellectual problem, a problem of understanding. Thus, one should resist the inclination to dismiss the above regress with the claim that perception obviously does yield knowledge. Of course it does. The problem is to understand how it can do so. To dismiss the problem by simply insisting that perception yields knowledge would be to see only one side of what, like many other philosophical problems, is basically an antinomy.

I shall conclude this section by disposing of an argument that might be thought to show that the regress is not a vicious one. The argument goes as follows. The more perceptions S has confirming his original perception of x as F, the less probable it becomes that the latter was not veridical. For example, suppose that S perceives a piece of paper to be pink. Now if S suspects that perhaps the paper is not really pink, he can check the light to make sure that it is not reddish or otherwise unusual. Suppose that S does this and perceives the light to be standard, white electrical illumination. Now, you may say, the probability that S was misperceiving the color of the paper has decreased very significantly. And if S fears that his color vision is off today, causing him to misperceive both the color of the paper and the light, he can appeal to memory: he can assure himself that the lights and other objects in the room do not look any different today than the way they looked on previous occasions when his vision was normal. Finally, if S is unsure whether his vision was really normal on those occasions or whether his memory of them is accurate, he can appeal to still other current and remembered perceptions. It may well seem that with each additional present or remembered corroborating perception, the probability that S is misperceiving the color of the paper diminishes until it becomes negligible.

The decisive objection to this line of defense is that it begs the question. To see this, let us begin by stating it a bit more formally. The idea is that S can perceptually know that x is F when his perception of x as F can be supported by an inductive argument whose schema is:

(1)   If I am correctly perceiving x to be F (e.g. the paper to be pink), then I can perceive u to be G (e.g. the light to be standard), and v to be H, and. . . , and I can remember perceiving y to be I (e.g. the walls to be white), and z to be J, and . . . .

(2)   I can perceive u to be G, and v to be H, and . . . , and I can remember perceiving y to be I, and z to be J, and . . .

In all probability, I am correctly perceiving x to be F.

Let us call an argument that conforms to this schema a 'form-A' argument. The proposal, then, is that condition (3) of the analysis be replaced by the following condition:

(3$'$)   S's perception of x as F can be supported by a form-A argument.

We can now show that the proposal is question-begging. Notice first that *if* a form-A argument presupposes that perceiving x to be F is sometimes a way of knowing that x is F, then the reformulated analysis is circular. For it will then turn out that

> S's perception of x as F can be supported by a form-A argument only if in some cases S perceptually knows that x is F (i.e. knows that x is F by perceiving x to be F).

But perceptual knowledge that x is F is precisely what we are attempting to analyze. So we would be analyzing perceptual knowledge in terms of perceptual knowledge, i.e. going in a circle.

But it should be clear that form-A arguments do presuppose that perceiving x to be F sometimes yields knowledge that x is F. For premiss (1) of a form-A argument assumes that we can correlate cases of correctly perceiving x to be F with certain obtainable and remembered perceptions. But in order to establish such correlations, we must obviously be able to identify cases of *correctly* perceiving x to be F. But we cannot identify cases of correctly perceiving x to be F unless we know that in those cases x is F. And since perception is ultimately the only way we have of acquiring such knowledge, we cannot know that in those cases x is F unless we sometimes know that x is F by perceiving x to be F, or sometimes know that y is G by perceiving y to be G and infer that x is F from our perceptual knowledge that y is G. Therefore, a form-A argument does presuppose that perceiving x to be F sometimes yields knowledge that x is F;[6] and so the reformulated analysis (the analysis in which [3'] is substituted for [3]) is circular. Hence, it provides no way to halt the regress generated by condition (3) of the original analysis.

4. AN ATTEMPT TO AVOID THE REGRESS:
THE SENSE-DATUM THEORY

We have just seen that the vicious regress generated by condition (3) of our analysis of perceptual knowledge cannot be turned into a benign one by appealing to probability. It would appear, therefore, that the vicious regress can be avoided only by preventing it from starting in the first place. And there seems to be only one way in which this could be done, short of simply rejecting condition (3) and, thus, falling back on the analysis of perceptual knowledge (given in Section II) that we found good reason to reject. This would be to show that perception can yield knowledge regardless of whether the conditions of observation are normal or abnormal. In other words, if it could be shown that *something* can always be *known* in a case of perception, regardless of the conditions of observation, then the regress would not arise. At first sight, however, this may seem like an impossible requirement to satisfy. For how could perception possibly yield knowledge even if it were occuring under abnormal conditions of observation, when things are often perceived otherwise than they really are?

There is an answer to this question which until quite recently was widely accepted by philosophers: the sense-datum theory. Sense-data were supposed to be objects of a special kind, perceived in a special way. The kind of object and mode of perception intended can be elucidated only in connection with the methods that philosophers used in order to introduce sense-data. These methods were quite varied. Some philosophers, such as Moore and Price, introduced sense-data by giving us directions or instructions for picking them out within our own perceptual experience. Others, such as Russell and Lovejoy, introduced them by means of arguments whose premises referred to scientific facts about the perceptual process. Still other philosophers, such as Ayer and, before him, the Classical Empiricists, used the so-called 'Argument from Illusion'. In the years just before the sense-datum theory fell into general disfavor, the favored method of introducing sense-data was by means of certain linguistic moves with the terms 'seems', 'appears', and 'looks', a procedure ingeniously defended by H. P. Grice as recently as 1961.[7] Actually, most advocates of the sense-datum theory made use of several of these methods more or less simultaneously. Thus, the literature in favor of the sense-datum theory contains a bewildering variety of arguments and analyses, in which it is difficult to find a unifying theme except for the thesis that we 'immediately perceive' or 'directly perceive' sense-data.

Nevertheless, I believe that a single theme does run through the various attempts to introduce sense-data. This unifying theme is the epistemological purpose of the sense-datum theory, which is: to explain how perception can be a source of knowledge. The connection betweeen this question and the sense-datum theory is as follows. If we assume that the only objects that could be perceptually known are the physical things that exist in our environment and act upon our sense-receptors, then the possibility that some abnormality in the conditions of observation is causing an illusion or perceptual error forces us to require that the perceiver know that the conditions of observation are normal. But this requirement, as we have seen, leads us into a vicious regress. However, suppose that there are objects of perception such that no abnormality in the conditions of observation can fool us about their properties. Suppose these are objects about which we could be mistaken, if at all, only because of failing to pay close enough attention to them or due to some conceptual confusion on our part. In order to obtain knowledge of such objects by perceiving them, we would not need to know anything about the conditions of observation. So the vicious regress would not arise with respect to these objects. Obviously these objects could not be the physical things in our environment and acting upon our sense-receptors. So they would have to be objects possessing a special status and perceived in a special way: sense-data.

In the following chapter, I shall try to show that one of the classical arguments for introducing sense-data, the Argument from Perceptual Relativity, supports this interpretation of the sense-datum theory. My strategy will be to show that the argument's main premiss *both* (a) calls attention to the facts about the conditions of observation that prevent perceiving x to be F from constituting knowing that x is F if x is assumed to be a physical object or event in the perceiver's environment, *and* (b) covertly asserts that every case of perceiving is, nonetheless, a case of knowing the character of *some* object. If this is correct, then this argument should not be seen, in the usual way, as a straightforward attempt to *prove* that there are sense-data; for then it is simply question-begging. Rather, it should be viewed as posing the following alternative: *either* admit that there are no objects whose nature can be perceptually known regardless of the conditions of observation – in which case you will run into a vicious regress when you attempt to specify the conditions under which perception yields knowledge – *or* admit that there are special objects, sense-data, which are perceived in an epistemologically privileged way, i.e. in such a way that their nature can be known regardless of whether the conditions of observation are normal or abnormal.

In the ensuing chapters, I shall argue that a similar analysis applies to the other two classical arguments for sense-data, the Argument from Causation and the Argument from Hallucination. Moreover, as noted in the Introduction, analyzing these arguments will deepen our understanding of the *problem* of perception. For these arguments (unlike the argument advanced in this chapter and the Argument from Perceptual Relativity) show that perceiving *x* to be *F* is not even a sufficient condition for knowing that *x exists*, and this leads to be a second vicious regress, which it is also the purpose of the sense-datum theory to avoid.

After we have analyzed the three classical arguments for the introduction of sense-data, we will be ready to turn to the question, whether introducing sense-data enables us to explain how perception can yield knowledge of the physical things in our environment. For, as noted in the Introduction (and as will be argued more fully in Section 2 of the following chapter), it is upon the answer to this question that the acceptability of the sense-datum theory ultimately turns.

NOTES

[1] A number of philosophers have defined senses of 'S perceives *x* to be *F*' which imply that *x* is *F* and, indeed, that S knows that *x* is *F*. (See for example R. M. Chisholm, *Perceiving: A Philosophical Study* (Cornell University Press, Ithaca, 1957), and Fred I. Dretske, *Seeing and Knowing* [University of Chicago Press, Chicago, 1969].) Although this use of 'S perceives *x* to be *F*' may accord with one ordinary use of that locution, the locution carries no such implication in its most common uses. In any case, no substantive issues are decided by adopting the stronger use. Rather, the definition of 'S perceives *x* to be *F*' must then incorporate both 'perceives' in my weaker sense *and* certain additional conditions which I prefer to represent as conditions that, in conjunction with 'S perceives *x* to be *F*', imply 'S knows that *x* is *F*'.
[2] Peter Unger, 'An Analysis of Factual Knowledge', *The Journal of Philosophy* 65 (1968), pp. 157–170.
[3] Unger would now hold that it provides only a necessary condition. See his *Ignorance: A Case for Scepticism* (Oxford University Press, London, 1975), Chapter 2, Note 4.
[4] S might know that the conditions were normal by perceiving something else to be the case, from which he could reliably infer that they are normal. But this obviously would not alter the logic of the issue.
[5] Less awkwardly: S knows that the conditions of observation, under which he perceives to be normal the conditions under which he perceives the (original) conditions of observation to be normal, are normal.
[6] I am here treating '*x*' and '*F*' as variables, such that '*x*' and '*F*' in this sentence can represent the same thing and property as either '*x*' and '*F*' or '*y*' and '*G*' in the previous sentence.

[7] H. P. Grice, 'The Causal Theory of Perception', *Proceedings of the Aristotelian Society* **35** (1961), pp. 121–168. As will be seen in Chapter Five, however, Grice did not intend to rehabilitate the sense-datum theory in the classical form favored by Moore, Price, and Russell.

CHAPTER TWO

THE ARGUMENT FROM PERCEPTUAL RELATIVITY

Perhaps the best-known method of introducing sense-data is by means of the Argument from Perceptual Relativity. This argument can be found in the writings of philosophers from antiquity to present times, and there are many different ways of formulating it.[1] I shall begin by expounding (only) what seems to me to be the strongest version of the argument; then I shall present the most important contemporary objection to the argument; and finally I shall try to specify the considerations on the basis of which the issue raised by this objection should ultimately be resolved.

1. EXPOSITION OF THE ARGUMENT

The Argument from Perceptual Relativity, in its strongest form, is not a putative proof that there are sense-data. Rather, it is a proof that sense-data have a special status; that they are, in H. H. Price's phrase, "not identical with parts of the surfaces of physical things". Obviously, such a conclusion is of little interest unless sense-data have first been introduced in such a way that their *existence* is not a matter of controversy. But how can this be accomplished by an argument which draws a conclusion solely about the *nature* of sense-data? The answer is that the argument as a whole is intended to function as an *ostensive* definition of sense-data. This will be evident if we consider the exceptionally clear statement of the argument given by G. E. Moore in Chapter 2 of *Some Main Problems of Philosophy*, originally presented by Moore as a lecture to his students at Cambridge.[2] As Moore goes through the argument, he is attempting to give the members of his audience a set of directions for picking out the sense-data within their own perceptual experience. Thus his argument is intended simultaneously to call our attention to sense-data and to demonstrate a truth about their nature.

Since Moore's procedure is partly ostensive, I shall describe what he did as well as what he said. Moore began by holding up an envelope in front of the members of his audience, and asking them to look at it for a few moments while he did the same. He then asked: "What happened to each of us, when we saw that envelope?" He said that he would begin by describing part of what happened to him.

I saw a patch of a particular whitish colour, having a certain size, and a certain shape, a shape with rather sharp angles or corners and bounded by fairly straight lines. These things; this patch of a whitish colour, and its size and shape, I did actually see. And I propose to call these things, the colour and size and shape, *sense-data*, things *given* or presented by the senses – given, in this case, by my sense of sight.[3]

In a footnote added when Moore revised his lecture for publication, he corrects this statement. He says that it is the seen patch itself, with its color, size and shape, which is the sense-datum; rather than the color, size and shape taken separately. Let us take it, then, that the sense-datum Moore says he sees as he looks at the envelope is the particular colored patch he has described – one that has not only a specific color but also a certain size and shape.

Before continuing the demonstration Moore pauses to insist that it would be an error to call this colored patch, as some other philosophers would do, a sensation. Since the continuation of the demonstration leads to the conclusion that sense-data are not identical with physical things or their surfaces, this insistence may seem puzzling. Why does Moore refuse to call sense-data 'sensations' if his own argument shows that they are sensations or at least something very like sensations? The most important reason, I suggest, is that Moore wants the term 'sense-datum' to be a metaphysically neutral one – one that does not necessarily imply, for example, that sense-data are subjective entities.[4] This is why he makes it clear that he does not want to build into the *meaning* of the term 'sense-datum' either (*a*) that sense-data do not continue to exist unperceived, or (*b*) that sense-data do not exist in the same place as the physical thing they belong to (e.g. the envelope).[5] Moore's idea, I believe, is that so long as no metaphysical assumptions are built into the notion of a sense-datum, the existence of sense-data is beyond any question; for it is undeniable that Moore himself, as well as the members of his audience, do each see a certain colored patch upon looking at the envelope.

These things; this patch of a whitish colour, and its size and shape, I did actually see. . . And I have no doubts whatever that this is part, at least, of what happened to all of you. You also saw certain sense-data; and I expect also that the sense-data which you saw were more or less similar to those which I saw. You also saw a patch of colour which might be described as whitish, of a size not very different from the size of the patch which I saw, and of a shape similar at least in this that it had rather sharp corners and was bounded by fairly straight lines.[6]

The metaphysical status of the colored patch, on the other hand, is a matter to be settled not by definition but by argument – indeed, by the argument Moore goes on to develop.

Moore next introduces the first premiss of this argument. He says: "But now, what I want to emphasize is this. . . no two of us, in all probability, saw exactly the *same sense-data".*[7] Why is this? Well, consider just the color of the patch seen by Moore and each member of his audience. In all probability, no two of them saw exactly the same color; for there were slight differences in the way the light fell on the envelope relative to each of them and probably also slight differences in their color-vision. Again, consider the size of the patch seen by Moore and each member of his audience. In all probability, no two of them saw a patch of exactly the same size, because they were situated at different distances from the envelope. Finally, consider the shape. Certainly, Moore and the members of his audience did not all see a sense-datum having exactly the same shape. Persons situated obliquely from the facing surface of the envelope saw various rhomboidal shapes, while persons situated more directly in front of it saw more nearly rectangular shapes. As Moore put it, at the same time facing the envelope in appropriate directions:

Those on my left will have seen a figure more like this which you in front now see, and which you see is different from *this* which you then saw. And those in front of me will have seen a figure like that which you on the left now see, and which, you see, is different from *this*, which you saw before.[8]

To shift for a moment to a more famous illustration, had Moore held up a penny rather than an envelope, persons close to the walls of the room would have seen skinny ellipses, those somewhat closer to the center would have seen fatter ellipses, while those directly in front would have seen circles. Had the persons held pieces of transparent plexiglass before their eyes while looking at the penny and traced onto them the outlines of the shapes they saw, these shapes would have differed among themselves (though admittedly more so than the shapes seen, because shape-constancy corrects to some extent for perspective distortion). Thus, Moore and the members of his audience saw sense-data that differed with respect to their colors, sizes, and shapes; this is why they did not all see the same sense-data.

But from this it clearly follows, Moore points out, that the sense-data seen by himself and the members of his audience cannot all have been identical with the envelope (or its surface). For an envelope cannot simultaneously have several different colors, sizes, or shapes. No physical thing or surface can simultaneously be of several different colors, sizes, or shapes. But the sense-data seen by Moore and the members of his audience did have many different colors, sizes, and shapes — probably as many, Moore implies, as there were persons looking at the envelope. Therefore these sense-data cannot all have been identical with the envelope or its surface.

Moore's argument, in its general form, can be put as follows:

(1)   The sense-data belonging to a physical thing or surface (e.g. to an envelope or its surface) have many incompatible qualities.

(2)   A physical thing or surface cannot have incompatible qualities.

∴ (3)   The sense-data belonging to a physical thing or surface are not all identical with that thing or surface.

Before discussing this argument something must be said to explain the term 'belonging to'. It designates the relationship between a sense-datum and the physical thing which stands to it in the same relation as the envelope stands to any of the colored patches (visual sense-data) mentioned by Moore. Some of the sense-data perceived by the members of Moore's audience, such as those they saw in looking above or below the envelope and those they heard in listening to Moore's voice, did not stand in this special relation to the envelope and so did not belong to it. The correct definition of 'belonging to' is of course not settled by these remarks. In his classic treatise on the sense-datum theory, *Perception*, H. H. Price treats the definition of 'belonging to' as one of the main questions to be answered by a theory of perception. What the above argument shows is that 'belongs to' can in any case not be defined as 'is identical with'. Should it, then, be defined roughly as 'is caused by', as the Causal Theory of Perception would hold? Or should it be defined roughly as 'is a member of a collection of sense-data of type —', as Phenomenalism would hold? The attempt to make these definitions precise and to work out their epistemological implications can be viewed as being identical with the task of formulating and evaluating these two theories when they are cast, as they traditionally have been, within the framework of a sense-datum epistemology.

It should be evident that the argument, as developed so far, does not show that *all* of the sense-data belonging to a physical thing or surface are distinct from it: on the contrary, (3) allows that some sense-data may actually be identical with the physical thing or surface to which they belong. It would be perfectly consistent with (3), for example, to hold that the sense-datum seen by an observer placed directly in front of and only a few feet away from Moore's envelope is identical with the facing surface of the envelope (in virtue of having the very color, size and shape of that surface). Moore himself admits this, though he adds that he is inclined to disbelieve it. As he puts it, "it seems very probable that *none* of the colours seen was really a part of the envelope; and that *none* of the sizes and shapes seen were the size or the

shape of the real envelope".[9] Sense-datum theorists do characteristically hold
that none of the sense-data belonging to a physical thing or surface are identical with it. But this clearly does not follow from (1) and (2) alone; further
argumentation is needed. I shall complete my exposition of the Argument
from Perceptual Relativity by summarizing the additional argumentation that
is typically given (e.g. by both H. H. Price and A. J. Ayer), postponing all
critical remarks until Section 2.

Typically, the move from 'not all the sense-data belonging to a physical
thing or surface are identical with it' to 'none of the sense-data belonging to
a physical thing or surface are identical with it' is mediated by the following
premiss, which can be regarded as beginning the second stage of the argument
summarized above.[10]

(4)   If the sense-data belonging to a physical thing or surface are not
        all identical with the thing or surface but some of the sense-data
        belonging to the thing or surface are identical with it, then there
        must be a special, discernible qualitative difference between the
        sense-data which are identical with the thing or surface and the
        sense-data which are not identical with it.

The rationale offered for this premiss is as follows. If some of the sense-data
belonging to a physical thing or surface are literally identical with the thing
or surface, then these sense-data have a very different status from those that
belong to the thing or surface but are not identical with it. For while the
latter are evidently subjective entities akin to Berkeleyan 'sensations or ideas',
the former are perceiver-independent, physical existents. Hence, there ought
to be some special, inspectable difference between these sense-data, answering
to and signaling their different metaphysical statuses. For example, if the sense-
datum seen from three feet directly in front of Moore's envelope is identical
with the envelope's facing surface, then this 'privileged' sense-datum has a
very different status from those seen from various distances and angles. So,
there ought to be some distinctive qualitative difference setting it off from
the others. But no such difference can be found. Accordingly, we must conclude that even the sense-datum seen from the privileged vantage point is distinct from the envelope's facing surface. Obviously this reasoning can be reiterated for any of the sense-data belonging to the envelope. The second stage of
the argument, then, can be completed in two steps. First, we add the premiss:

(5)   There is no special, discernible qualitative difference among the
        sense-data belonging to a physical thing or surface.

We can now conclude from (3), (4), and (5) that

(6)   None of the sense-data belonging to a physical thing or surface
        are identical with that thing or surface.

A variant formulation of the argument's second stage (also mentioned by
both Price and Ayer) appeals to the continuity between the members of a
series of sense-data belonging to a physical thing.[11] Suppose for example
that an observer, starting from directly in front of Moore's envelope, backs
steadily away from the envelope. If he keeps on looking at the envelope, he
will perceive a continuous series of sense-data diminishing in size. But, it is
argued, if any one of these sense-data were identical with the envelope's
facing surface, then there ought to be a greater difference between it and the
next member of the series than between any two consecutive members of the
series neither of which are identical with the envelope's surface. As Price puts
it,

We should expect at least a jerk or a flicker as the one [i.e. the sense-datum which we
are supposing to be identical with the envelope's surface] is replaced by the other [i.e.
the next member of the series, which, since it has a different size, cannot also be identical with the envelope's surface].[12]

But again, no such difference can be found. So it must be concluded that
there is no difference of metaphysical status between the members of the
continuous series of sense-data. And since the first stage of the argument has
proved that some — indeed at least *virtually* all — of these sense-data are
special entities distinct from the envelope's surface, it follows that all of them
are entities of this special kind.

2. EVALUATION OF THE ARGUMENT

We have seen that the Argument from Perceptual Relativity is a valid proof
that not all sense-data are identical with the physical things or surfaces to
which they belong.[13] Does this mean that the phenomenon of perceptual
relativity logically *requires* us to accept the view that we perceive sense-data
(at least some of) which are distinct from physical things or surfaces? No, it
does not. For the question, whether the sense-data we perceive are identical
with physical things or surfaces, arises only if we accept the view that we
perceive sense-data. But we do not have to accept this view. For recall how
sense-data were introduced. Moore did not offer any argument to prove that
we see sense-data when we look at the envelope. Rather, he gave us a set of
directions for picking out the sense-data within our own perceptual experience. Moore said, in effect,

if you consult your experience as you look at the envelope I am holding, you will become aware of a colored patch whose color, size, and shape probably differ from those seen by every other person in the room and can be altered merely by changing your own distance or direction from the envelope. This patch or expanse is an example of what I mean by a 'sense-datum'.

It is only if this introduction of sense-data is legitimate that Moore can legitimately formulate the first premiss of his argument, i.e. that the sense-data belonging to an envelope have several different colors, sizes, and shapes.

However, we do not have to describe our experience in the way Moore suggests. We are free to respond to Moore as follows.

When I follow your instructions and look at the envelope, the *only* thing I see is a physical object – i.e. an envelope – which *seems* white or greyish depending on how the light is falling on it, which *looks* rectangular or rhomboidal depending on the angle from which it is viewed, which *appears* larger or smaller depending on the distance from which it is viewed. I do *not* see *any* object which actually depends for its color, shape, and size on the conditions of observation or the identity of the observer. Likewise, when I look at a penny from a certain angle, what I see is a round penny which *looks* elliptical from that angle. I do not see any object which actually *is* elliptical.

This negative response to the introduction of sense-data has been made by virtually every recent critic of the theory and is quite commonly regarded as decisive. For example, J. L. Austin quotes H. H. Price as saying, "a distant hillside which is full of protuberances, and slopes upwards at a quite gentle angle, will appear flat and vertical. . . . This means that the sense-datum, the colour-expanse which we sense, actually *is* flat and vertical." To this Austin responds: "But why should we accept this account of the matter? Why should we say that there is *anything* we see which *is* flat and vertical, though 'not part of the surface' of any material object?"[14] And Gilbert Ryle writes in *The Concept of Mind*:

Let us consider the . . . instance of a person looking at a round plate tilted away from him, which he may therefore describe as looking elliptical . . . . The question is whether the truth of his report that the plate looks elliptical implies that he is really espying, or scanning, an object of sense which, not being the plate itself, can claim to be entitled 'a look' or 'a visual appearance of the plate'. We may grant that if we are bound to say that he has come across an object of sense which is really elliptical . . . then this elliptical object . . . is a sense-datum and therefore that there are sense-data . . . [But] in saying that the plate looks elliptical, he is not characterizing an extra object, namely 'a look' as being elliptical, he is likening how the tilted round plate does look to how untilted elliptical plates do or would look. He is not saying 'I am seeing a flat elliptical patch of white', but 'I might be seeing an elliptical and untilted piece of white china . . . . When we say that someone has a pedantic appearance, we do not mean to suggest that there are two kinds of pedantic beings, namely some men and some appearances of men. We mean that he looks rather like some pedantic people look. Similarly there are not two kinds of elliptical objects, namely some platters and some looks; there are some platters which are elliptical and others which look as if they were elliptical.[15]

The point Austin and Ryle are both making is that in order to describe the phenomenon of perceptual relativity, it is not necessary to reify the ways things appear to us under various conditions by introducing sense-data. Rather, the phenomenon can be adequately described by means of such words as 'looks', 'seems', 'appears'.

This crucial point is incisively made by R. M. Chisholm in his influential book, *Perceiving*. Chisholm points out that the argument form

S perceives a . . . which appears . . . to him

∴ S perceives an appearance which is . . .

is simply invalid. There are many counterexamples to such an argument. For example 'S perceives a painting which appears several hundred years old to him' does not entail 'S perceives an appearance which is several hundred years old'; since the premiss could be true but the conclusion is obviously false. Chisholm adds that there is no true premiss which, in conjunction with 'S perceives an x which appears F to him', yields the conclusion 'S perceives an appearance (sense-datum) which is F'. He accordingly dubs this form of argument 'The Sense-Datum Fallacy'.[16] In an article titled 'The Myth of Sense-Data', Winston Barnes makes essentially the same criticism as Chisholm: " . . . I cannot infer . . . merely from the three facts that I am seeing something, that it looks pink and that it is red, that there is a pink something where the thing appears pink to me".[17]

The bearing of these objections on Moore's attempt to introduce sense-data is clear. Austin, Ryle, Chisholm, Barnes and many others would say that Moore assumes that he can legitimately reformulate, for example,

S perceives an envelope which appears rhomboidal to him

as

S perceives a sense-datum which is rhomboidal.

However, this is an instance of the Sense-Datum Fallacy — an elementary error in reasoning. It is clear that if this is the correct response to Moore's attempt to introduce sense-data, then the Argument from Perceptual Relativity collapses. For, as we have seen, the argument does not prove that we perceive sense-data; it assumes this in its opening premiss. All the argument proves is that *if* we perceive sense-data, *then* these are not identical with physical things or their surfaces. But if, following contemporary critics of the sense-datum theory, one simply rejects the notion of a sense-datum as an illegitimate reification of the ways in which physical objects appear to us under different conditions of observation, then Moore's conclusion, though it follows from his premisses, is of no interest or importance.

Accordingly, let us look closely at the logic of the situation between Moore and the opponents of sense-data. We must begin by granting the point that 'S perceives something which appears *F* to him' does not entail 'S perceives a sense-datum which is *F*'. This inference is certainly fallacious. Moore, however, did not attempt to introduce sense-data by means of this or any other inference. Rather, as I have been at pains to emphasize, his procedure was an ostensive one. He said, in effect: "if you attend carefully to your experience while looking at the envelope from an angle you will really *see* a rhomboidal patch of color. Thus if you pay attention to your experience you will see for yourself that there are sense-data." To this the opponents of sense-data retort: "When I consult my experience all I see is a rectangular envelope that can be made to look or appear rhomboidal by viewing it from a certain angle. I do not see any object which really is rhomboidal." Our question is, how should we decide who is right here?

We cannot decide by evaluating some argument attempting to prove that there are sense-data, since no such argument has been offered. Nor have the critics made an attempt to disprove the existence of sense-data. Rather, they have offered an alternative way of describing the facts Moore appeals to, with the implication that theirs is the better or indeed the only correct way to describe those facts.

Can the matter then be settled by appealing to ordinary language? I do not think that it can, because ordinary language pulls both ways. On the one hand, it is quite natural to say that when one looks e.g. at a penny from an angle, all one sees is a round penny that looks elliptical from that angle; one doesn't see anything which *is* elliptical. On the other hand, it is certainly no misuse of language to insist that when I look at a penny from an angle, I see a brownish ellipse that gets fatter or skinnier depending on the angle. And it can be added that this ellipse surely exists since I see it. What is seen must exist. So the brownish ellipse exists, though it is not identical with the penny or its surface since that is round. All of this accords completely with the ordinary use of language.

Should the issue then be settled by appealing to Occam's razor? As many philosophers have pointed out, once sense-data are introduced certain puzzling questions arise about their nature. How does one count sense-data? How many sense-data do I see, for example, when I look at my hand? Do sense-data, like physical objects, "have surfaces, as well as parts which are behind or beneath these surfaces, and rear surfaces which face away?"[18] When a sense-datum is called 'elliptical' or 'brown' or 'small', do these terms have the same meanings as when they are applied to physical objects? In light of these puzzling questions, should we conclude that since introducing sense-data multiplies entities and difficulties beyond necessity, they ought not to be introduced?[19]

The appeal to Occam's razor is both relevant and important. However, it is not decisive. For in the first place, *some* of the puzzling questions about sense-data can reasonably be rejected by a resourceful sense-datum theorist. For example, A. J. Ayer argues effectively that any definite answer to the question as to how many sense-data one sees on a given occasion would, like a definite answer to certain questions about physical things, be arbitrary. The passage is worth quoting at some length.

How . . . are we to determine what is to count as one sense-datum? At the present moment it seems to me that I see the walls of a house, covered with virginia creeper, and a rose tree climbing to an open window, and two dogs asleep upon a terrace, and a lawn bespeckled with buttercups and clover, and many other things besides . . . How many visual . . . sense-data am I sensing? And at what point are they replaced by others? If one of the dogs seems to stir in its sleep does this create a new sense-datum for me or merely transform an old one? And if it is to be new, do all the others remain the same? Clearly the answers to these questions will be arbitrary; the appearance of the whole frontage of the house may be treated as one sense-datum, or it may be divided into almost any number . . . . The correct reply may, therefore, be that these questions do not admit of a definite answer, any more than there is a definite answer to the question how many parts a thing can have, or how much it can change without altering its identity.[20]

In the second place, there is a more fundamental reason why considerations of simplicity are not decisive here. Sense-data are introduced for a certain purpose; namely, to solve a fundamental problem concerning the relation between perception and knowledge. So if that problem can indeed be solved in this way, then the introduction of sense-data may well be justified despite the increased ontological complexity that results from it. Simplicity, here as elsewhere, is only one desideratum; another equally important desideratum is an answer to the very fundamental question how perception can be the source of knowledge we all take it to be. Considerations of simplicity may provide a good reason — perhaps even a decisive one — not to countenance sense-data if they cannot help answer this question. But if they can, then it may well be reasonable to countenance sense-data despite Occam's maxim (which counsels us not to multiply entities *unecessarily*).

Finally, the epistemological purpose of the sense-datum theory may itself provide a way to answer questions about the nature of sense-data that cannot reasonably be rejected. Concerning the question whether sense-data have rear surfaces or parts that face away, for example, Chisholm writes:

> It is important to realize that we cannot avoid such puzzling questions merely by redefining the word 'appearance'. We could define 'appearance' in such a way that we could say of any appearance, as Professor Price has said, that its goods "are entirely in the shop-window". We could define 'the appearance of a piece of coal' as being something which has just those attributes which the coal appears to have. And then, of course, we could be sure that the appearance of the coal doesn't have a rear surface or any parts which face away. But now we may ask of *a* — the something which is blue when the coal looks blue — whether *a is* an appearance, as just defined, of the piece of coal. And this question can be answered only by deciding whether *a* has a rear surface or any parts which 'face away'.[21]

It is quite true that whether *a* is an appearance (sense-datum) would depend upon whether it has a rear surface or parts that face away. But this does not mean that this question must be answered in a straightforward empirical manner, say in the way one would discover whether the other side of a coin was tarnished. For the question might be answered in the light of theoretical considerations related to the purpose of the sense-datum theory. Thus, suppose it turned out that we could account for the fact that perception yields knowledge only by supposing that color-patches such as those Moore describes do "have their goods entirely in the shop-window" and so do not have rear surfaces or parts that face away. Then we might justifiably conclude that *a* — the blue patch of color seen upon looking at the coal — does not have a rear surface or parts that face away.

I contend, then, that the only way of coming to a reasoned decision concerning sense-data is to determine whether they can provide a solution to the problem of perception and knowledge. Let us recall the general contours of the problem, as we have developed it so far, in order to see exactly how Moore's introduction of sense-data suggests a solution. On the one hand, it is obvious that perception is our fundamental way of acquiring factual knowledge. But on the other hand, when we attempt to formulate the conditions under which 'S perceives *x to be* F' implies 'S knows that *x* is *F*', we run into difficulty. For in the first place, we cannot simply equate perceiving *x* to be *F* with knowing that *x* is *F*, since it is possible to perceive *x* to be *F* though *x* is not *F*. Furthermore, we cannot equate perceiving *x* to be *F* under normal conditions of observation with knowing that x is F, even after having partially defined 'normal conditions' as those in which S wouldn't perceive x to be F unless x really were F. For S can know that x is F only if it is not at all accidental, coincidental, or lucky that S is right about x's being F. But even when the conditions of observation are normal, it is somewhat accidental or lucky that they are, and so that S is perceiving x as it really is; just as even when the abnormally fluctuating heat-sensitivity of the man we imagined earlier (in Chapter One, Section 2) happens to match that of an average perceiver at most times, it is accidental or lucky that it does, and so that he perceives the water's temperature accurately. Therefore, S can know that x is F by perceiving x to be F only if S *knows* that the conditions of observation are normal. But this requirement leads to a vicious regress. For the only way S can know that the conditions of observation are normal is by perceiving them to be normal. However, the chance that some abnormality in the conditions of observation is producing a perceptual error or an illusion attaches to S's perceiving the conditions of observation to be normal no less than to S's perceiving x to be F. So even if the conditions of observation under which S perceives the original conditions of observation to be normal are normal, it is somewhat accidental or lucky that they are, and so that S perceives the original conditions of observation as they really are. Therefore, S can know that the original conditions of observation are normal by perceiving them to be normal only if S *knows* that the conditions of observation under which he perceives the original conditions of observation to be normal are themselves normal. But S can know this only by still other perceptions, that themselves constitute knowledge only if S knows that they are occurring under normal conditions of observation, which S can know to be the case only by still other perceptions ... etc. *ad infinitum.*

This regress, as I argued in Section 3 of Chapter One, cannot be avoided by appealing to probability. Therefore it can be avoided only by preventing it from arising in the first place. But this cannot be done, compatibly with the principle that one cannot know something if it is partly a matter of luck that one is right about it, simply by resisting the requirement that the conditions of observation be known to be normal. Hence it can be done only by establishing that something can be known in a case of perception regardless of whether the conditions of observation are normal or abnormal.

But regardless of the conditions of observation, I can know that I am seeing a colored patch of the kind to which Moore calls attention. No matter what the light, the medium, the acuity of my vision, my angle of view etc. are, I can know by inspection that I am seeing "a patch of a particular whitish

color, having a certain size, and a certain shape . . . with rather sharp angles
or corners and bounded by fairly straight lines". Even if — to anticipate considerations to be introduced in subsequent chapters — I were suffering from a
hallucination and there were no envelope there at all, I could still know that I
was seeing this sense-datum. As Price put the same point in a famous passage:

When I see a tomato there is much that I can doubt. I can doubt whether it is a tomato
that I am seeing, and not a cleverly painted piece of wax. I can doubt whether there is
any material thing there at all. Perhaps what I took for a tomato was really a reflection;
perhaps I am even the victim of some hallucination. One thing however I cannot doubt:
that there exists a red patch of a round and somewhat bulgy shape, and having a certain
visual depth, and that this whole field of colour is directly present to my consciousness.
What this patch is, whether a substance, or a state of a substance, or an event, whether it
is physical or psychical or neither, are questions that we may doubt about. But that
something is red and round then and there I cannot doubt.[22]

Notice that it would not do to express what Price is here claiming to know
as 'I see a tomato which *looks* red, round, and bulgy'. For this would imply
that Price knows that what he is seeing is a *tomato*. But Price cannot know
that something is a tomato by perceiving it to be a tomato regardless of what
the conditions of observation are. For some abnormality in the conditions of
observation could cause him to perceive something to be a tomato though it
was not a tomato. In order to express what can be known by perception
regardless of the conditions of observation, the notion of a sense-datum or
something very like it must be employed: 'I see a red patch of a round and
somewhat bulgy shape . . .'

Unlike Price, Moore does not explicitly refer to what can or cannot be
doubted when he introduces sense-data. Nevertheless, suppose we interpret
Moore's question concerning 'what exactly . . . happens when (as we should
say) we *see* a material object', or what we 'actually see' upon looking at the
envelope, to mean: what do we see in such a way that we can *know* its nature
regardless of what the conditions of observation are? Then the answer cannot
be: an *envelope* which looks whitish and angular; since under certain conditions of observation one can perceive something to be an envelope though it
is not an envelope. At this point someone may say that it should be obvious
that *nothing at all* is ever seen in such a way that its nature can be known
regardless of whether the conditions of observation are normal or abnormal.
But if we accede to this, then we shall be unable to account for the fact that
perception is a source of knowledge, because of the regress that arises unless
something can be known by perception regardless of the conditions of
observation. So in accordance with our hypothesis that every method of

introducing sense-data seeks to avoid this regress by *assuming*, overtly or covertly, that every case of perceiving is a case of knowing, let we suppose that Moore is making this assumption. Then we can explain why he formulates the main premiss of his argument in terms of the concept of a sense-datum rather than in terms of the envelope's seeming, appearing, or looking whitish, angular, etc. The reason is that Moore intends to characterize something whose nature can be known by perception regardless of the conditions of observation; and that for this purpose he must like Price refer to colored patches or the like — to sense-data or something similar. Thus the Argument from Perceptual Relativity ultimately turns on the assumption that every case of perceiving is a case of knowing; or more precisely, of knowing the character of some *object*. As David Hamlyn puts it:

Moore does not explicitly say, as Price did, that the reason for invoking sense-data was that these are things over which there is no possibility of doubt. But his use of the phrase 'actually see' and the notion of 'direct apprehension' certainly suggests some such idea. Otherwise, why should not the members of the audience say that what they actually saw was an envelope? Why restrict the answer to something about patches of color? The only possible answer is that it might not have been an envelope after all, while there could be no doubt about patches of color.[23]

The assumption that every case of perceiving is a case of knowing also lies behind the second stage of the Argument, in which the inference is made from 'not all the sense-data belonging to a physical thing or surface are identical with the thing or surface' to 'none of the sense-data belonging to a physical thing or surface are identical with the thing or surface'. The premiss on which this inference is made to rest — that if some though not all the sense-data belonging to a physical thing or surface are identical with the thing or surface, then there must be a special, discernible qualitative difference between the sense-data that are identical with the thing or surface and those that are not — has been vigorously attacked by J. L. Austin.

[I]f ... I had never seen a mirror, but were told (*a*) that in mirrors one sees reflections of things, and (*b*) that reflections of things are not 'generically the same' as things, is there any reason why I should forthwith *expect* there to be some whacking big 'qualitative' difference between seeing things and seeing their reflections? Plainly not; if I were prudent, I should simply wait and see what seeing reflections was like. If I am told that a lemon is generically different from a piece of soap, do I 'expect' that no piece of soap could look just like a lemon? Why should I? ... [W]hy on earth should it not be the case that, in some few instances, perceiving one sort of thing is exactly like perceiving another?[24]

Austin is right: there is no reason why different kinds of things cannot be qualitatively alike or even indistinguishable. But Austin misses the underlying point. Suppose that in a case of perception P the sense-datum d is perceived, and that we do identify d with the physical thing or surface to which it belongs. Then we deprive d of the epistemological function which provides the sole reason for introducing sense-data; for no physical thing or surface is such that its nature can be known by perception regardless of the conditions of observation. Therefore P, contrary to the assumption that in every case of perceiving something can be known, is not a case of knowing. This result would be avoided only if d had some special perceptible feature signaling that unlike the other sense-data belonging to the thing or surface it was both (a) identical with the thing or surface yet (b) such that its nature could be known merely by perceiving it, regardless of the conditions under which it was perceived — a feature which would necessarily distinguish it from all the other sense-data belonging to the thing or surface. Pointing to the lack of a special qualitative difference among the sense-data belonging to a physical thing or surface is a way of pointing out that none of these sense-data do have such a distinguishing feature. I shall have more to say about the principle that generically different things must be qualitatively different in Chapter Four in connection with the Argument from Hallucination, which turns on this principle.

How, in light of the foregoing discussion, should we assess the Argument from Perceptual Relativity? The argument shows, I believe, that we *can* describe our perceptual experience in terms of perceiving (or sensing) sense-data, that this is a possible way of describing what we perceive.[25] But it does not show that we *must* introduce sense-data or even that we *should* do so. For the phenomenon of perceptual relativity can be described just as well in terms of physical things' appearing to us in various ways under different conditons. Thus, whether sense-data should be introduced turns on the broader implications of the sense-datum theory. Introducing sense-data does make it possible to maintain that something can be known in every case of perceiving regardless of the conditions of observation. This seems to be an advantage given the regress that arises otherwise. But this advantage could yet turn out to be illusory. For the objects about which such knowledge can be had — sense-data — are not the physical things and events in our environment. But what an adequate solution to the problem of perception and knowledge must do, after all, is to show how perception can provide the kind of knowledge we all think it does provide: knowledge of the physical world. Can the sense-datum theory help to show this? In other words, can knowledge of the physical world be based upon or derived from knowledge of sense-data? It is to this traditional question that we must turn in order to come to a reasoned decision concerning the sense-datum theory.

Before turning to this question, however, I want to examine two other classical arguments for the introduction of sense-data: the Argument from Causation and the Argument from Hallucination. I shall try to show that both of these arguments, like the Argument from Perceptual Relativity, beg the question if they are interpreted as attempts to *prove* that there are sense-data. We shall also see that these two arguments draw attention to another dimension of the *problem* of perception and knowledge.

NOTES

[1] Three classic presentations of the argument are Plato, *Theaetetus*, 152ff; Berkeley, *Three Dialogues Between Hylas and Philonous*, the First Dialogue; Bertrand Russell, *The Problems of Philosophy*, Chapter I. I analyze Berkeley's argument in 'Two Arguments from Perceptual Relativity in Berkeley's Dialogues Between Hylas and Philonous', (unpublished).

[2] The lecture was first delivered by Moore in 1910. But *Some Main Problems of Philosophy* did not appear until 1953, at which time Moore, apart from some minor changes in the characterization of sense-data (signaled in his footnotes), still held to the sense-datum theory.

[3] G. E. Moore, *Some Main Problems of Philosophy* (Collier Books, New York, 1966), p. 44.

[4] Compare H. H. Price, *Perception* (Methuen, London, 1932), pp. 18–19.

[5] G. E. Moore, *Some Main Problems of Philosophy*, p. 45.

[6] *Some Main Problems of Philosophy*, pp. 44, 46.

[7] *Some Main Problems of Philosophy*, p. 46.

[8] *Some Main Problems of Philosophy*, p. 46–47.

[9] *Some Main Problems of Philosophy*, pp. 52–53.

[10] See H. H. Price, *Perception*, pp. 31–32; A. J. Ayer, *The Foundations of Empirical Knowledge* (MacMillan, London, 1940), pp. 5–8, and Ayer, *The Problem of Knowledge* (Penguin Books, London, 1956), p. 88.

[11] Price, *Perception*, p. 32; Ayer, *The Foundations of Empirical Knowledge*, pp. 8–9.

[12] Price, *Perception*, p. 32.

[13] Initially I confine my evaluation of the argument to its first stage. At the end of the section I shall discuss the second stage, in which the move is made from the O proposition that "not all the sense-data belonging to a physical thing or surface are identical with that thing or surface" [(3), above], to the E proposition that "none of the sense-data belonging to a physical thing or surface are identical with that thing or surface" [(6), above].

[14] J. L. Austin, *Sense and Sensibilia* (Oxford University Press, New York, 1962), p. 28.

[15] Gilbert Ryle, *The Concept of Mind* (Barnes & Noble, New York, 1949), pp. 216-218.

[16] R. M. Chisholm, *Perceiving: A Philosophical Study* (Cornell University Press, Ithaca, 1957), pp. 151–152. See also Chisholm's *Person and Object: A Metaphysical Study* (George Allen & Unwin, London, 1976), pp. 47–48.

[17] Winston H. F. Barnes, 'The Myth of Sense-Data', p. 153. Reprint in R. J. Swartz (ed.), *Perceiving, Sensing, and Knowing* (University of California Press, Los Angeles, 1976), pp. 138–167.

[18] R. M. Chisholm, *Perceiving*, p. 119.

[19] R. M. Chisholm, *Theory of Knowledge* (Prentice-Hall, Englewood Cliffs, 1966), p.95.

[20] A. J. Ayer, *The Problem of Knowledge*, pp. 109–110.

[21] R. M. Chisholm, *Perceiving*, pp. 119–120.

[22] Price, *Perception*, p. 3.

[23] D. W. Hamlyn, *The Theory of Knowledge* (Doubleday & Company, Inc., Garden City, New York, 1970), p. 156.

[24] J. L. Austin, *Sense and Sensibilia*, pp. 50, 52.

[25] For some doubts about this, see O. K. Bouwsma, 'Moore's Theory of Sense-Data', reprinted in G. J. Warnock (ed.), *The Philosophy of Perception* (Oxford University Press, 1967), pp. 8–24. Bouwsma argues that Moore fails to make clear how to pick out sense-data within one's experience. However, Bouwsma addresses himself to a brief passage in Moore's 'Defense of Common Sense'. I can only say that in the much fuller discussion of sense-data in *Some Main Problems of Philosophy*, Moore seems to me to make the matter sufficiently clear.

CHAPTER THREE

THE ARGUMENT FROM CAUSATION

In this chapter I shall consider the main 'scientific' argument for the introduction of sense-data, the argument from Causation. I shall try to show that the argument has force only insofar as it is really an *epistemological* argument, and that its force derives from its calling attention to a dimension of the epistemological problem of perception that we have so far not considered.

1. SOME INEFFECTIVE VERSIONS OF THE ARGUMENT

The starting point of the argument is that perception requires an extremely complex causal chain from the stimulus-object to the perceiver's brain. In visual perception, for example, the stimulus-object reflects light of a certain frequency into the eyes of the perceiver, causing certain chemical changes in the retina, which in turn cause nervous impulses to travel up the optic nerve so that the visual areas of the cerebral cortex are affected, at which point the perceiver finally has the visual experience which we call 'seeing the object'. This is, of course, the merest sketch of what happens in visual perception; at each stage of the process, there occur many complicated changes which are by no means completely understood by modern neurophysiology. However, the specific nature of these changes is, except in some variants of the argument to be mentioned presently, irrelevant to its logic. For certain important conclusions are supposed to follow simply from the fact that perception requires a very complicated causal chain from the stimulus-object to the perceiver's brain, regardless of the specific nature of the links in the chain.

What, if anything, does follow from this fact? Well, it is sometimes inferred that the perceiver does not really perceive the stimulus-object. The fact that the object is at the far end of a causal chain terminating in the perceiver's brain is supposed to show that the object is not really perceived at all. But this is an absurd conclusion to draw from the facts cited. For these facts constitute a causal explanation of *how* we are able to perceive the physical things stimulating our sense-receptors. To take these facts as proving that we cannot really perceive those things is therefore absurd. It is to take the explanation of a thing as a proof of the impossibility of that very thing. Why

47

should perceiving X require the absence of the very things that make it possible to perceive X?

Sometimes certain specific causal facts about perception are singled out as being especially significant. For example, it is pointed out that light and sound waves transmitted from objects to the eyes and ears are very different from the nervous impulses which convey the stimuli to the brain, and that these impulses are themselves much more alike or homogeneous (differing primarily in the paths they take) than the various colors, sounds, smells etc. we say we perceive.[1] But what this shows is that the perceptual process has complicated aspects of which we are unaware in perception. It does not follow that we do not really see the colors and hear the sounds we think we do; anymore than it follows from the fact that the process of understanding a sentence has complicated aspects of which we are unaware that we do not really understand the sentence.

Again, the facts that perception does not occur until a measurable (though usually very small) interval of time after light or sound waves are emitted from an object, and that sometimes it even occurs after the object (e.g. a distant star) has ceased to exist, are cited as proof that we do not really perceive the things we think we do. Indeed, these facts have been regarded by distinguished philosophers such as Bertrand Russell and A. O. Lovejoy as providing an important, independent argument proving that we can never perceive the physical things in our environment. Although this 'Time-Gap' or 'Time-Lag' Argument is an interesting one, I shall not discuss it at length; for it has been well discussed in recent literature and is in any case unsound.[2] It is unsound because the scientific considerations concerning the finite speed of light etc. to which it appeals can validly yield the desired conclusion only if they are combined with a premiss expressing some version of the idea that perception must be simultaneous with its object, e.g. with the premiss (*a*) that we cannot perceive a thing in a state in which it *was* an instant (or longer) before we perceived it, or (*b*) that we can perceive a thing only if it exists at the time we perceive it. But the conclusion of a logically valid argument can be rejected if the premisses from which it is deduced are false; and what the relevant scientific facts show is simply that (*a*), (*b*) and other premisses expressing the same basic idea are false. Yet any version of the time-gap argument, no matter how subtly formulated, must employ some such premiss.

The conclusion which is most commonly drawn from the fact that perception involves a complex causal chain is that the objects stimulating our sense-receptors are not *immediately* perceived. The main difficulty that arises in evaluating this inference concerns the meaning of its conclusion. The key term, 'immediately perceived', (or some cognate such as 'directly perceived') is typically introduced into the argument without any prior explanation, as though its meaning were already clear. But, as ordinary-language philosophers have insisted *ad nauseam*, the meaning of this term is obscure.[3] Thus, the first step toward an adequate appraisal of the Argument from Causation is to explain the meaning of its conclusion, that physical things are never immediately perceived. In the absence of such an explanation, that conclusion's meaning must be elicited entirely from the premiss from which it is derived; namely, that perception requires a complex causal chain from the object to the perceiver's brain. But then, since the notion of immediate perception has been given no sense independent of that premiss, the argument collapses into triviality. From the premiss that

> Perceiving a physical thing requires a complex causal chain from the thing to the perceiver's brain

the conclusion is drawn that

> No physical thing is ever immediately perceived

But when we ask what this conclusion means, the only answer forthcoming is

> No physical thing is ever perceived except by means of a very complex causal chain from the thing to the perceiver's brain

which is equivalent to the premiss. So the argument reduces to the triviality that:

> Perceiving a physical thing requires a complex causal chain from the thing to the perceiver's brain.

∴   Perceiving a physical thing requires a complex causal chain from the thing to the perceiver's brain.

To see that the difficulty I am here raising is not a merely fictitious one, consider a couple of sample passage from the literature. R. J. Hirst writes:

Perception cannot be the direct contact or immediate confrontation with an external object it seems to be, since it requires this causal chain from object to the percipient's brain and is prevented if that is interrupted. Directness or immediacy, in this context, must mean no intermediary, no possibility of interruption, as well as no inference.[4]

What does the conclusion that "perception cannot be [a] direct contact or immediate confrontation with an external object . . ." mean? Well, it seems to mean nothing more than the premiss that "[Perception] requires this causal chain from object to the percipient's brain and is prevented if that is interrupted". But then the argument collapses into the redundancy that since perception requires this causal chain from object to the percipient's brain, therefore it requires this causal chain from object to the percipient's brain. Again, consider the following passage by D. M. Armstrong:

The argument [from Causation] bases itself on the scientific discovery that, before we can perceive anything, a chain of processes must begin in the object, travel through our sense-organs, and reach the brain . . . . Until these complex processes occur, perception cannot occur. It is inferred from this that there can be no *immediate* perception of the physical object or happening we say is perceived. The only possible *immediate* object of perception is the last link in the chain of processes. This last link is usually identified with a sense-impression whose immediate cause is a happening in the brain. [Armstrong's emphasis] [5]

This passage, on examination, also seems to be adumbrating a tautology — indeed, two tautologies. For saying that there can be no immediate perception of the physical object or happening seems to be a way of repeating in different words that there can be no perception of the object or happening unless certain complex processes beginning in the object and terminating in the brain have occurred. And no sense has been given to the conclusion that the only possible *immediate* object of perception is the last link in the chain of processes except that it — the *last* link in the chain — is the only thing that can be the *last* link in the chain.

Perhaps the best way to dispel the illusion that the conclusion that physical things are not immediately perceived takes us somewhere beyond the premiss that physical things are not perceived without a complex causal chain is to ask: what is the conclusion supposed to *contrast* with, i.e. what would perceiving a physical thing 'immediately' or 'directly' consist in? Would it consist in perceiving the thing *without* there being a complex causal chain from it to the brain? How simple then must the causal chain be? Or would it consist in perceiving the thing without there being *any* causal chain from it to the perceiver? In that case, one should be able to perceive physical things without the benefit of sense-organs or a nervous system!

One quite common definition of 'immediately perceived' is 'perceived without any inference'. As Berkeley makes Hylas say at the beginning of the First Dialogue: ". . . in truth the senses perceive nothing which they do not perceive immediately, for they make no inferences".[6] Now Hylas is supposed to be a fairly unsophisticated thinker, who must certainly not be assumed to be familiar with the fine points of Berkeley's theory of perception at the outset of the *Dialogues*. Accordingly, his statement should be understood in the most obvious and straightforward way, as making a point of introspective psychology or phenomenology. Hylas means that sense-perception has a characteristic immediacy that sets it off from reasoning or inferring. Thus the notion of immediate perception Hylas is invoking can be defined as follows, where the subscript 'p' indicates that the notion being defined is a psychological one:

X is immediately perceived$_p$ = $_{df}$ X is perceived without going through any process of reasoning or performing any (conscious) inference.

It is important to note that given this meaning for 'immediately perceived', Hylas's statement, that whatever is perceived by the senses is immediately perceived, is *true*. In sense-perception as such there is no experienced movement from any data to a conclusion, nor any conscious transition from sign to signified. (Compare for example seeing George across the field with inferring that it is George who is across the field from the color of his shirt, or seeing a ship move with inferring that it has moved from its altered position relative to a fixed object.) As Chisholm has recently put the same point:

. . . surely no perceiver, on opening his eyes in the morning, can be said to 'infer' that he is surrounded by familiar objects . . . . Use of the technical psychological terms 'unconscious inference' and 'interpretation', in this context, serves only to obscure the fact that perceiving is *not* an inference, in the ordinary sense of the word 'inference'.[7]

Since, then, whatever is perceived by the senses is immediately perceived$_p$, it follows that *if* a philosophical argument proved that physical things are never immediately perceived$_p$, that argument would also prove the paradoxical conclusion that physical objects are never perceived by the senses at all. This point, as we shall see in Section 3, and in Chapter Five, Section 3, lies behind certain serious errors in the philosophy of perception. For the time being, however, it will be sufficient to establish that the Argument from Causation certainly does not prove that physical things are not immediately perceived$_p$. The fact that perceiving a physical thing requires a complex causal chain from the thing to the perceiver's brain obviously does not show that the thing cannot be perceived without performing an inference or going through some process of reasoning. Indeed, these matters are quite unrelated, especially since the complex mechanisms of perception are unknown to most of us. In any case, we certainly do not infer that our surroundings contain various physical things from premisses about what is happening in our sense-organs, nervous system, and cerebral cortex. Defenders of the scientific argument are themselves fond of *contrasting* the complexity of the mechanisms involved in perceiving with the phenomenological immediacy of perceiving. As one proponent of the argument puts it

What natural philosophy and anatomy therefore show is that our sense organs play a different and more complicated role in the process of perception than we directly experience them as playing. In order that we should perceive external objects these organs must themselves be affected, and must then transmit physical effects. . . . However, it is to be noted that it does take inquiry . . . to establish such a causal chain: direct experience frequently seems to suggest the contrary notion, that our senses are like open windows and doors through which the outside world makes direct contact with our minds.[8]

It would be quite *inconsistent* for a philosopher who appreciates this contrast to argue that since perceiving a physical thing requires a complex causal chain, physical things are not immediately perceived$_p$. For his position is rather that *despite* the fact that perceiving a physical thing requires a complex causal chain, physical things *are* immediately perceived$_p$.

In summary, then, the fact that perception requires a complex causal chain does not show that we cannot really perceive the physical things that stimulate our sense-receptors; nor have we found any non-trivial meaning for 'immediately perceived' on which it shows that we cannot immediately perceive those things. I suggest that nothing of philosophical interest follows from the sole premiss that perception requires a complex causal chain.

2. AN EPISTEMOLOGICAL VERSION OF THE ARGUMENT

There is more to the Argument from Causation, however, than fallacious attempts to draw philosophical conclusions from the premiss that perception requires a complex causal chain from the stimulus-object to the perceiver's brain. Proponents of the argument frequently make a point that I have not yet mentioned. This is that the stimulus-object is not causally required for the perceiver to have the kind of perceptual experience that it produces by stimulating his sense-receptors. For an exactly similar experience could be caused by producing any of the intermediate members of the causal chain in some other manner, say by electrically stimulating the optic nerve or even the brain itself. Thus, for example, the page now in front of you is not causally required for you to have the kind of visual experiences you are having as you look at it; experiences which you could not distinguish from these could be produced though there were no page stimulating your eyes, by producing in some other manner one of the intermediate links in the causal chain between the page and your brain. To put the point generally, any perceptual experience can be duplicated though no physical thing is stimulating the appropriate sense-receptors, by producing in some other way one of the intermediate members of the causal chain that terminates in that experience. After all, this is precisely what happens in a realistic hallucination: some disturbance in the nervous system produces an experience which is normally caused by some physical thing(s) stimulating the sense-receptors. This point was very clearly (if somewhat archaically) put by Descartes in his *Meditations*.

... [I]n the cord ABCD (which is in tension) if we pull the last part D, the first part A will not be moved in any way differently from what would be the case if one of the intervening parts B or C were pulled, and the last part D were to remain unmoved. And in the same way, when I feel pain in my foot, my knowledge of physics teaches me that this sensation is communicated by means of nerves dispersed through the foot, which, being extended like cords from there to the brain, when they are contracted in the foot, at the same time contract the inmost portions of the brain which is their extremity and place of origin, and there excite a certain movement which nature has established in order to cause the mind to be affected by a sensation of pain represented as existing in the foot. But because these nerves must pass through the tibia, the thigh, the loins, the back and the neck, in order to reach from the leg to the brain, it may happen that although their extremities which are in the foot are not affected, but only certain ones of their intervening parts (which pass by the loins or the neck), this action will excite the same movement in the brain that might have been excited there by a hurt received in the foot, in consequence of which the mind will necessarily feel in the foot the same pain as if it had received a hurt. And the same holds good of all the other perceptions of our senses.[9]

Let us express the point to which Descartes is calling attention in the following proposition:

(1)   In order for a perceiver to have any given perceptual experience, it is not necessary that there be a physical thing stimulating his sense-receptors.

From this proposition it is supposed to follow that

No physical thing is ever immediately perceived.

However, this conclusion obviously does not follow from (1) alone. In order to derive the conclusion from (1), certain other propositions must be used as premisses. Let us try to supply these additional premisses.

We may begin by noting that premiss (1) raises an epistemological question. If in order for a person to have a given perceptual experience it is not necessary that there be a physical thing stimulating his sense-receptors, then how on any given occasion can the person *know* that he is really perceiving a physical thing? If the only condition which is necessary for any given perceptual experience to occur is (direct) stimulation of the person's brain, then how can he know that certain other, specific factors (such as stimulation of his sense-receptors by a physical thing) are at the origin of the causal chain leading to his present experience? For example, how can you know that the cause of the visual experiences you are now having is a sheet of paper, since your visual experiences could be exactly the same if there were no sheet of paper, provided your brain were being stimulated in a certain way? It seems that the only thing you can know on the basis of your present visual experience alone is that you are having that experience, and perhaps also that certain events are taking place in your brain. But of course this does not show that there is a sheet of paper in front of you reflecting light into your eyes: you could be having the very same kind of visual experience due to some abnormal condition of your nervous system, drugs, or even direct stimulation of your brain. Accordingly, we may add as a second premiss:

(2)   If (1), then no perceiver can know solely on the basis of a given perceptual experience that he is really perceiving a physical thing.

In other words, if any given perceptual experience can be duplicated though no physical thing is stimulating the appropriate sense-receptors, then the subject cannot possibly know *solely* on the basis of a given perceptual experience that he is really perceiving a physical thing.[10]

The conclusion that physical things are never immediately perceived still does not follow from the premisses given. Moreover, it is difficult to think of any considerations not already discussed that would link premisses (1) and (2) to this conclusion, because we still have no suitable definition of 'immediately perceived' to guide us in constructing the argument. (Premisses (1) and (2) plainly bear no relation to whether physical things are immediately perceived in the purely psychological sense defined in the previous section.) Accordingly, let us complete the argument by adding the simplest premiss that will serve to connect premisses (1) and (2) with the desired conclusion. This is

(3)   If no perceiver can know solely on the basis of a given perceptual experience that he is really perceiving a physical thing, then no physical thing is ever immediately perceived.

Premisses (1), (2), and (3) now validly yield the conclusion that

(4)   No physical thing is ever immediately perceived.

But what does this conclusion mean? What is being asserted when we are told that we never *immediately* perceive, say, a chair? In the absence of a suitable definition of 'immediately perceived', our only clue to the meaning of this conclusion lies as before in the premisses from which it is deduced. This time, however, the conclusion does not simply repeat in different words that perceiving a physical thing requires a complex causal chain from the thing to the perceiver's brain. For the point on which the argument now turns is rather that the last member of the causal chain — e.g. the visual experience associated with seeing a chair — can occur even when the first member of the chain, the chair, is absent. But the only thing that follows from this is that having this visual experience does not by itself amount to knowing that one is really seeing a chair — a point which already follows from (1) and (2) and whose generalization is expressed by the antecedent of (3). It appears, therefore, that the consequent of (3) does not differ significantly in meaning from its antecedent, i.e. that (3) is an analytic proposition establishing a meaning-connection between its antecedent and its consequent. In other words, it appears that in this argument the term 'immediately perceived' functions as an epistemological one, which may be correctly applied only to whatever objects (if any) *can* be known solely on the basis of a given perceptual experience.

This hypothesis is confirmed when we remember what the ultimate purpose of the Argument from Causation is: to support the introduction of sense-data. We know from previous discussion that a sense-datum is supposed to be an object whose nature can be known simply by perceiving the sense-datum, provided only that one is attentive to one's perceptual experience and able to apply the requisite concept. Accordingly, one part of the definition of 'X is immediately perceived' ought to be that x is perceived in such a way that its nature can be known solely on the basis of a given perceptual experience. But this is not all. For the conclusion of the Argument from Causation means that the *existence* of a physical thing cannot be known solely on the basis of a given perceptual experience; since the nerve of the argument is that the physical thing is not necessary in order to account for the experience. Therefore, the other part of the definition of 'X is immediately perceived' ought to be that X is perceived in such a way that its existence *can* be known solely on the basis of a given perceptual experience. Indeed, when we said earlier that sense-data such as Moore's colored patches are supposed to be objects whose nature can be known simply by perceiving them, we were certainly assuming that their existence is also supposed to be knowable simply by perceiving them. Let us accordingly adopt the following definition of an *epistemological* notion of immediate perception:

> X is immediately perceived$_e$ = $_{df}$ X is perceived in such a way that its existence and nature can be known solely on the basis of a given perceptual experience.

Given this epistemological meaning for 'immediately perceived', I submit that the Argument from Causation is not only a formally valid, but also a sound argument, for the conclusion that physical things are never immediately perceived. Simply put, the fact that any given perceptual experience had by perceiving a physical object can be duplicated though there is no physical object stimulating the appropriate sense-receptors does prove that one cannot know, *solely on the basis of a given perceptual experience*, that there exists a certain physical object in one's environment.

However, this is a purely negative conclusion. How does one get from this conclusion to the positive thesis that sense-data are immediately perceived? Well, the argument would presumably continue as follows:

(5)   If no physical thing is ever immediately perceived, then sense-data are immediately perceived.

(6)   Sense-data are immediately perceived. (from (4) and (5) by *Modus Ponens*)

But premiss (5) is obviously questionable. For it says that if physical things are not perceived in such a way that their existence and nature can be known solely on the basis of a given perceptual experience, then objects of another kind — i.e. sense-data — are perceived in this special manner. But why should we accept the idea that *any* objects are perceived in such a way that their existence and nature can be known solely on the basis of a given perceptual experience? That there are such immediate objects of perception is simply *assumed* in premiss (5) — quite gratuitously it might seem. Here again, then, we find the characteristic pattern of arguments for the introduction of sense-data: their premisses imply that perceiving is never a sufficient condition for knowledge concerning physical things, yet also assert that perceiving is a sufficient condition for knowledge of *some* object. In the present case this assertion is packed into the assumption that there are objects which are immediately perceived$_e$ — an assumption which is virtually identical with the affirmation of the sense-datum theory itself.

We have already discussed at length the grounds for this assumption: Unless *something* can be known merely by perceiving, it is difficult to see how perception can be the source of knowledge we all take it to be, because of the vicious regress that arises concerning knowledge of the conditions of observation. However, the Argument from Causation adds a new dimension to the problem of perception and knowledge. The negative conclusion (4) threatens, in a way that we have not yet considered, our fundamental conviction that perception is a source of knowledge. For it implies that perceiving a physical thing x to be F does not even amount to knowing that x *exists*, since one's perceptual experience could be exactly similar if x did not exist (in which case, of course, one would not really be perceiving x nor, *a fortiori*, be perceiving x to be F, but only seeming to perceive x). This is a more radical difficulty than the one we have discussed so far; namely that perceiving a physical thing x to be F does not amount, even when the conditions of observation are normal, to knowing that it is F. For while the latter difficulty concerns knowledge of x's properties, the former pertains to knowledge of x's very existence. In the light of this new difficulty, premiss (5) is not the gratuitous assumption it may seem to be. Let us see why this is so.

There is a very natural way to respond to the threat presented by (4). This is to concede that while it is of course true that perceiving a physical thing at a given time does not by itself provide knowledge of the thing's existence or nature, it ultimately does yield such knowledge provided that the original case of perception is corroborated by others. After all, if there is any doubt whether I really see a chair, then the obvious way to resolve that doubt is to corroborate my visual perception by touching the chair, obtaining other views of it, hearing other persons say that they see it too, and so forth. Initially, this may seem to take the sting out of (4). For is there really anything surprising about the fact that a given case of perception, considered in isolation from other cases of perception, does not amount to knowledge of the existence and nature of any physical thing? Of course not. Only a little reflection is needed to show that it is only by means of a set of successive perceptions that we can go from what Price calls 'perceptual acceptance' (on first seeing a chair I spontaneously accept the fact that there is a chair before me) to 'perceptual assurance' (on obtaining other views of the chair, touching it, etc. I come to know, or in any case to believe rationally, that there is a chair before me).[11]

However, it is this very appeal to corroborating perceptions that seems to require the introduction of sense-data. The reason is that a corroborating perception must itself constitute knowledge of some sort. We cannot possibly corroborate anything by appealing to something we do not know. Consider an analogy. Suppose a scientist were to claim that the results of an experiment he performed were corroborated by the results of a similar experiment performed in a different laboratory. But when asked what the results of this other experiment were, suppose the scientist conceded that he did not know what they were. This would obviously be absurd. One experiment cannot corroborate another for a scientist unless he knows what the results of the corroborating experiment are. Likewise, one case of perception cannot corroborate another for a perceiver unless he knows *something* by means of the corroborating perception. Otherwise that perception is simply a surd which cannot possibly serve to corroborate anything. But what then is known by means of the corroborating perception? Well, what is known by means of the corroborating perception cannot be that some physical thing(s) or event(s) exists and has certain properties. For the epistemological version of the Argument from Causation that we have developed applies to any case of perception, and so to the corroborating perception(s) as well as the original perception. The perceptual experience had in the corroborating case of perception can, just as easily as the one had in the original case of perception, be duplicated though no physical thing is stimulating the appropriate sense-receptors. The upshot is that we are threatened by a new vicious regress: a case of perception P can yield knowledge only if it is corroborated by another case of perception P_1, but P_1 can corroborate P only if P_1 is itself corroborated by another case of perception P_2, but P_2 can corroborate P_1 only if P_2 is in turn corroborated by still another case of perception P_3, and so on *ad infinitum*. How, then, can sense-perception be the source of knowledge we all take it to be?

It is at this point that the sense-datum theorist enters the picture. He says, in effect, the following: There is a kind of knowledge yielded by every case of perception despite the fact that no such case amounts to knowing the existence or nature of any physical thing. This knowledge, which can really be had by any case of perception independently of all other cases of perception, is knowledge of the existence and nature of certain sense-data. The Argument from Perceptual Relativity showed that we can pick out such immediate objects of perception within our own perceptual experience, and to some extent also elucidated their nature. So the thesis that we immediately perceive sense-data is an intelligible one. Furthermore, in light of the vicious regress generated by (4), we have just found further reason to think that the sense-datum theory is the only way to justify our fundamental conviction that perception is a source of knowledge. Therefore this theory acquires a new measure of attractiveness. And this is why premiss (5) of the Argument from Causation, though it is not an obvious truth and has not been proved, is by no means a purely gratuitous or arbitrary assumption.

The Argument from Causation, then, does not, anymore than the Argument from Perceptual Relativity, *prove* that there are sense-data. Interpreted in that manner it is simply question-begging. Rather, the function of the argument is to present opponents of the sense-datum theory with the following by-now familiar challenge: if you deny that there are sense-data, then you will be unable to justify our fundamental conviction that perception is a source of knowledge. Accordingly, the appropriate response to the argument is (as the criterion for evaluating the sense-datum theory advocated in the final section of the previous chapter implies) the counterchallenge: *Show* that the sense-datum theory can explain how perception yields the kind of knowledge we all believe it does yield, namely knowledge of the physical world. For only if the sense-datum theory can perform this function should premiss (5) of the Argument from Causation, and the conclusion it allows us to deduce, be accepted.

3. PSYCHOLOGICAL AND EPISTEMIC IMMEDIACY: A CRUCIAL DISTINCTION

I have argued that if the Argument from Causation is interpreted as an attempt to demonstrate that there are sense-data, then it simply begs the question. If this is correct, then it should be somewhat surprising that the argument *has* generally been understood in that way both by its defenders and its detractors. In this section, I shall put forward a hypothesis to explain why the argument has been so interpreted.

No doubt part of the explanation is that philosophers and scientists have been taken in by the fallacious versions of the argument criticized in Sec. 1 of this chapter. But I believe that there is also another, more interesting reason. This is that philosophers who use the term 'immediately perceive' (or any of its cognates, such as 'directly perceive') have conflated two different meanings of that term. One is the epistemological meaning defined in the previous section, on which 'X is immediately perceived' means 'X is perceived in such a way that its existence and nature can be known solely on the basis of a given perceptual experience' ('immediately perceived$_e$'). The other is the psychological meaning defined in Section 1, on which 'X is immediately perceived' means 'X is perceived without going through any process of reasoning or performing any (conscious) inference' ('immediately perceived$_p$').

We shall see that the epistemological meaning is of fundamental importance in the philosophy of perception. Indeed, I have already shown that 'immediately perceived' must be understood in the epistemological sense in order to make good sense of the Argument from Causation; this both reveals the epistemological nature of this 'scientific' argument and supports my general interpretation of the sense-datum theory and its supporting arguments. And in the following chapter, I shall show that the Argument from Hallucination also turns on the epistemological notion of immediate perception. The psychological notion, on the other hand, would not be very important for the philosophy of perception, had it not been persistently conflated (at least since Berkeley, and I think largely as a result of his influence) with the epistemological one.[12] Specifically, the conflation has taken the form of assuming that psychological immediacy is a *sufficient* condition for epistemic immediacy, i.e. of assuming that:

(A)   For any x, if x is immediately perceived$_p$, then x is immediately perceived$_e$.

This assumption has led, as we shall see, to a number of serious errors in the philosophy of perception. And among these errors, as I shall now show, is the idea that the Argument from Causation proves that there are sense-data.

To see how (A) can make the Argument from Causation look like a proof that there are sense-data, let us first note that it follows from (A), by contraposition and by letting 'x' range over physical things, that:

(B)   If no physical thing is ever immediately perceived$_e$, then no physical thing is ever immediately perceived$_p$.

Now (B), in conjunction with the negative conclusion drawn in step (4) of the Argument from Causation to (to wit, that no physical thing is ever immediately perceived$_e$), entails that:

(C)   No physical thing is ever immediately perceived$_p$.

But (C) readily leads to the view that there must be sense-data. To see this, let us recall Hylas's claim that:

(D)   Whatever is perceived by the senses is immediately perceived$_p$.[13]

This proposition, as we noted in Section 1 above, is true. Sense-perception does have a characteristic immediacy that sets it off from reasoning or inferring. This is a purely phenomenological point about perceiving, one which holds true true regardless of the epistemological status of perception and the metaphysical status of its objects. It follows from (D), however, that:

(E)   If nothing is immediately perceived$_p$, then nothing is perceived by the senses.

Now the consequent of (E) is simply too incredible to be believed: surely perception, even if it does not necessarily amount to knowledge of its objects, *has* objects. In other words, we can hardly deny that:

(F)   Something is perceived by the senses.

Now it is a tautological truth that:

(G)   If no physical thing is ever immediately perceived$_p$, then either objects of some other kind are immediately perceived$_p$ or nothing is immediately perceived$_p$.

But it follows from (E), (F), and (G) that:

(H)   If no physical thing is ever immediately perceived$_p$, then objects of some other kind are immediately perceived$_p$.

In other words, if physical things are never immediately perceived$_p$, then it appears that we must introduce some alternative objects of immediate perception$_p$ in order to avoid the patent absurdity that we never perceive *anything* by our senses. But what kind of objects would these be? Well, they can very plausibly be identified with sense-data, because sense-data appear to be the only objects other than physical things that we can actually find or pick out within our perceptual experience. Thus, it seems reasonable to maintain that:

(I)   If objects of some other kind (i.e. of some kind other than physical things) are immediately perceived$_p$, then sense-data are immediately perceived$_p$.

But now, it follows from (C), (H), and (I) that:

(J)   Sense-data are immediately perceived$_p$,

from which it follows that:

(K)   There are sense-data.

The upshot is that if one assumes that psychological immediacy is a sufficient condition for epistemic immediacy, then the Argument from Causation takes on the appearance of an acceptable proof that there are sense-data.

But this appearance is a specious one, because the assumption in question is false. One instructive way of showing this is to show that (B) implies something which is obviously false, and so must itself be false, in which case (A) is false too, since it implies (B). For the sake of perspicuity, let us begin by rewriting (B) with each occurrence of 'immediately perceived' replaced by its appropriate *definiens*. This yields:

(B)   If no physical thing is ever perceived in such a way that its existence and nature can be known solely on the basis of a given perceptual experience, then no physical thing is ever perceived without going through a process of reasoning or performing an inference.

Next, let us rewrite premiss (3) of the Argument from Causation in a similar fashion:

(3)   If no perceiver can know solely on the basis of a given perceptual experience that he is really perceiving a physical thing, then no physical thing is ever perceived in such a way that its existence and nature can be known solely on the basis of a given perceptual experience.

It follows from (B) and (3) that:

(L)   If no perceiver can know solely on the basis of a given perceptual experience that he is really perceiving a physical thing, then no physical thing is ever perceived without going through a process of reasoning or performing an inference.

Now (L) is a general principle which implies, among other particular instances, that:

(M)   If no perceiver can know solely on the basis of a given perceptual experience that he is really perceiving a tomato, then no tomato is ever perceived without going through a process of reasoning or performing an inference.

But (D) — the principle that whatever is perceived by the senses is immediately perceived$_p$, i.e. perceived without going through a process of reasoning or performing an inference — implies that:

(N)   If no tomato is ever perceived without going through a process of reasoning or performing an inference, then nobody ever visually perceives a tomato, i.e. ever sees a tomato.

In other words, (D) implies that if, contrary to fact, tomatoes could be perceived only by performing some inference, as a person's motives are perceived when they are inferred from his behavior, then tomatoes would never be perceived by vision (or by any of the other senses). Finally (M) and (N) imply that:

(O)   If no perceiver can know solely on the basis of a given perceptual experience that he is really perceiving a tomato, then nobody ever visually perceives a tomato, i.e. ever sees a tomato.

But (O), I submit, is obviously false. The *antecedent* of (O) is, indeed, shown to be true by the Argument from Causation: Since a perceptual experience had upon really perceiving a tomato can be exactly duplicated though there is no tomato stimulating one's sense-receptors, it is true that a perceiver cannot *know*, solely on the basis of such an experience, that he is really perceiving a tomato. But it does not follow that when a tomato is actually stimulating one's eyes and thereby causing one to have the sort of visual experience associated with seeing a tomato, one does not *in fact see* a tomato. That would be an absurd claim: what more is required for a person to see a tomato than that a tomato be causing him to have such a visual experience by stimulating his eyes?[14] Rather, what follows is that one can *see* a tomato without thereby *knowing* that one is really seeing a tomato. And there is nothing absurd about that claim. For it is no different in principle from the unexceptionable claim that one can see a real, botanical tomato without knowing that it is a real, botanical tomato. Furthermore, the reason why the latter claim is true is no different in principle from the reason why the former is true: since one's visual experience could be exactly the same if it were caused by a wax tomato that looked just like a real one, one cannot know, solely on the basis of this visual experience, that one is seeing a real tomato. But of course this doesn't mean that one cannot see a real tomato. It only means that one can see a real tomato without knowing that one is seeing a real tomato.

What is especially instructive here, however, is that the falsity of (O), by showing the falsity of (B) and hence of (A), illustrates the importance of distinguishing between 'immediately perceived$_e$' and 'immediately perceived$_p$'.[15] The former is a special notion whose application to *something* seems to be required in order to deal with the epistemological problem generated by the two regresses that arise when we reflect on the relation between perception and knowledge; the latter applies to all sense-perception regardless of the epistemological status of perception. To confuse the two can only lead to various absurdities.

Perhaps the chief of these absurdities is the view that physical things are unperceivable. To see how (A) leads to this view, consider the following pair of syllogisms, in which (A) is reformulated as a categorical proposition and appears as premiss (2):

(1)   Whatever is perceived by the senses is immediately perceived$_p$.

(2)   Whatever is immediately perceived$_p$ is immediately perceived$_e$.

∴ (3)   Whatever is perceived by the senses is immediately perceived$_e$.

(4)   No physical things are immediately perceived$_e$.

∴ (5)   No physical things are perceived by the senses.

Notice that the argument can easily be modified to yield the conclusion that only sense-data are perceivable. This can be accomplished by substituting for (4) the premiss that

(4′)   Only sense-data are immediately perceived$_e$.

The conjunction of (3) and (4′), or alternatively, the conjunction of (1), (2), and (4′), then entails that

(5′)   Only sense-data are perceived by the senses.

I believe that Locke had (4) and (4′) in mind when he insisted that the only *immediate* objects of perception are ideas. I know of no evidence, however, that indicates that he was committed to the false assumption, (2), or its consequence, (3). And I do not think that anything else in the logic of his position commits him to the paradoxical conclusions, (5) and (5′), which he accepts only waveringly but which Berkeley evidently supposed must follow from a causal theory of perception such as Locke's. I shall return to this point in Chapter Five, Section 3, where I shall argue that the conflation of psychological and epistemic immediacy lies behind the common but mistaken idea that a causal analysis of perceiving implies the unperceivability of physical things.

Although it is essential to distinguish between the epistemic and psychological senses of 'immediately perceived' if certain errors are to be avoided, making this distinction does not of itself advance the solution of the epistemological problem of perception. If the introduction of sense-data can ultimately provide a solution to this problem, then this will justify introducing them. But the fact remains that the Argument from Causation does not demonstrate that there are sense-data; the idea that it does stems from conflating psychological and epistemic immediacy. Thus the argument provides no reason to modify our earlier conclusion that whether sense-data should be countenanced depends upon whether the sense-datum theory can successfully perform its epistemological function.

NOTES

[1] See for example Chapter I of Sir Russell Brain's *Mind, Perception and Science* (Blackwell, Oxford, 1951), and J. Eccles, *The Brain and the Unity of Conscious Experience* (Cambridge University Press, Cambridge, 1965), pp. 17–18.

[2] Brief but helpful critical discussions are included in A. J. Ayer, *The Problem of Knowledge*, pp. 93–95 and in R. M. Chisholm, *Perceiving: A Philosophical Study*, p. 153. A fuller, very careful discussion, as well as further bibliographical references, can be found in James W. Cornman, *Materialism and Sensations* (Yale University Press, New Haven and London, 1971), pp. 218–227 and pp. 341–342.

[3] See for example J. L. Austin, *Sense and Sensibilia*, pp. 14–19 and 135–136. I find Austin's own discussion of 'directly perceive' versus 'indirectly perceive' unhelpful, because Austin contents himself with showing that sense-datum philosophers' uses of these and cognate expressions are not identical with their ordinary uses (which would be freely admitted by these philosophers). It does not follow, however, that the philosophers' usages are "first obscurely metaphorical, but ultimately meaningless". (p. 15) For, as I shall show, they can be adequately explained by analyzing the arguments in which they function.

[4] R. J. Hirst (ed.), *Perception and the External World* (Macmillan, New York, 1965), p. 11. In fairness to Hirst, I should point out that this is not his fullest statement of the argument. But he does seem to regard the mere fact that perception requires a complex causal chain as *an* argument showing that physical things are not immediately perceived.

[5] D. M. Armstrong, *Perception and the Physical World* (Humanities Press, New York, 1961), p. 141. Armstrong does not accept the argument. I quote his statement for its exceptional clarity.

[6] Berkeley, *Three Dialogues Between Hylas and Philonous*, p. 112. In C. M. Turbayne (ed.), *Principles, Dialogues, and Philosophical Correspondence* (Bobbs-Merrill, Indiannapolis and New York, 1965).

[7] R. M. Chisholm, *Perceiving: A Philosophical Study*, pp. 158–159.

[8] Maurice Mandelbaum, *Philosophy, Science, and Sense Perception* (The Johns Hopkins Press, Baltimore, 1964), pp. 138–139. See also the above quotation from R. J. Hirst (page 49).

[9] Descartes, *Meditation VI*, pp. 196–197. In *The Philosophical Works of Descartes*, Vol. I, translated by Elizabeth S. Haldane and G. T. R. Ross (Dover Publications, New York, 1955).

[10] Premiss (2), as well as the rhetorical questions raised in this paragraph, assumes that a perceiver can know that he is really perceiving a physical thing only if he can know that the thing is (one of) the cause(s) of his present perceptual experience. Although I think this assumption is obviously true, the causal analysis of perceiving that underlies it will be defended in Chapter Five, Section 2 and the assumption itself in Chapter Seven, Section 3.

[11] H. H. Price, *Perception*, Chapter VI and VII. For a good summary statement of the distinction, see pp. 170–173.

[12] I try to show textually that Berkeley conflates these two notions, and that this conflation plays an important role in Berkeley's case for immaterialism, in 'The Concept of Immediate Perception in Berkeley's Immaterialism', forthcoming in C. M. Turbayne (ed.), *Berkeley: Critical and Interpretative Essays* (University of Minnesota Press, Minneapolis).

[13] The reader will no doubt have noticed that (C) and (D) entail that physical things are not perceived by the senses. This is indeed one of the chief paradoxes that follows from (A). I shall return to this point below (p. 64).

[14] The Causal analysis of perceiving underlying this rhetorical question will be defended in Chapter Five, Section 2.

[15] The logic involved may be summarized as follows. Since (O) is false, either (M) or (N) is false; but (N) is true, so (M) is false. Since (M) is false, (L) is false. Since (L) is false, either (B) or (3) is false; but (3) is true, so (B) is false. Therefore, (A) is false.

CHAPTER FOUR

THE ARGUMENT FROM HALLUCINATION

In this chapter I want to consider a final argument for the introduction of sense-data, the Argument from Hallucination. I shall begin by discussing a formulation of the argument given by D. M. Armstrong in his book, *Perception and the Physical World*. Armstrong's formulation is an instructive one for two reasons. First, it does not confuse hallucinations with other phenomena such as illusions and perceptual relativity, as do some other, looser presentations of the argument.[1] Second (and more significantly, from the point of view being developed here), Armstrong is careful to point out that the purpose of the argument is to show that the *immediate* object of perception is always a sense-datum. Unlike many other writers, Armstrong recognizes that the sense-datum theory need not deny that physical things are perceived, but only that they are immediately perceived. He correctly insists that unless this point is kept clearly in mind, philosophers who accept the sense-datum theory will seem to be defending the absurd view that we never perceive physical objects, while those who reject the theory will seem to be defending the platitude that we do perceive physical objects. Armstrong's own words are worth quoting:

[S]ome modern philosophers seem to assume that the issue between Direct Realism, on the one hand, and Representationalism and Phenomenalism, on the other, is simply the question 'Do we perceive physical objects or not?' 'Do we ever see trees, touch stones, or hear trains?' The only answer can be given is that of course we do, and so Direct Realism has been taken as true but perfectly trivial, while its opponents have been taken to be saying something so absurd that only a philosopher would be capable of taking it seriously. And it must be admitted that some Representationalists and Phenomenalists have been so naive as to assert that we do not perceive physical objects, while some Direct Realists have been deceived by these assertions into thinking that they are simply defending the triviality that we *do* perceive physical objects. But the real question at issue is 'What is the *direct* or *immediate* object of awareness when we perceive?'[2]

Accordingly, before stating the Argument from Hallucination, Armstrong tries to elucidate its key term, 'the *immediate* object of perception'. He attempts to elicit the meaning of this term from Berkeley's discussion, in the First Dialogue between Hylas and Philonous, of hearing the sound of a coach. Armstrong rightly sees that the notion of immediate perception on which the

67

argument turns is the same as the one implicit in Berkeley's example. However, Armstrong does not succeed in clearly defining this notion. For the notion of immediate perception involved in both the argument and the coach example is the epistemological one defined in the previous chapter. But Armstrong does not succeed in disentangling this notion completely from the psychological one with which Berkeley conflates it.[3] This prevents him from giving a fully adequate analysis of the Argument from Hallucination.[4]

My discussion will proceed as follows. In Section 1, I shall analyze Armstrong's version of the Argument from Hallucination, and show that its main premiss is acceptable only if the notion of immediate perception it invokes is understood in the epistemic sense. We shall also see that once this fact is recognized, it becomes evident that a proposition which Armstrong treats as a premiss of the argument should actually be regarded as part of its conclusion. Accordingly, in Section 2 I shall reformulate the argument in a way that brings out its logic more accurately than does Armstrong's formulation. The present chapter is intended to complete the case for my general interpretation of the sense-datum theory and its supporting arguments.

1. ANALYSIS OF THE ARGUMENT FROM HALLUCINATION

Armstrong formulates the first premiss of the Argument from Hallucination in the following manner, which is quite typical:

(1)   In a hallucination the immediate object of perception is a sense-datum.

This premiss is commonly supported by appealing to phenomenological considerations. From a purely phenomenological point of view, a hallucination isn't an experience of nothing at all. Rather, in a hallucination there is something manifestly present to consciousness. Thus H. H. Price, in discussing a hallucinatory pink rat, says: "This rat is not real. Still, [a person who is hallucinating a pink rat] does have perceptual consciousness of it, in exactly the same way in which he has a simultaneous perceptual consciousness of his table or his boot".[5] And Armstrong explains the premiss as follows:

Suppose, e.g., I am suffering from auditory hallucinations and I wrongly think I am hearing a sound, or I have experiences as if I were hearing a sound, although there is no sound being made. Now surely, in some sense, am I not *perceiving*? The sound that I hear may not be a physical object. It may be wrong to speak of it as a *sound* or of *hearing* it. But surely it is there in my sensory field. It cannot be conjured away. If we are not allowed to say that we hear it we shall just have to find another word. Perhaps

we should say that we are aware of it or that we sense it? But the overwhelming resemblance to perception makes it natural to ignore ordinary usage and to talk about perception instead. It is utterly natural to be driven along this path, and so to come to say
that when we have an auditory hallucination we immediately perceive an auditory *sense-
impression* ['sense-impression' is Armstrong's word for 'sense-datum'].[6]

Notice that despite what Armstrong says here about ignoring ordinary usage,
ordinary language does support premiss (1), to a certain extent. A man who is
having visual hallucinations of pink rats, for example, can be said to 'see pink
rats', in some legitimate and non-technical sense of 'see'. Indeed, in this sense
of 'see', it would be false to say that the man sees nothing at all: this would
imply that his visual field is empty or blank, whereas in fact it contains pink
rats.[7]

On the other hand, it can be argued that neither the phenomenological nor
the linguistic considerations mustered in behalf of (1) are compelling. For we
can do justice to the former by saying that in a hallucination it only *seems* to
us that we are perceiving something — it is *as if* we were perceiving something
— but in fact we are not really perceiving anything.[8] And this is arguably a
stricter or less misleading way of describing what takes place in a hallucination than by the unqualified use of perceptual verbs like 'see'. Furthermore, it
can be objected against (1) that even if we grant that something is perceived
in a hallucination, we do not also have to grant that this is a sense-datum. We
can say, instead, that it is a hallucinatory object or entity, e.g. a hallucinatory
pink rat, a hallucinatory ringing in the ears, etc. (This is not merely a verbal
point, because if it were conceded, the argument's third premiss would become an obvious falsehood, as we shall see.)

Which is the correct view here: the view that in a hallucination something
is perceived even though this is not a physical object, or the view that in a
hallucination nothing is really perceived though it seems as if something were
being perceived? Moreover, even if we were to grant that something is perceived in a hallucination, why should we also grant that this is a sense-datum?
If we restrict ourselves to the facts that Armstrong and Price cite — i.e. to the
obduracy and 'overwhelming resemblance to perception' of certain hallucinatory experiences — then I believe that we shall find no way of answering
either of these two questions. On the other hand, once we shall have fully
stated Armstrong's version of the Argument from Hallucination, we will find
that the argument can be reformulated in such a way that premiss (1) becomes part of its *conclusion*. Accordingly, let us go on to the next premiss of
the argument, keeping in mind that so far we have seen no good reason to
accept premiss (1).

The second premiss in Armstrong's version of the argument is:

(2)   A hallucinatory perceptual experience may be indistinguishable from a non-hallucinatory perceptual experience.

This premiss does not mean, of course, that there may be no difference at all between a hallucinatory and a non-hallucinatory perceptual experience. This would be obviously false, since there must be a difference, for example, in the way that the experiences are caused. Rather, (2) should be understood as asserting that a person's hallucinatory perceptual experience can, while the hallucination lasts, be phenomenologically indistinguishable to the person from the experience that he would have if he were perceiving some physical object(s). This assertion must be granted by anyone who acknowledges the causal facts of perception discussed in the previous chapter; in particular, the fact that a perceptual experience caused by a physical object stimulating the sense-receptors can be exactly duplicated by producing in some other manner one of the intermediate members of the causal chain between the object and the perceiver's brain. For in many such cases the resulting experience would be a hallucination (in other cases it might be a realistic dream). Furthermore, even those of us who have never had a realistic hallucination may accept premiss (2) on the basis of empirical evidence, because there is good experimental evidence for the premiss. For example, the neurologist Sir Russell Brain points out that in experiences which are only partly hallucinatory, the subject may be unable to distinguish between the hallucinatory and the non-hallucinatory elements of his experience. Extreme cases of this are 'apparitions', which cast shadows, block real objects from view, become smaller as they move away from the perceiver and dimmer when they move into poorer light, etc. Also, a hallucination can involve more than one sense, as in the case of a man who hallucinates a coin on the floor and reports that he feels its milled edge when he stoops to pick it up.[9] In the light of these considerations, premiss (2) is surely acceptable.

The third and final premiss in Armstrong's formulation is the one on which his argument turns. The premiss is:

(3)   If the immediate object of perception in a hallucination is a sense-datum and a hallucinatory perceptual experience may be indistinguishable from a non-hallucinatory perceptual experience, then even in a non-hallucinatory perceptual experience the immediate object of perception is a sense-datum.

From premisses (1)–(3), we can now deduce the argument's desired conclusion that:

> Even in a non-hallucinatory perceptual experience the immediate object of perception is a sense-datum.

Clearly, however, premiss (3) calls for justification. The principle which underlies the premiss is, evidently, that if hallucinatory and non-hallucinatory experiences may be indistinguishable, then their immediate objects must be entities of the *same kind*. [This is why I said earlier that substituting 'hallucinatory object' for 'sense-datum' in premiss (1) would turn premiss (3) into an obvious falsehood. For the premiss's consequent would then have to read: "even in a non-hallucinatory perceptual experience the immediate object of perception is a hallucinatory object".] But why should we accept this principle? Surely it is not generally true that if two things are perceptually indistinguishable, they must be of the same kind: recall the example of the wax tomato which is visually indistinguishable from a real one. As Austin says in a remark that I have already had occasion to quote, "why on earth should it *not* be the case that, in some few instances, perceiving one sort of thing is exactly like perceiving another?"[10] Why not say, then, that the immediate object of perception in a hallucination is a sense-datum, while the immediate object of perception in a non-hallucinatory perceptual experience is a physical object? Armstrong considers this objection and replies:

But it seems clear that this compromise is unacceptable. When I suffer auditory hallucination it is logically possible for me to be having a veridical perception of an actual noise. My perceptual experience will be absolutely identical in both cases. Now if it be admitted that in auditory hallucination the immediate object of perception is an auditory sense-impression, and if it be admitted that the very same experience could be a veridical perception, it can hardly be denied that even in a veridical perception the *immediate* object of perception is a sense-impression. This result can be generalized to apply to all immediate perception. Whenever I have a veridical perception, it is possible that I should have had exactly the same experience, yet the perception have been illusory. My immediate object of perception in the hallucinatory case would have been a sense-impression, so my immediate object of perception is always a sense-impression. [Armstrong's emphasis][11]

What is interesting here is that this passage really gives no additional support to premiss (3): It consists only in insisting on the very claim that Austin denies; namely, that if hallucinatory and normal perception may be indistinguishable, then their immediate objects must be of the same kind. Yet, the passage may be felt as quite persuasive. Why is this? What really is behind "the curious general principle . . . that if two things are not 'generically the same', the same 'in nature', then they can't be alike . . . ?"[12] Notice also that

Armstrong has not even considered the question we raised concerning premiss
(1), as to why, even if we grant that in a hallucination there is an 'immediate
object of perception', this should be called a 'sense-datum' (or, in Armstrong's
terminology, a 'sense-impression') rather than a 'hallucinatory - - - ". Why
should it be "admitted that in an auditory hallucination the immediate object
of perception is an auditory sense-impression?"

The answers to these questions can be found only be examining the way in
which the term 'immediate object of perception' functions in the argument.
Suppose that this term were taken in a psychological sense corresponding to
'immediately perceived$_p$', i.e. that it were taken to mean, 'object perceived
without performing any inference'. Then premiss (3) of the argument would
be equivalent to:

(3_p) If the object perceived without performing any inference in a
           hallucination is a sense-datum and a hallucinatory perceptual
           experience may be indistinguishable from a non-hallucinatory
           perceptual experience, then even in a non-hallucinatory perceptual
           experience the object perceived without performing any inference
           is a sense-datum.

But there would be no reason to accept (3_p). Why should we not maintain
instead that the object perceived without performing any inference in a hallucination is a sense-datum, while the object perceived without performing
any inference in a non-hallucinatory perceptual experience is a physical thing?
Further, such a psychological definition of 'immediate object of perception'
would not enable us to answer our question concerning premiss (1). There is
no reason to hold that the object perceived without performing any inference
in a hallucination must be a sense-datum, as opposed to a hallucinatory object
or entity.

Suppose, on the other hand, that we take the term 'immediate object of
perception' in an epistemological sense corresponding to 'immediately per-
ceived$_e$', i.e. that we take it to mean, "object whose existence and nature can
be *known* solely on the basis of one's present perceptual experience".[13] Then
premiss (3) of the argument becomes equivalent to:

(3_e) If the object whose existence and nature can be known solely
           on the basis of one's present perceptual experience in a hallucina-
           tion is a sense-datum and a hallucinatory perceptual experience
           may be indistinguishable from a non-hallucinatory perceptual

experience, then even in a non-hallucinatory perceptual experience the object whose existence and nature can be known solely on the basis of one's present perceptual experience is a sense-datum.

Now I submit that (3_e) is true. The object whose existence and nature can be known solely on the basis of one's present perceptual experience in a non-hallucinatory perceptual experience cannot be of a different kind from the object whose existence and nature can be known solely on the basis of one's present perceptual experience in a hallucination, if the two experiences can be indistinguishable. For obviously the indistinguishability of the two experiences would make it impossible to *know* of any difference in kind between their objects solely on the basis of the experiences themselves. But this would mean that the nature of the objects was not knowable solely on the basis of the experiences themselves, after all. Therefore, the object whose existence and nature can be known solely on the basis of one's present perceptual experience in a non-hallucinatory perceptual experience must be of the same kind as the object whose existence and nature can be known solely on the basis of one's present perceptual experience in a hallucination. So if it is true that the latter is a sense-datum, then likewise the former must be a sense-datum.

The epistemological meaning of the term 'immediate object of perception' in the argument also explains why the term 'sense-datum' is used in premiss (1), rather than 'hallucinatory object' or some such term. The *immediate* object of perception in a hallucination cannot be (characterized as) a *hallucinatory* object. For the indistinguishability of hallucinatory and non-hallucinatory experiences cuts both ways. Not only does it prevent the object whose existence and nature can be known solely on the basis of one's present perceptual experience in a non-hallucinatory perceptual experience from being a physical thing, but it also prevents the object whose existence and nature can be known solely on the basis of one's present perceptual experience in a hallucination from being a hallucinatory object. For, from all one can tell from one's present perceptual experience alone, that experience may be being produced in a way quite incompatible with its being a hallucination, even if it is in fact a hallucination. The upshot is that the immediate object of perception — the object whose existence and nature can be known *solely* on the basis of one's present perceptual experience — can never be *either* a physical thing or a hallucinatory entity. It can only be that pattern of sensuously given characters which, to speak metaphorically, can be skimmed off from either a hallucinatory or a non-hallucinatory perceptual experience —

i.e. a sense-datum. Or, to cash the metaphor, it can only be an entity of the kind that was defined ostensively in presenting the Argument from Perceptual Relativity.

2. A REFORMULATION OF THE ARGUMENT

In the light of the foregoing analysis, it is worth reformulating the Argument from Hallucination in a way that brings out its structure more clearly than does Armstrong's formulation. The starting point of the argument is the true premiss that:

(1)   A hallucinatory perceptual experience may be indistinguishable from a non-hallucinatory perceptual experience.

The principle on which the argument turns is that:

(2)   If a hallucinatory perceptual experience may be indistinguishable from a non-hallucinatory perceptual experience, and there is an immediate object of perception in both hallucinatory and non-hallucinatory perceptual experiences, then this object must be of the same kind in both sorts of experiences.

This principle is true for reasons that I have discussed, provided of course that 'immediate object of perception' means 'object whose existence and nature can be known solely on the basis of one's present perceptual experience'. The *assumption* on which the argument rests is that:

(3)   There *is* an immediate object of perception in both hallucinatory and non-hallucinatory perceptual experiences

where, again, 'immediate object of perception' means 'object whose existence and nature can be known solely on the basis of one's peresent perceptual experience'. From (1)–(3), it follows that:

(4)   The immediate object of perception is of the same kind in both hallucinatory and non-hallucinatory perceptual experiences.

What kind of object would this be? Well, the only suitable objects that we seem to be able to find or pick out within our perceptual experience are objects of the kind to which Moore directs our attention in presenting the Argument from Perceptual Relativity and which, following him, we are calling 'sense-data'. Thus, it seems legitimate to employ the further premiss that:

(5)   If the immediate object of perception is of the same kind in both hallucinatory and non-hallucinatory perceptual experiences, then in both sorts of experiences the immediate object of perception is a sense-datum.

We may now conclude from (4) and (5) that:

(6)   In both hallucinatory and non-hallucinatory perceptual experiences the immediate object of perception is a sense-datum.

Notice that the first premiss of Armstrong's formulation of the argument ("In a hallucination the immediate object of perception is a sense-datum") is now, as I said earlier, entailed by the conclusion of the argument.

It should be clear that the Argument from Hallucination is not different in its basic thrust from the other arguments for the introduction of sense-data. It resembles the Argument from Causation especially closely. For its premisses simultaneously entail that physical things are not immediately perceived and assume that nevertheless something *is* immediately perceived. In Armstrong's formulation this assumption is made when the phrase 'the immediate object of perception' is used denotatively in the argument's premisses; in my reformulation the assumption is explicitly asserted in premiss (3). Thus the Argument from Hallucination, like the other arguments for the introduction of sense-data, should not be regarded as an attempt to demonstrate that there are sense-data: so interpreted it simply begs the question. Rather, the argument should be regarded as yet another way of calling attention simultaneously to (*a*) an epistemological problem concerning perception, and (*b*) the possibility of dealing with this problem by introducing sense-data. The epistemological problem here is the same as the one to which the Argument from Causation gives rise: perceiving x to be F does not even amount to knowing that x exists, because the perceptual experience had in perceiving x to be F could be exactly duplicated if x did not exist. This means, as I argued in the previous chapter, that corroboration must be sought from other cases of perception. But the Argument from Hallucination, like the Argument from Causation, can be reiterated for any case of perception. How, then, are we to ensure that the corroborating perceptions constitute some sort of knowledge, as they must if they are to corroborate anything? This can be done, it would seem, by introducing sense-data. And whether this solution should be accepted depends, as I have argued, on whether by introducing sense-data one can ultimately account for the fact that perception provides us with knowledge of the physical world.

NOTES

[1] This is true despite the fact that Armstrong calls the argument, 'The Argument from Illusion'. For the argument turns entirely on what Armstrong calls 'immediate sensory illusion', which turns out to be the same thing as hallucination. See pp. 21–22 of *Perception and the Physical World* (Humanities Press, New York, 1961).

[2] *Perception and the Physical World*, pp. xi–xii. Cf. also p. 24.

[3] Support for the parts of these claims bearing on Berkeley is provided in my 'The Concept of Immediate Perception in Berkeley's Immaterialism', forthcoming in C. M Turbayne (ed.), *Berkeley: Critical and Interpretative Essays* (University of Minnesota Press, Minneapolis).

[4] No doubt this is also because Armstrong himself rejects the argument, and his rejection of it depends upon his own analysis of immediate perception, on which its first premiss is simply false. Thus, Armstrong never gives a satisfactory answer to the question I want to ask: what meaning for 'immediate object of perception' would be needed to make the argument's premisses true?

[5] H. H. Price, *Perception*, p. 147.

[6] *Perception and the Physical World*, p. 26.

[7] This sense of 'see' will be discussed more fully in Chapter Five, Section 2.

[8] This is the line that Armstrong himself ultimately takes. In Chapter Seven, Section 2, I shall also defend such a position; although the analysis of hallucination I will give is very different from Armstrong's.

[9] Russell Brain, 'Hallucinations', reprinted from *The Nature of Experience* in R. J. Hirst (ed.), *Perception and the External World*, pp. 51–60.

[10] J. L. Austin, *Sense and Sensibilia*, p. 50. See above, p. 43.

[11] *Perception and the Physical World*, p. 27.

[12] J. L. Austin, *Sense and Sensibilia*, p. 50.

[13] For the sake of perspicuity, I am here using the phrase 'known solely on the basis of one's present perceptual experience', rather than the phrase 'known solely on the basis of a given perceptual experience' (used in defining 'immediately perceived$_e$'). This substitution is harmless, because 'given perceptual experience' means 'perceptual experience occuring at a given time', and 'present' can be taken arbitrarily to denote any given time. Nor does the term 'one's' beg any disputed questions, since it presupposes the existence of a perceiver in perception but does not presuppose any particular view concerning the nature of the perceiver.

CHAPTER FIVE

THE CAUSAL THEORY OF PERCEPTION

A causal theory of perception has been held by many philosophers, e.g. by Descartes, Locke, Kant, and Russell, to mention only a few. Yet these philosophers' theories of perception differ greatly — so greatly that it would be misleading to say that they held 'the same theory of perception'. But since my aim is to analyze the epistemological problem of perception and to appraise possible solutions to it (rather than to expound the views of any particular philosopher), I shall not go into special features of individual philosophers' versions of the causal theory except insofar as this serves my purpose. Rather, I shall seek to formulate the fundamental features of the causal theory — fundamental in the sense that ignoring them would lead to overlooking either some aspect of the problem or some possible solution to it. In this task, I shall be guided by H. P. Grice's valuable article, 'The Causal Theory of Perception'.[1] In this article Grice provides an excellent definition of the theory's fundamental features.

1. GENERAL FORMULATION OF THE CAUSAL THEORY

On Grice's formulation, the causal theory consists of two logically independent parts (or 'clauses', as he calls them). The first part is a definition or analysis of perceiving in causal terms; I shall call this part 'the analytic thesis'. The second part specifies how a person could justify a belief or claim to be perceiving some physical thing; this part I shall call 'the justification thesis'. A preliminary formulation of the analytic thesis is:

> AT: S perceives M if and only if M is a part-cause of S's present perceptual experience.

The justification thesis may be put as follows:

> JT: S could justify the belief or claim that he perceives M by an argument showing that M is causally required to account for the character of some of S's perceptual experiences.

Notice that these two theses are logically independent. The analytic thesis might be a correct definition though the justification thesis were false (e.g. if there were *no* way to justify the claim to perceive M); the justification thesis might be true though the analytic thesis were incorrect.

Unlike Grice I have not used the term 'sense-datum' in this formulation.[2] My reason for not doing so is as follows. In discussing the various arguments for introducing sense-data, I have given the notion of a sense-datum a particular interpretation. Sense-data are supposed to be the objects we immediately perceive, i.e. the objects whose existence and nature we can know solely on the basis of our present perceptual experience. Apart from giving reasons why sense-data cannot be identical with physical things or surfaces, I have said little about their ontological status. But I have consistently treated them, in the traditional way, as objects or entities of some sort. Moreover, I have argued that whether such objects should be countenanced depends upon whether they can successfully serve their epistemological function. So if I were now to formulate the causal theory in terms of the notion of a sense-datum, I would be committed to holding that the acceptability of the causal theory depends upon the success or failure of the traditional sense-datum theory. But this would be a mistake. For Grice is right, I believe, in holding that at least part of the causal theory is correct in any case. We shall see that the analytic thesis, qualified in certain ways to be explained presently, is, as Grice puts it, "an acceptable bit of philosophical analysis" in its own right, i.e. whether or not the traditional sense-datum theory is acceptable.[3] Thus, the correctness of the analytic thesis must not be made to turn on the acceptability of the traditional sense-datum theory: that is why I have avoided the term 'sense-datum' in formulating this thesis.

The reason that Grice himself does formulate the analytic thesis in terms of the notion of a sense-datum is that he gives this notion a very broad interpretation. For Grice, to say that someone senses or has a sense-datum is only another way of saying that the person has a perceptual experience. It is just an elliptical way of making a statement of the type illustrated by, 'it looks to S as if there is an elephant approaching', 'it feels to S as if there is something soft touching his hand', 'it sounds to S as if . . .', etc. Statements of this sort Grice calls 'sense-datum statements'; and all he means by saying that S has or senses a sense-datum is that some sense-datum statement is true of S.[4] To be sure, Grice is committed to holding that such a statement reports a certain state of affairs — one for which a physical object M (e.g. an elephant, a feather, an airplane) may be 'causally responsible'. But he is not committed to any particular analysis of such states of affairs. Whenever I want to refer to such states of affairs without implying any particular analysis of them, I shall say that 'S has a perceptual experience'. I shall continue to reserve the term 'sense-datum' for a particular (metaphysical) analysis of S's having a perceptual experience, according to which this state of affairs consists in S's immediately perceiving$_e$ certain sense-data. Thus, were I to formulate the (preliminary version of the) analytic thesis in terms of the notion of a sense-datum, it would read:

AT_{sd}: S perceives M if and only if M is a part-cause of S's immediately perceiving certain sense-data.

While the truth of AT is a necessary condition for the truth of AT_{sd}, it is not sufficient; in order for AT_{sd} to be true it must also be the case that the particular analysis of perceptual experience given by the sense-datum theory is correct. So AT does not, while AT_{sd} does, depend for its truth on the acceptability of the traditional sense-datum theory.

It may well be asked, however, why I have not at least formulated the justification thesis in terms of the sense-datum theory, as follows:

JT_{sd}: S could justify the belief or claim that he perceives M by an argument showing that M is causally required to account for the fact that S is immediately perceiving or has immediately perceived a certain set of sense-data.

After all, the task we set for ourselves in the previous chapters was to appraise the sense-datum theory by considering whether it can explain how perception yields knowledge of the physical world. One of the two main ways in which sense-datum theorists have attempted to do this is by adopting a causal theory of perception (the other is by adopting phenomenalism); and JT_{sd} is a fair summary of the position they have defended. Indeed, the conjunction of AT_{sd} and JT_{sd} is a fair summary of the fundamental features of the causal theory when it is cast, as it traditionally has been, within the framework of the sense-datum theory; and so I shall henceforth refer to this conjunction as 'the *classical* causal theory of perception'. Nevertheless, I have a reason for not using the notion of a sense-datum in formulating even the justification thesis of the causal theory. I want to call attention to the possibility of formulating both the analytic thesis and the justification thesis — and so the causal theory as a whole — outside the framework of the traditional sense-datum theory. In other words, I wish to call attention to the fact that the causal theory of perception does not *have* to be linked with the sense-datum theory, even though it traditionally has been so linked. This point is of some importance in itself, but its main significance will be seen only at a later stage. For ultimately I intend to argue that the causal theory as a whole is defensible, provided that the sense-datum theory is dropped in favor of a different analysis of perceptual experience. For it then becomes possible to combine the causal theory with an epistemological version of phenomenalism in a way that offers a plausible solution to the problem of perception.

Before arguing in favor of this combined theory, however, I shall examine the causal theory (as well as phenomenalism) in its classical form. So when I consider the justification thesis in Section 4 and 5 of the present chapter, it is JT_{sd} that I shall discuss. And when I consider phenomenalism, I shall begin with the earlier, ontological version of that theory on which it too is formulated within the framework of the traditional sense-datum theory. In appraising the classical causal theory of perception and ontological phenomenalism, I shall at the same time be appraising the sense-datum theory. The conclusion I shall seek to establish is that neither the classical causal theory nor ontological phenomenalism provides a satisfactory solution to the problem of perception. The classical causal theory is sound in its basic metaphysics but fails on epistemological grounds, because JT_{sd} cannot be successfully defended. Ontological phenomenalism, on the other hand, is very attractive from a purely epistemological point of view but fails because it generates metaphysical paradoxes. Thus, the strengths and weaknesses of the two traditional theories are complementary. Schematically:

	causal theory	phenomenalism
epistemology	W	S
metaphysics	S	W

Having noted the strengths and exposed the weaknesses of the two theories in their classical forms, however, I shall be in a position to put forward a constructive hypothesis. This is that it is possible to combine the metaphysics of the causal theory with the epistemology of phenomenalism in a way that yields a unified and plausible theory, provided that the sense-datum theory is rejected in favor of an 'averbial' analysis of perceptual experience that preserves the epistemological function of sense-data without reifying the ways in which things appear to perceivers.

2. THE ANALYTIC THESIS

In this section, I shall argue that AT, properly qualified to rule out certain counterexamples, is true. It should be borne in mind that although AT must be true in order for AT_{sd} to be true, even if AT is true the question whether AT_{sd} is also true can be settled only by deciding whether sense-data are to be countenanced.

I have already claimed that Grice is right in holding that the analytic thesis is true. Now this is a substantive claim. For the analytic thesis has perfectly clear metaphysical implications. It entails that the things we perceive are distinct from our perceptual experiences of them. For a cause, even a part-cause, cannot possibly be identical with any effect that it helps to produce. Thus, the analytic thesis entails common-sense realism with respect to the objects we perceive. In defending the analytic thesis, therefore, one is defending the realist metaphysic implicit in any version of the causal theory of perception.

I shall first argue that it is a necessary condition of S's perceiving M that M be a part-cause of S's present perceptual experience. Assuming, as seems reasonable, that in this context one can safely generalize from one sense-modality to the others, this is the case if and only if the following statement is analytically (conceptually) true:

(S_1)   If I taste a potato chip, then a potato chip is one of the causes of my present gustatory experiences.

Now (S_1) is analytically true if and only if its negation, namely

(S_2)   I taste a potato chip, but it is not the case that a potato chip is one of the causes of my present gustatory experiences

is self-contradictory. But I submit that (S_2) is self-contradictory; *unless* the perceptual verb 'taste' is being used in a somewhat special sense which the causal theory is not intended to cover. This 'unless' is necessary for the following reason. Suppose that A has knowingly (perhaps as part of a scientific experiment) taken a drug that causes him to have gustatory experiences exactly like tasting potato chips. Then S could report his experiences by saying 'I taste a potato chip', and he could consistently add 'but of course I realize that there is no potato chip causing my present gustatory experiences'. Indeed, it is a fact that people who are having realistic hallucinations and who know that they are hallucinating report their experiences with such locutions as 'I see. . . ', 'I hear', etc.; as opposed to 'I seem to see . . .', 'I seem to hear . . .', etc.[5] It must be admitted, then, that there is an interpretation of (S_2) on which (S_2) is consistent. But this does not count against the causal theory. For the perceptual verb 'taste' is normally used in a sense in which the statement 'I taste a potato chip' entails that there *is* a potato chip which I taste. But the causal theory is intended to provide the truth-conditions of that

statement only when 'taste' is being used in this normal sense. And provided
that 'taste' in (S_2) is understood in that sense, (S_2) is self-contradictory. So
the fact that there is a different sense of 'taste', on which (S_2) is consistent,
does not count against the causal theory.

It may be objected that this is to save the analytic thesis by the questionable maneuver of multiplying senses of words. I can only reply that perceptual verbs such as 'see', 'hear', 'taste', 'smell', and 'feel' do have these two
senses. Suppose that S is hallucinating spots on what is in fact a blank wall. If
the perceptual verb 'sees' is taken in its normal sense, then it is simply false
that S sees spots on the wall. (Rather, S only seems to see spots on the wall.)
For this would entail the falsehood that there *are* some spots on the wall.
Nevertheless, there is also an ordinary, though somewhat special, sense of
'sees' in which it is *true* to say that S sees spots on the wall (and in which S
can truly report, 'I see spots on the wall'). For on that sense of 'sees', the
statement that S sees spots on the wall does not falsely entail that there are
some spots on the wall. (That it does not entail this is why 'sees' is being used
in a rather *special* sense.)[6] The fact that 'sees' can be used in these two ways
— i.e. either such that statements of the form 'S sees X' entail, or such that
they do not entail, that there exists an X which S sees — and that parallel
considerations apply in a systematic way to other perceptual verbs, warrants
saying that these are two different senses of 'sees'. Therefore it is legitimate
to maintain that the analytic thesis of the causal theory covers 'sees' (and
other perceptual verbs) in only one of these two senses: the sense in which
'S sees M' entails 'There exists an M which S sees'. And on that sense of 'sees',
the statement

(S_3)   S sees M, but it is not the case that M is one of the causes of S's
          present visual experience

is self-contradictory.

Grice offers a different demonstration of the proposition that S can perceive M only if M is a part-cause of S's present perceptual experience. Suppose
that S is having a visual experience exactly like seeing a clock on the shelf; or
as Grice puts it, that it looks to S as if there is a clock on the shelf. Furthermore, suppose that there really is a clock on the shelf within S's field of view,
before his eyes. Is this sufficient for it to be true that S sees the clock? No, it
is not. For suppose that S's visual experience is being produced by an expert
directly stimulating S's brain or by some kind of post-hypnotic suggestion; so
that even if the clock's position on the shelf were altered or the clock were
entirely removed, S's visual experience would remain unchanged: it would

continue to look to S as if there is a clock on the shelf. In that case S does not *see* the clock, even though it is there before his very eyes. And the reason he does not see it is that it plays no role in causing his visual experience.[7] I think that Grice's example shows clearly that S does not see M unless M is a part-cause of S's present visual experience. And it seems safe to generalize from what is here true of vision to perception in general.

Let me now turn to the question of whether M's being a part-cause of S's present perceptual experience is a sufficient condition for S's perceiving M. A moment's reflection suffices to show that the answer is 'no'. The reason is that perception always occurs under a complex set of conditions: there are always many causes helping to cause one's perceptual experience other than the object perceived. For example, light rays are one of the causes of the visual experience I have when I look at a chair. But although I do see the chair I do not see the light rays. Again, certain complex events in my nervous system and in my brain are among the causes of the visual experience I have when I see the chair. But although these events are no less part-causes of my visual experience than the chair, I certainly do not see them. So 'M is a part-cause of S's present perceptual experience' is not a sufficient condition for 'S perceives M': this would imply that we perceive many things which we obviously do not perceive. Therefore, as it stands AT is too broad an analysis of perceiving; it must be restricted so as to rule out such M's as light rays and S's own physiological processes.

It would appear that the most promising way of so restricting AT is, as Grice suggests, to incorporate into the analysis some specification of the *way* in which M must contribute to the causation of S's perceptual experience. And one possible way of doing this is, as he says, "to introduce into (the analysis) some part of the specialist's account, for example to make a reference to the transmission of light-rays to the retina. . .".[8] Some philosophers, notably R. M. Chisholm in *Perceiving*, have given causal analyses of this kind. Chisholm's analysis of visual perception, for example, invokes certain rudimentary concepts of physiology and physics, such as that of M's being 'a *proper* visual stimulus of S' (a notion which itself is defined in terms of the transmission and reflection of light), and of S's "sensing in a way that is functionally dependent upon the stimulus energy produced in S by [M]".[9] A number of philosophers, however, have objected to such analyses. Their objection is that there are people who know nothing about the physics or physiology of perception, but who nevertheless understand perfectly well what it means for a person to perceive an object — to see, touch, hear, taste or smell something. Therefore, it is argued, the concept of perception must not be analyzed in terms of any notions of physics or physiology.

If this objection is taken to show, as its proponents apparently believe, that any analysis of perceiving akin to Chisholm's is in principle mistaken, then I think the objection is unjustified.[10] For the objection, when taken in this heavy-handed way, assumes that there is *no* conception of perceiving that includes any material of which a person who understands the term 'perceive' might be ignorant. But this assumption seems untrue. Consider e.g. the fact that seeing requires the transmission of light from the object seen to the perceiver's eyes. Admittedly, some people who understand the term 'see' are ignorant of this fact. Does it follow that there is no conception of seeing that includes a reference to the transmission of light? Surely not. For suppose that a new type of perception was discovered, which occurred without any transmission of light from the object perceived. It would be quite legitimate to hold, on conceptual grounds, that this new type of perception could not really be seeing, i.e. could not really be *visual* perception, even if it resembled vision in other respects.

If, on the other hand, the objection is taken to show only that analyses such as Chisholm's cannot serve as analyses of the *ordinary* conception of seeing, then the objection seems to be sound. For, as Grice puts its,

if we are attempting to characterize the ordinary notion of perceiving, we should not explicitly introduce material of which someone who is perfectly capable of employing the ordinary notion might be ignorant.[11]

Accordingly, the objection suggests a question: Is it *impossible* to give an analysis of perceiving without explicitly including material unknown to many people? That is very implausible. It should be possible to give an adequate analysis of perceiving that does not presuppose any specialized knowledge. For if this is not possible, then it follows that people who lack such knowledge do not know what perceiving is (what 'perceives' means). In *Perceiving*, Chisholm actually accepts this implication:

Using perception words in the way they are defined here, we must say that there are people who perceive things, who see, hear, feel, or touch them, without *knowing* that they are perceiving anything, without knowing that they are seeing, hearing, feeling, or touching anything. For there are people who perceive things without knowing anything about the physical processes in terms of which we have defined the nonpropositional senses of perception words.[12]

Chisholm does go on to add that such people

may say that they see, hear, feel or touch things, but, in so saying, they use perception words in ways other than those defined here. If we wished our definitions to be adequate to their uses . . . we would replace the definition . . . which we finally settled upon, with one of the simpler definitions we had rejected.[13]

However, since the simpler definitions to which Chisholm is referring were rejected by him on the grounds that there are counterexamples to them, this seems to imply that such people are *confused* or *mistaken* about what perceiving is (about what 'perceives' means). And indeed Chisholm remarks that "people who do not know that they are perceiving anything may yet *say* that they do".[14] Now if this remark is intended, as it seems to be, to characterize people who are ignorant of the scientific notions employed in Chisholm's final definition, then surely the remark is mistaken. For it is clear that people who are ignorant of physics and physiology can know what it is for a person — themselves or someone else — to see, touch, smell, hear or taste an object. And when such people *say* that they perceive something, they may *know* perfectly well that they do. Nor need they be confused about what perceiving is, just because they are ignorant of its physics and physiology. Rather, such people have a less detailed, more schematic conception of perceiving than people who understand something of the physics and physiology involved; but this is not to say that their conception of perceiving is unclear. (In Cartesian terms, it may be 'clear' without being 'distinct'.)

The best way to support this claim is to give a satisfactory analysis of the ordinary conception of perceiving. This can be accomplished, I believe, by using the method proposed by Grice. He suggests that the way in which the perceived object contributes to the causation of a perceptual experience be indicated by means of examples. For instance, seeing can be defined as follows:

> S sees *M* if and only if *M* is a part-cause of S's present visual experience, in the same kind of way in which e.g. one's hand is a part-cause of one's visual experience when one looks at it in good light, *whatever that kind of way may be.*

Likewise, hearing could be defined as follows:

> S hears *M* if and only if *M* is a part-cause of S's present auditory experience, in the same kind of way in which e.g. a ringing telephone is a part-cause of one's auditory experience when one is a few feet away from it, *whatever that kind of way may be.*

Similar definitions could be given for touching, tasting, and smelling; and the general formulation of the analytic thesis would be:

AT_2:   S perceives M if and only if M is a part-cause of S's present perceptual experience, in the same kind of way in which e.g. one's hand is a part-cause of one's visual experience when one looks at it in good light, or in which a ringing telephone is a part-cause of one's auditory experience when one is a few feet away from it, or in which . . . etc., *whatever that kind of way may be.*[15]

Grice adds that further specification of the manner of causation can be left to specialists in the relevant fields, presumably psychology or physiology. He sees "nothing absurd in the idea that a non-specialist concept should contain, so to speak, a blank space to be filled in by the specialist".[16] This certainly seems correct. For we are able to apply the concept of perception without knowing how the 'whatever that kind of way may be' is spelled out by specialists. Moreover, as Grice points out, we are prepared to say that the same kind of mechanism is involved in e.g. all cases of vision, without being able to describe (in any detail) the mechanism. Finally, if we were in doubt as to whether a certain organism could correctly be said to *see* objects, then we might well settle the doubt by finding out from a specialist whether it possessed sense-organs similar in kind to the human eye.[17]

Grice's remarks suggest a certain view of the relation between his own analysis and more technical ones such as Chisholm's — a view according to which both types of analyses can be seen to be legitimate. One can have a more or less detailed conception of perceiving. A layman has a fairly schematic and undetailed conception while a specialist has a more refined and detailed one. But there is an overlap between the layman's and the specialist's conceptions: the specialist's conception includes what is included in the layman's but not vice-versa.[18] (If there were no overlap, then they could not be conceptions of the same thing.) Accordingly, we can place Grice's and Chisholm's analyses on a scale going from the layman's schematic and undetailed conception of perceiving (analyzed by Grice) to more detailed conceptions (such as the one analyzed by Chisholm) embodying various degrees of firmly-established but specialized knowledge concerning perception. There is no need to choose between these analyses except relative to one's purposes. If one's purpose is to analyze the ordinary (i.e. the layman's) conception of perceiving, then Grice's analysis is quite adequate. If one's purpose is to analyze a specialist's conception of perceiving, perhaps for the sake of answering conceptual questions about perceiving that arise in light of scientific knowledge concerning perception, then a more technical analysis may be both appropriate and illuminating.

Our own purpose is to analyze the epistemological problem of perception, and to seek an adequate solution to it. For this purpose, we do not need an analysis more detailed than Grice's: the problem of perception and knowledge arises at a basic level of understanding. In what follows, therefore, I shall presuppose only the correctness of Grice's formulation of the analytic thesis (AT_2) – with one slight modification.

The modification is that I wish to make explicit in the analysis that M must contribute to the causation of S's present perceptual experience *by stimulating S's sense-receptors*, specified non-technically as S's eyes, ears, nose, skin, or tongue and palate. Thus, for example, if M causes S to have a visual experience by directly stimulating his optic nerve or his cerebral cortex, then S does not *see M*; for the causal connection between M and S's visual experience is not of the kind necessary for S to *see M*. This remains true even if the character of S's visual experience is 'veridical'; e.g. even if a computer wired directly to S's brain causes it to look to S exactly as if there is a computer wired to his own brain. For in such a strange case S would not *see* the computer; rather, the computer would be causing S to have a visual hallucination whose content corresponds to reality. It is part of the *ordinary* conception of perceiving that we see with our eyes, hear with our ears, smell with our noses, etc. I suspect that Grice intends his analysis to cover this point: the examples chosen to indicate the manner of causal connection between M and S's perceptual experience would all be cases in which M stimulates a sense-receptor of S. But be that as it may, my reason for making this point explicit in the analysis is that it has epistemological significance. For as we have seen in connection with the Argument from Causation, and as will be emphasized in our critique of the justification thesis of the causal theory, the possibility that S's present perceptual experience is *not* being produced by stimulation of his sense-receptors poses an epistemological difficulty. Accordingly, the formulation of the analytic thesis whose correctness I shall henceforth presuppose is the following:

AT_3:   S perceives M if and only if M, by stimulating S's sense-receptors, is a part-cause of S's present perceptual experience, in the same kind of way in which e.g. one's hand, by stimulating one's eyes, is a part-cause of one's visual experience when one looks at it in good light, or in which e.g. a ringing telephone, by stimulating one's ears, is a part-cause of one's auditory experience when one is a few feet away from it, or in which . . . etc., *whatever that kind of way may be.*

3. DOES THE CAUSAL THEORY IMPLY THAT PHYSICAL
OBJECTS ARE UNPERCEIVABLE?

There is a certain picture of what perceiving is that has come to be associated with the causal theory of perception. According to this picture, we perceive only our own ideas or sense-data, which are caused in us by physical things that are themselves unperceivable in principle. Our sense-data constitute a kind of screen, veil, or barrier that prevents us from ever perceiving the physical world. But since these sense-data to a certain extent resemble or duplicate the physical objects that cause them (by 'copying' the objects' primary qualities), perception can give us knowledge of the physical world.

Once this picture is adopted, a multitude of questions and absurdities is generated. To begin with the most obvious question, if physical things are unperceivable, then how can we know that they are really the causes of our sense-data? Perhaps there are no physical things at all, and our sense-data are caused instead by a powerful arch-deceiver as Descartes suggested, or by God himself as Berkeley maintained. Further, even if we could know that our sense-data are caused by physical things, how could we possibly tell which of the sense-data caused by a physical thing resembled it and which did not? Consider for example the sense-data belonging to Moore's envelope. Clearly they cannot *all* resemble it, since they have incompatible qualities. How, then — if the envelope itself is unperceivable — can we tell which of these sense-data are genuine representations of it? Indeed, how can we ever know that any sense-data resemble any physical things, if the latter are unperceivable in principle? By hypothesis we can never *compare* the sense-data with the things in order to verify the resemblance or lack of resemblance. But what other way is there to determine whether the postulated resemblance actually obtains? Finally, does it even make sense to maintain that sense-data resemble things which are unperceivable? Berkeley gives an ingenious argument to show that such a claim makes no sense. If physical things are unperceivable, he argues, then they must be invisible, intangible, *etc*. Sense-data, on the other hand, being perceivable, must be visible, or tangible, *etc*. But how can something visible *resemble* something invisible, or something tangible *resemble* something intangible, etc.?[19]

Although it is true that causal theorists such as Locke have often said that physical things are unperceivable and that we perceive only sense-data, nevertheless the foregoing questions and criticisms are directed largely against a straw man. In the first place, neither Locke nor his more recent followers consistently or unequivocally hold the view in question: Locke, for example, notoriously vacillates between holding that we perceive only ideas and that we perceive objects.[20] More importantly, nothing in the logic of the causal theory implies that physical objects are unperceivable. It should be obvious that the Justification Thesis does not imply the unperceivability of physical things, since it explicitly asserts that claims to perceive such things can be justified. To see that the Analytic Thesis does not have this implication either, we may consider what Grice says about the matter. He first allows that it would not be *inconsistent* to combine a causal analysis of perceiving with the view that it is in principle impossible to perceive a physical thing. In other words, one could hold, without self-contradiction, both that

(1)   S perceives M if and only if M is a part-cause, in a way to be indicated by example, of S's present perceptual experience

and that

(2)   It is in principle impossible for M to be a part-cause of S's present perceptual experience.

Since (1) and (2) are not inconsistent, Grice grants that a critic who holds that the causal theory implies the unperceivability of physical things is at least not guilty of inconsistency; though, as he adds, "this position, even if internally consistent, would seem to be open to grave objection" [(2) being wholly devoid of plausibility].[21] However, even if (2) is consistent with (1), (2) is certainly not a logical *consequence* of (1)! Therefore, the proposition that physical things are in principle unperceivable does not follow from a causal analysis of perceiving. Nor does the logic of the situation change when the Analytic Thesis is formulated in terms of sense-data (i.e. on the model of AT_{sd} rather than AT). It would not be inconsistent to hold both that

(1')   S perceives M if and only if M is a part-cause, in a way to be indicated by example, of S's immediately perceiving certain sense-data

and that

(2')   It is in principle impossible for M to be a part-cause of S's immediately perceiving certain sense-data.

But again, while (1') and (2') are logically consistent, (2') certainly does not follow from (1'). [And besides, (2') has nothing to recommend it.]

Why, then, is the causal theory of perception so commonly thought to imply that physical things are unperceivable? When one looks to the literature for an answer to this question, one finds a rather surprising situation. On the one hand, the picture I described above, according to which physical things are beyond or behind the 'veil of perception' constituted by our sense-data, is standardly associated with the causal theory. Open almost any philosophy textbook, and you will find the causal theory expounded in terms of this picture and criticized in terms of the absurdities it obviously involves. Yet, if you search for an argument or chain of reasoning that would explain just how the unperceivability of physical things is supposed to follow from the theory, you will find almost nothing that fits the bill. Rather, it seems that philosophers have simply assumed that the causal theory must have this consequence.

Still, one can discern, largely implicit in the literature, three different considerations that help to explain this assumption.

(1) The literature makes it abundantly clear that many philosophers have been influenced by the so-called 'scientific' argument that I discussed in Chapter Three. The fact that perceiving requires a complicated causal chain from the object to the perceiver's brain has been taken to show that the objects cannot really be perceived. Despite its invalidity, this argument seems to have a perennial appeal, especially to philosophers and scientists who are impressed by certain specific features of the causal chain, such as the 'time-gap' and the contrast between the homogeneity of neural processes and heterogeneity of the perceptual experiences thereby produced.[22] The argument may also acquire plausibility when the last member of the causal chain is conceived in certain ways. Locke, for example, conceived of the 'sensation' or 'idea' in which the chain terminates as a kind of image or picture of the stimulus-object. But if the immediate object of perception is an image of the stimulus-object, then it may well seem that we do not *need* to perceive the latter in order to acquire knowledge of it by perception. Thus, the representationalism which Locke built into his version of the causal theory may encourage us to think of physical objects as being unperceivable. It should be noted, however, that representationalism does not entail the unperceivability of physical things. There would be no *inconsistency* in holding that (1) only ideas are *immediately* perceived, (2) physical things are perceived by the senses (though not immediately perceived), and (3) ideas resemble physical things.[23] The most that can be said is that representationalism *suggests* that the objects represented are not themselves perceived. Moreover, even if representationalism did imply the unperceivability of physical things, it still would not follow that even the *classical* causal theory had that implication. For, since representationalism is not entailed by either AT_{sd} or JT_{sd} or their

conjuction, it is not an essential feature of the theory, but rather a special feature of the Lockean version of the theory. What the classical causal theory does entail is (1) that the sense-data obtained by perceiving a physical thing M are partly caused by M, and (2) that a person could justify the claim to perceive M by an argument showing that M was causally required to account for certain of his sense-data — contentions which are not *prima facie* implausible, and which do not imply that any of the person's sense-data resemble or copy M.

(2) On phenomenological grounds, it may seem simply false to hold that whenever one perceives a physical thing, one perceives *both* the thing *and* the sense-datum that it causes. For example, on looking at Moore's envelope, one does not see both the envelope and, somewhere adjacent to it, an envelopish sense-datum; unless, perhaps, one is suffering from double vision. Thus, it may seem that we must *choose* between holding that we see the envelope and holding that we see a sense-datum; so that if we accept the (classical) causal theory's contention that we see a sense-datum caused by the envelope, then we must deny that we see the envelope. But this overlooks the crucial point that the envelope and the sense-datum are perceived in *different ways*: the sense-datum is immediately perceived$_e$, the envelope is not. Once this is remembered, the apparent difficulty in maintaining that we perceive both the envelope and the sense-datum vanishes. For there is nothing odd in the view that, upon looking at an envelope from an angle, I perceive, in such a way that I can know its existence and nature solely on the basis of my present visual experience, a rhomboidal, whitish patch or expanse; and I also perceive, though not in such a way that I can know its existence and nature solely on the basis of my present visual experience, an envelope. Furthermore, I can focus my attention on the envelope or on the sense-datum; and shifting my attention from the envelope to the sense-datum does not require that I look above or below or to the side of the envelope. Rather, shifting my attention from the one to the other is more like (though not exactly like) shifting from seeing side 1 of the figure as its front side to seeing it as its back side.

(3) The conflation of psychological and epistemological immediacy that was discussed in Chapter Three, Section 3, also helps to explain the assumption in question, as can be seen by considering the following argument.

(1)   Whatever is perceived by the senses is immediately perceived$_p$.

(2)   Whatever is immediately perceived$_p$ is immediately perceived$_e$.

∴ (3)   Whatever is perceived by the senses is immediately perceived$_e$.

(4)   No part-causes of any perceptual experience are immediately perceived$_e$.

∴ (5)   No part-causes of any perceptual experience are perceived by the senses.

(6)   If some physical things are perceived by the senses, then some part-causes of some perceptual experiences are perceived by the senses.

∴ (7)   No physical things are perceived by the senses.

We have seen that premiss (1) is true: it is true that whatever is perceived by the senses is perceived without any process of reasoning or (conscious) inference.[24] Premiss (2) expresses the conflation of psychological and epistemic immediacy, in the form that this conflation ususally takes: namely, assuming that psychological immediacy is a *sufficient* condition of epistemic immediacy. Premiss (4) is true because of the considerations canvassed in connection with the Argument from Causation: since a perceptual experience having a certain part-cause (e.g. stimulation of the sense-receptors by a physical thing) could be duplicated by the action of a different part-cause (e.g. direct stimulation of the brain), one cannot know what the correct part-cause is on the basis of a given perceptual experience alone. Premiss (6) is an immediate corollary of the analytic thesis of the causal theory. The premiss follows by *Modus Ponens* from the conjunction of the analytic thesis with the tautological proposition that

(P)   If (S perceives M if and only if M, by stimulating S's sense-receptors in a way to be indicated by example, is a part-cause of S's present perceptual experience) then (if S perceives M, then S perceives a part-cause of his present perceptual experience).[25]

Here, then, is an argument that leads from a causal analysis of perceiving [invoked in premiss (6)], *via* some by-now familiar premisses concerning immediate perception, to the conclusion that physical things are unperceivable — thereby seeming to show that this paradoxical proposition follows from such an analysis.

Although this argument is formally valid, it is certainly unsound. For premiss (2), as I have already argued, is false.[26] Its falsity can also be shown by counterexamples. Consider for instance the case of a man who has frequent, realistic hallucinations of tomatoes. At a given time t, however, he is seeing the real thing: he is looking directly at a real tomato which is reflecting light into his eyes and thereby causing it to look to him exactly as if there is a tomato before him. At time t, then, he immediately perceive$_p$ a real tomato. However, at time t he does not immediately perceive$_e$ a real tomato. For since he frequently hallucinates realistic tomatoes — since it frequently looks to him exactly as if there is a tomato before him although there is really no tomato before him — even when he sees a real tomato he does not see it in such a way that he can know it to be a real tomato solely on the basis of his present visual experience. Therefore premiss (2) is false, and so the argument fails to show that the causal theory of perception implies that physical things are unperceivable.

Why have philosophers conflated psychological and epistemic immediacy, thereby accepting the falsehood expressed in premiss (2)? Part of the explanation, I believe, is that Berkeley, whose influence on the perceptual vocabulary of other philosophers is second to none, conflated the two notions.[27] But there is another reason as well. Consider premiss (3) of the above argument. This premiss spells out the consequence of combining the truism expressed by premiss (1) with the conflation involved in premiss (2). This consequence boils down to the claim that perceiving always constitutes knowledge. In other words, the first three steps of the argument amount to this: given the truism that sense-perception has psychological immediacy, then if only we can collapse this psychological immediacy with epistemic immediacy, we can say that perceiving constitutes knowing. Now the temptation to do just this is very strong. For we all believe that perceiving is our fundamental way of acquiring knowledge about the world, and (3) seems to do justice unequivocally to this conviction. Furthermore, the collapsing of the two notions of immediacy that leads to (3) has a plausibility of its own. For consider again the man who is immediately perceiving$_p$ a tomato. One wants to say: the tomato is really there before his eyes; he sees it; from a psychological point of view his awareness of it could not be more direct or unmediated than it is; so he must know that he's seeing a tomato. It is only when we recall that this man frequently hallucinates realistic tomatoes that we realize that there is a gap between psychological and epistemic immediacy. And when we remember that anyone's perceptual experiences can be caused in a number of different ways, then we are reminded that this gap applies not only to a man who frequently hallucinates but to normal perceivers as well. The upshot is that we are pulled in opposite ways: in one direction by our conviction that perceiving is our fundamental way of knowing, in the other direction by our realization on reflection that perceiving does not always constitute knowing, and that we run into difficulties when we try to specify the conditions under which perceiving does yield knowledge. Thus the conflation of 'immediately perceived$_p$' and 'immediacy perceived$_e$' is an attempt to escape from the antinomy that is generated when we reflect on the relation between perception and knowledge, by ignoring the very considerations which both give rise to the antinomy and make the conflation illegitimate.

We may safely conclude that the causal theory of perception does not imply, either in its general or its classical formulation, that physical things are unperceivable. The theory leaves us free to maintain that we see, touch, hear, taste, and smell physical things. But this does not mean that there is no epistemological problem of perception. To assume that it does would be to make just the converse mistake of the one made by those who think that the causal theory does imply the unperceivability of physical things. They assume that because physical things are not immediately perceived$_e$, therefore they are not immediately perceived$_p$ and so are not perceived by the senses. We would be assuming that just because physical things are perceived by the senses and so are immediately perceived$_p$, therefore they are immediately perceived$_e$. But the assumption that perceiving constitutes knowing, whether it is put negatively or positively, is mistaken. This means that a standard way of conceiving the problem of perception and knowledge is mistaken. The problem is put as: "Do we perceive physical things or do we perceive sense-data? If we must say that we perceive sense-data — if we must accept 'epistemological dualism' — then we have an epistemological problem on our hands because physical things become unperceivable. But if we can defend saying that we perceive physical things — if we can maintain 'direct realism' ('naive' realism) — then the problem is dissolved because there is no screen of sense-data to hide the things from us." It should now be clear that this way of conceiving the problem is radically mistaken. A very brief formulation of the problem should rather go as follows: "Granting that we can and do perceive physical things, *how*, given the regresses that arise when we attempt to specify the conditions under which perception yields knowledge, do we *know* that we perceive them? If this knowledge can be accounted for on the theory that it is based on immediately perceiving sense-data, then this epistemological problem can be solved by introducing sense-data. But if this knowledge cannot be accounted for on the theory that it is based on the immediate perception of sense-data, then we have an unsolved epistemological problem on our hands." Accordingly, it is time to turn to the justification thesis of the classical causal theory, which purports to specify how our knowledge that we perceive physical things can be derived from our knowledge of the sense-data we immediately perceive.

4. THE JUSTIFICATION THESIS. (I)

It will be remembered that the justification thesis of the classical causal theory goes as follows:

JT_{sd}:   S could justify the claim or belief that he perceives M by an argument showing that M is causally required to account for the fact that S is immediately perceiving or has immediately perceived a certain set of sense-data.

Simply put, JT_{sd} asserts that a perceptual claim or belief can be justified by means of a causal argument or inference. This argument proceeds from effects to causes, like the inference from smoke to fire. When one sees or smells smoke, one can reliably infer that there is fire. Likewise, according to JT_{sd}, when we immediately perceive certain sense-data, we can reliably infer that there is a physical thing of a particular sort stimulating our sense-receptors, thereby producing these sense-data.

Before considering whether such a causal inference is legitimate, let us clear away a possible misunderstanding. The justification thesis does not imply that we go through a process of reasoning or perform an inference from our sense-data to their causes whenever we believe that we are perceiving a physical object. This would be simply false. Rather, the justification thesis asserts that such a belief *could be justified* by a causal argument. Thus, suppose that you were asked to justify your belief that on a certain occasion you are hearing someone talking. Then, according to JT_{sd}, you could appeal to a causal argument. You could say something of the following sort: "I am immediately perceiving certain auditory sense-data of a particular sort. Now I am not producing those sense-data myself; nor are they being caused by any of the other sense-data (visual, tactual, etc.) that I am immediately perceiving or have immediately perceived. So their cause must be some physical thing. Furthermore, sense-data of this particular sort are not caused by inanimate objects or by any of the lower animals. Therefore, what I am hearing is a person speaking." Notice, however, that supposing it is true that you could justify your perceptual belief in some such way as this, it does not in the least follow that whenever you believe that you are hearing someone speaking, you must actually go through some process of causal reasoning. The proposition that S could justify the belief that he perceives M by a causal inference is perfectly compatible with the proposition that in believing that he perceives M S performs no inference. The justification thesis is an epistemological one; not a psychological one.[28]

In examining the justification thesis, it will be useful to divide the question as follows:

(1)   Can the causal argument show that S's sense-data are caused by something other than *other* sense-data S has immediately perceived?

(2)   Can the causal argument show that S's sense-data are caused in the particular manner required by the analytic thesis, i.e. by specific physical objects stimulating S's sense-receptors?

I shall begin by stating the argument in favor of an affirmative answer to (1). Then I shall raise an objection to this argument but will not attempt to settle the difficult issue raised by this objection. Rather, I shall argue that even if we grant for the sake of the argument that (1) can be answered in the affirmative, (2) must be answered in the negative.

The argument in favor of an affirmative answer to (1) is as follows.[29] If you consider the sense-data you immediately perceive through a given period of time, you will be struck by the fact that they are generally quite discontinuous and chaotic. Consider just your visual sense-data. When you change the direction in which you are looking, or change your location by a few feet or more, your visual sense-data usually alter completely. In time a set of similar sense-data may recur, but it will not always be preceded or followed by similar sense-data. For example, visual sense-data as of a certain building may on one occasion be preceded by sense-data as of a field and followed by sense-data as of a river; on another occasion they may be preceded by sense-data as of a river and followed by sense-data as of a field; on yet another occasion they may be neither preceded nor followed by sense-data as of a river or field but by quite different visual sense-data instead. And if you go into a dreamless sleep or are blindfolded before or after having the sense-data as of the building, then there will be no visual sense-data preceding or following them. This illustrates a very general point about sense-data; namely, that our sense-data do not themselves exhibit the kind of temporal ordering or regularity that they would have to exhibit in order for it to be true that sense-data are caused by other sense-data. This would require that similar sense-data always be followed by similar sense-data; for just this kind of ordering in time is necessary for there to be a cause-effect relationship. Therefore, the argument goes, our sense-data are not caused by other sense-data, and so question (1) can be answered in the affirmative. For the only other alternative would be to hold that our sense-data occur without any causal explanation, and that is absurd.

Let me now raise the objection to this argument. The objection is that the argument presupposes the truth of the causal principle, i.e. of the principle that every event must have a cause (except perhaps for certain specially restricted classes of events). But one is not entitled to presuppose the truth of the causal principle in giving an argument for the justification thesis. For the principle is a generalization from what we know about the operations of physical things. It is not a generalization from what we know about sequences of sense-data, for the very reason that sense-data do not themselves exhibit causal order. Therefore, appealing to the principle of causality in order to justify the belief that we perceive physical things puts the cart before the horse. We can only be justified in accepting the principle of causality if we are already justified in believing that we perceive physical things.

I shall not attempt to evaluate the force of this objection, because it raises a difficult and controversial issue. Some philosophers would deny that the causal principle is merely a generalization from what we know about the operations of physical things. They would admit that this is true of particular causal laws, such as the law that water at sea level will boil if heated to 212 degrees Fahrenheit. But they would hold, following Kant, that the general principle that every event must have *some* cause is an *a priori* truth (though *what* the particular causes of any event are can be known only empirically). Attempting to determine whether this view is tenable would be a major task in its own right, which I shall not undertake here. Rather, I propose to grant for the sake of the argument that our sense-data have causes. Given this assumption, and given also that sense-data do not themselves exhibit the sort of temporal order that they would have to exhibit for these causes to be other sense-data, it follows that our sense-data are caused by something other than other sense-data, i.e. that question (1) above may be answered in the affirmative. However, as Price puts it, "as to the *character* of this something other than sense-data, the argument so far tells us nothing . . . We cannot even say whether it is one or many."[30] Our question accordingly becomes: assuming that an affirmative answer to (1) is warranted, can we go on from this to the stronger claim that an affirmative answer to question (2) is also warranted? Can we get from the proposition that our sense-data are caused by *something* other than other sense-data, to the proposition that they are caused (in many cases) by particular physical objects stimulating our sense-receptors? It is here, I believe, that the classical theory fails us.

Let us begin by asking: how do we establish particular causal connections, such as the connection between smoke and fire? Roughly speaking, the answer is that we establish them by determining that in every case the event we call the cause is accompanied or followed by the event we call the effect. In other words, we determine that there is a strict correlation between one type of event and another. Such a correlation entitles us to conclude that there is a causal connection between events of the two types. Now let me call attention to a crucial feature of this procedure. It presupposes that there is some way to ascertain the occurrence of each member of the pair of correlated events *independently* of the other member of the pair. Thus, for example, establishing that there is a causal connection between smoke and fire presupposes that there is some way to ascertain the presence of fire *other* than by noting the presence of smoke and vice-versa. If there were no tests for the presence of fire other than the presence of smoke or vice-versa, we could not even begin to correlate the two so as to establish that there is a causal connection between them.

Let us apply this to the case where the members of the pairs of events to be correlated are (*a*) the occurrence of certain sense-data, and (*b*) the stimulation of our sense-receptors by a certain physical object. Clearly, there is a way of ascertaining (*a*) independently of (*b*). For sense-data are supposed to be immediate objects of perception, i.e. objects whose existence and nature can be known *solely* on the basis of a given perceptual experience. So in order to ascertain the occurrence of certain sense-data, one need not ascertain that any physical thing is stimulating one's sense-receptors; one need only attend to one's perceptual experience. On the other hand, there is no way to ascertain (*b*) independently of (*a*). For, given the two vicious regresses that arise when we reflect on the relation between perception and knowledge, there is no way of *knowing* that a certain physical object is stimulating one's sense-receptors *other* than by the occurrence of certain sense-data. Therefore, it seems quite impossible to establish the kind of correlation between the occurrence of sense-data and the presence of physical things stimulating our sense-receptors that must be established before a causal inference from the former to the latter can be warranted.

Notice that this criticism does not turn on the idea that physical things are in principle unperceivable. Rather, it turns on the point that there is in principle no way of *knowing* that one is perceiving a physical thing independently of immediately perceiving certain sense-data.[31] Thus the criticism is formally analogous to, but not identical with, the criticism of the causal theory which was first made by David Hume. Hume argued that we can only draw a causal inference from an event A to an event B if we have observed a 'constant conjunction' between such events, i.e. if we have observed that events of type A are invariably accompanied by events of type B. However, since we can never perceive physical things at all but only sense-data, it follows that it is impossible to draw any causal inference from sense-data to physical things.

But as no beings are ever present to the mind but perceptions [i.e. Humean 'impressions' and 'ideas'] ; it follows that we may observe a conjunction or a relation of cause and effect between different perceptions, but can never observe it between perceptions and objects. 'Tis impossible, therefore, that from the existence of any of the qualities of the former, we can ever form any conclusion concerning the existence of the latter, nor ever satisfy our reason in this particular.[32]

It is a question of fact whether the perceptions of the senses be produced by external objects resembling them. How shall this question be determined? By experience, surely, as all other questions of a like nature. But here experience is and must be entirely silent. The mind has never anything present to it but the perceptions, and cannot possibly reach any experience of their connection with objects. The supposition of such a connection is, therefore, without any foundation in reasoning.[33]

Hume regarded this as a perfectly decisive objection to the causal theory, and it has become the standard objection to it. Nevertheless, the objection is unsound, because it rests on the false doctrine that physical objects are unperceivable (that only sense-data are ever 'present to the mind'). But while the objection to the causal theory that I have just made — namely that a causal inference from the occurrence of sense-data to the presence of physical things stimulating our sense-receptors is unjustified because there is in principle no way of *knowing* the latter independently of the former — is structurally similar to the standard objection, it does not turn on the idea that physical things are unperceivable.

A defender of the classical causal theory, however, would certainly not concede that this criticism refutes the justification thesis. He would point out that causal theorists such as Locke or Russell have never supposed that the inference from the occurrence of sense-data to the presence of physical objects stimulating our sense-receptors is an ordinary causal inference like the one from smoke to fire. Rather, causal theorists hold that the inference is a special type of causal inference, called an 'inference to the best explanation'. This type of inference can be illustrated with an example from the history of science. Boyle discovered that for relatively low temperature, the pressure of a gas varies inversely with the volume of the gas. This led Boyle to anticipate the kinetic theory of gases, according to which the particles in a gas move freely and rapidly in straight lines and collide with each other, causing changes in their velocities and directions; and the pressure of the gas results from the impact of these particles (e.g. against the inner walls of the container). Now suppose we ask: how does the inverse relation between the pressure and volume of a gas justify or support the kinetic hypothesis? The answer is that the latter is the best explanation of the former. For if the particles constituting a given quantity of gas are perpetually moving, colliding, and so being diverted in new directions, then when the volume of gas is reduced the collisions will become more frequent and so more of the particles will simultaneously strike the retaining walls of the container (or anything within the container), resulting in an increase in pressure. And conversely, if the volume occupied by the gas is expanded, the collisions will become less frequent and so fewer of the particles will simultaneously strike the inner portions of the container, resulting in a decrease in pressure. Thus, the kinetic hypothesis explains very well why the pressure and volume of a gas vary inversely; that is why the inference from Boyle's Law to the kinetic hypothesis is justified or reasonable. But notice that this inference, unlike an ordinary causal inference, does not require that there be an independent way of ascertaining the presence of the cause, i.e. of the moving gas particles, to which indeed Boyle had no independent access since they were too small to be observed. This is a crucial point for the causal theorist. For he can now claim that the lack of any way to ascertain the presence of physical things stimulating our sense-receptors independently of the occurrence of sense-data does not vitiate the inference from the latter to the former. The inference is justified anyway, because the hypothesis that there are physical things stimulating our sense-receptors is the best explanation of our sense-data, just as the kinetic hypothesis was the best explanation of Boyle's Law.

This claim must be defended by showing that specific facts about our sense-data are best explained by the hypothesis that the sense-data are caused by physical objects stimulating our sense-receptors. In a section of his *Essay Concerning Human Understanding* that can well be regarded as the prototypical defense of the justification thesis, Locke appeals to the following facts ('concurrent reasons', as he calls them).[34]

(1) Whether a person obtains sense-data of a given sense-modality depends on whether the person possesses the corresponding sense-receptors. "It is plain those perceptions are produced in us by exterior causes affecting our senses; because those that want the *organs* of any sense can never have the ideas belonging to that sense produced in their minds."

(2) Most of our sense-data occur independently of our wills.

(3) Certain kinds of sense-data are sometimes accompanied by pain (or pleasure); sometimes not. "Many of those ideas are *produced in us with pain*, which afterwards we remember without the least offence."

(4) Our sense-data are mutually corroborative. "Our senses in many cases bear witness to the truth of each other's report, concerning the existence of sensible things without us. He that *sees* a fire, may, if he doubt whether it be anything more than a bare fancy, *feel* it too; and be convinced by putting his hand in it."

Locke's thesis is that each of these facts, and especially all of them taken together, are best explained by the hypothesis that our sense-data are generally produced by physical things stimulating our sense-receptors. Consider for example point (2). Here Locke can be understood as asking the question: why is it that although *some* of our sense-data depend on our wills, most of them do not? His answer is that the best explanation of this difference among our sense-data is that the former are produced by ourselves when we *imagine* or *remember* something, while the latter are produced by the action of physical things on us.

For though, when my eyes are shut, or windows fast, I can at pleasure recall to my mind the ideas of light, or the sun, which former sensations had lodged in my memory; so I can at pleasure lay by that idea, and take into my view that of the smell of a rose, or taste of sugar. But, if I turn my eyes at noon towards the sun, I cannot avoid the ideas which the light or sun then produces in me. So that there is a manifest difference between the ideas laid up in my memory (over which . . . I . . . have constantly the same power to dispose of them, and lay them by at pleasure), and those which force themselves upon me, and I cannot avoid having. And therefore it must needs be some exterior cause, and the brisk acting of some objects without me, whose efficacy I cannot resist, that produces those ideas in me, whether I will or no.[35]

Again, consider point (3). Here Locke can be interpreted as asking: why is it that similar sense-data are sometimes accompanied by pain (or pleasure), and sometimes not so accompanied? For example, suppose that on a certain occasion you have a visual sense-datum of a very bright yellow disk accompanied by smarting or pain. On another occasion, you have a similar sense-datum without any discomfort. How is this difference best explained? Locke's answer would be that on the first occasion a physical thing (e.g. the sun or a bright lightbulb) was actually stimulating your eyes, thereby causing pain as well as a certain visual sense-datum; while on the second occasion you were only having a memory-experience or some other sort of mental image.

How should we evaluate Locke's inference to the best explanation? Well, it would seem that the reasonable procedure is to ask the following question. Could Locke have *ruled out other possible explanations* of the facts to which he appeals, i.e. have shown that other possible explanations of those facts are

not as good as the hypothesis that our sense-data are caused by physical
objects stimulating our sense-receptors? For unless Locke could have done
this, his claim that this hypothesis provides the *best* explanation of (1)–(4) is
gratuitous and unjustified. Locke is aware of this. Thus, in connection with
point (1), he says,

> The organs themselves, it is plain, do not produce them [i.e. our sense-data]; for then
> the eyes of a man in the dark would produce colors, and his nose smell roses in the
> winter. . . .[36]

Here Locke is in effect answering the following challenge: "You say that we
do not obtain certain sense-data unless we possess the corresponding sense-
organs, and that this is best explained by the hypothesis that these sense-
data are caused by physical objects stimulating those sense-organs. But it
would be an equally good explanation of this fact to hold that the sense-data
are caused by the sense-organs themselves." Locke's reply is that this would
not be as good an explanation, because it would fail to explain why the sense-
organs do not produce the sense-data at all times.

Before considering whether Locke could have ruled out alternative explanations of (1)–(4), it must be pointed out that (1), as it stands, is not a
fact to which Locke is entitled to appeal. For his task is to show how our
knowledge that we perceive physical things can be derived, by an inference
to the best explanation, from knowledge about (*only*) certain facts concerning the sense-data we immediately perceive. But the fact that obtaining
certain sorts of sense-data requires having certain kinds of sense-organs is not
only a fact about the sense-data; it is partly a fact about the sense-organs,
which are themselves physical things known by perception. Therefore,
Locke's appeal to (1) is illegitimate: if one is trying to explain how any
knowledge that we perceive physical things is possible, then one must not do
so in terms of the very kind of knowledge one is trying to explain.

This point is important. For in defending the justification thesis there is a
strong temptation to appeal, as Locke does in (1), to various portions of our
common-sense or scientific knowledge; and such appeals lend a specious
plausibility to Lockean inferences to the best explanation. For example, if
we consider a certain sequence of visual sense-data, say those that would
lead us to think that we are successively viewing each of the sides and corners
of a cube, and if we take our knowledge that such a series of sense-data is
occurring *in conjunction with* knowledge of certain antecedent conditions
about the perceiver's physical surroundings and of the laws of perspective,
optics, etc., then no doubt the best explanation of the sequence of sense-

data will be that the perceiver is really seeing a cubical object. But if we are serious about and remain faithful to the program of showing that the best explanation of certain facts about (only) our sense-data is that they are caused by certain sorts of physical objects stimulating our sense-receptors, then we must forego any appeal to facts other than the qualities of and relations between sense-data themselves. To do otherwise is to give up the epistemological purpose of defending the justification thesis, which is to show that our knowledge that we perceive physical things can be derived from knowledge about (only) sense-data. Thus, the nearest thing to (1) that Locke could legitimately appeal to is certain facts about the relations between sense-data of a given modality and certain other sense-data, e.g. the fact that one does not obtain olfactory sense-data unless one at least sometimes also obtains sense-data as of one's nose being clear (uncongested). Locke might then argue that the best explanation of this fact is that olfactory sense-data are usually produced by physical objects affecting the nose in a certain way. Notice, however, that point (1) then becomes a special instance of point (4).

Could Locke have ruled out alternative explanations of (2)–(4)? Let us begin with (2). While one way to explain the difference between sense-data that do and those that do not depend on our will for their occurrence is to maintain that the latter unlike the former are caused by physical objects 'briskly acting' on our sense-organs, this is not the only possible explanation. In hallucinations and in dreams we also have sense-data that are not within our control: the sense-data obtained during a realistic and frightening nightmare (or drug-induced hallucination), for example, are quite as impossible to will away as any others. Perhaps, then, the sense-data that we "cannot avoid having" are always produced by some cause other than physical objects stimulating our sense-receptors. Perhaps, as Descartes suggested

... there is in me some faculty fitted to produce these ideas without the assistance of any external things, even though it is not yet known by me; just as, apparently, they have hitherto always been found in me during sleep without the aid of any external objects.[37]

Of course we do not *believe* this; rather, as Descartes also pointed out, we have an irresistible, spontaneous propensity to believe that our sense-data are produced by external objects.[38] But our question here is how this belief is *justified*; and in particular, whether it is justified because what we are naturally impelled to believe is a better explanation of (2) than any other possible explanation. And this, at least if (2) is taken by itself, seems not to be the case.

Does it help to add (3), i.e. the fact that similar sense-data are sometimes accompanied by pain (or pleasure), and sometimes not so accompanied? Again, while one possible explanation of this fact is that the sense-data 'produced in us with pain' are caused by objects impinging on our sense-receptors, this is not the only possible explanation. Many pains occur due to intra-organic causes rather than because some object is impinging on our sense-organs. There is also the case (pointed out by Descartes) of an amputee who feels pain 'in' the amputated limb long after his wounds have healed.[39] And there are purely psychosomatic pains. Perhaps, then, the explanation of certain sense-data's being accompanied by pain is always that some intra-organic mechanism or psychological faculty has come into play. Of course, if we consider this hypothesis in light of our knowledge of physiology and medicine, it is highly implausible and even quite absurd. But here it must be stressed once again that a defender of the justification thesis is not entitled to appeal to such knowledge. For his task is *not*: to show that, *given* a certain body of knowledge about human organisms and their physical environment (knowledge ultimately acquired by perception), the best explanation of certain facts about sense-data is that they are caused by physical objects stimulating our sense-receptors. Rather his task is: to show that, given *only* knowledge of certain features of our sense-data themselves, the sense-datas' occurrence is best explained by the hypothesis that they are caused by objects stimulating our sense-receptors. But it does not seem that this can be shown by appealing to (2) and (3) either separately or conjointly.

Does it help to appeal also to point (4), i.e. to the fact that our sense-data are mutually corroborative? One possible explanation of this fact is indeed that our sense-data are caused by certain sorts of objects, behaving in accordance with certain fixed principles (scientific laws), stimulating our sense-receptors. But again, this is not the only possible explanation. For in a hallucination or dream, the sense-data of one modality sometimes corroborate those of another, as in the case of a man who has a visual hallucination of a coin and a tactual hallucination of its milled edge when he tries to pick it up. And a hallucination can be quite prolonged and systematic: our man might go on to hallucinate inserting the coin in a juke-box, hearing dance music, inviting someone to dance, etc. Is it possible, then, that all of our sense-data, no matter how systematically they "bear witness to the truth of each other's report concerning the existence of sensible things without us", constitute a perpetual hallucination?

In his First *Meditation*, Descartes asks us to consider the following hypothesis. Suppose that there really are no physical objects and never have been. Instead, an extremely powerful and intelligent spirit, whose sole purpose is to deceive us continually, causes absolutely all of our sense-data. Yet the sense-data that he causes us to have are sufficiently vivid, systematic and orderly to give us an irresistible propensity to believe that they come from physical objects behaving in accordance with fixed laws and affecting our senses. As Descartes puts it:

. . . I have long had fixed in my mind the belief that an all-powerful God existed by whom I have been created such as I am. But how do I know that He has not brought it to pass that there is no earth, no heaven, no extended body, no magnitude, no place, and that nevertheless I possess the perceptions of all these things and that they seem to me to exist just exactly as I now see them? . . . But possibly God has not desired that I should be thus deceived, for He is said to be supremely good . . . . I shall then suppose, not that God who is supremely good and the fountain of truth, but that some evil genius not less powerful than deceitful, has employed his whole energies in deceiving me; I shall consider that the heavens, the earth, colours, figures, sound, and all other external things are nought but the illusions and dreams of which this genius has availed himself in order to lay traps for my credulity; I shall consider myself as having no hands, no eyes, no flesh, no blood, nor any senses; [i.e. sense-organs] , yet falsely believing myself to possess all these things . . .[40]

Later, Berkeley was to use the same hypothesis against Locke:

Suppose – what no one can deny possible – an intelligence without the help of external bodies, to be affected with the same train of sensations or ideas that you are, imprinted in the same order and with like vividness in his mind. I ask whether that intelligence has not all the reason to believe the existence of corporeal substances, represented by his ideas and exciting them in his mind, that you can possibly have for believing the same thing? Of this there can be no question – which one consideration is enough to make any reasonable person suspect the strength of whatever arguments he may think himself to have for the existence of bodies without the mind.[41]

Today, science-inspired variants of Descartes's hypothesis continue to haunt the pages of works on epistemology. For example:

Suppose that a group of psychologists, biophysicists, and neurologists have constructed an adequate explanation of the neurophysiology of perception, and to test their explanation they take a subject from birth and wire him into a computer which directly stimulates his brain in such a way as to give a coherent, but completely false, sequence of sensations. In the subject's own mind he would seem to live out a completely normal life, growing up, making friends, going to school, getting a job, marrying and raising a family, etc. And yet all those years he was really sealed into an experimental apparatus in which he was fed intravenously and never had any contact with the outside world. It is true that in the present state of neurophysiology this could not be done, but it is certainly a meaningful hypothesis and a logical possibility. Now, how do I know that I am not in the position of the subject of the above experiment? Perhaps a group of scientists have me hooked into such a computer, and all of the experiences that I think

I have had since birth are really figments of the computer. How can I possibly know that this is not the case?[42]

Of course, it might be argued that the hypothesis that all of my sense-data constitute a perpetual hallucination is not really coherent or meaningful. Indeed, this is what a phenomenalist would hold, and it is what I shall myself argue in Chapter Seven. The point I wish to make now, however, is that this would be to abandon the attempt to defend the justification thesis by an inference *to the best explanation*. Such a defense presupposes that the deceiver hypothesis (as I shall call Descartes's hypothesis and contemporary variants of it) is coherent or logically possible, but claims that it can be ruled out on the grounds that it does not provide as good an explanation of our sense-data as Locke's hypothesis of physical things stimulating our sense-receptors. The difficulty, however, is that if the only facts we are allowed to appeal to are facts about the qualities of and relations between sense-data, then it does not seem possible to show that the deceiver hypothesis is a less adequate explanation of our sense-data than Locke's hypothesis.

The reason for this difficulty in Locke's position, I suggest, is as follows. For an inference to the best explanation to be justified, there must be *in principle* some way of ascertaining the occurrence of the inferred cause independently of the effect from which it is inferred. This requirement was satisfied in the case of Boyle's explanation of the inverse relation between the volume and pressure of a gas in terms of the kinetic hypothesis. For the only reason Boyle could not ascertain the presence of the moving gas particles independently of noting variations in the gas's pressure (when its volume was expanded or reduced) was that these particles were too small to be observed even through the most powerful magnifying instruments available to him. But this meant only that there was *in fact* no way of ascertaining the presence of the gas particles independently of noting the variations in pressure. That this was merely a factual limitation due to the unavailability of more powerful magnifying instruments, rather than a limitation in principle, is shown by the fact that the limitation has now been overcome by the construction of magnifying instruments powerful enough for us to observe molecules and even smaller particles. On the other hand, in the case of Locke's explanation of our sense-data in terms of physical things stimulating our sense-receptors, there is in principle no way of ascertaining the existence of the cause independently of ascertaining the occurrence of the effect. For, as the regress arguments of Chapters One and Three show, there is in principle no way of knowing that one is perceiving a certain physical thing independently of knowing that one is immediately perceiving certain sense-data.[43] (This point, as we have seen, must not be confused with the false proposition that physical things are unperceivable in principle.) And this is why Locke's inference to the best explanation is unjustified.

At this point, however, it may well be asked *why*, in order for an inference like Locke's to be justified, there should have to be in principle some way to ascertain the existence of the cause independently of the effect. In other words, what justification, if any, is there for imposing this requirement on an inference to the best explanation? Why isn't the requirement a merely arbitrary one?

In order to answer this question, let us begin by noting another feature of Boyle's inference to the best explanation. This is that even in Boyle's own day, there were cases where the manner of causation was generically similar (the same in kind) to the one being inferred, and where there was *in fact* an independent way to ascertain the existence of the cause. For example, Boyle could certainly have observed angry bulls in a bull-pen running into the sides of the pen, causing these to shake, give way, *etc.* In this case, the manner of causation is generically similar to the one that Boyle inferred: there is an obvious generic similarity between the way in which pressure is exerted on the sides of the bull-pen, and the way in which pressure is exerted on the inner walls of the gas-container. In one case, some quite large objects are running into the retaining walls of a container; in the other, some very small objects are running into the retaining walls of a container. Of course, there are differences between the causes of the motions involved in each case: those causes are not generically similar. But the *proximate* cause of the pressure on the walls of the bull-pen is generically the same as the proximate cause of the pressure on the walls of the gas-container — impacting bodies. Further, in the case of the bulls (though not in that of the gas molecules), there was, in Boyle's own day, a way to ascertain the presence of the cause (the impacting bulls) independently of ascertaining the occurrence of the effect (the bull pen's shaking, giving way, *etc.*); namely, direct observation.

Having noted this feature of Boyle's inference to the best explanation, I want to put forward a proposition, which invokes the feature, about what makes such an inference legitimate. This proposition is:

(1)   In order for an inference to the best explanation to be justified, there must be cases in which (*a*) the manner of causation is generically similar to the one inferred, and (*b*) there is in fact a way to ascertain the occurrence of the cause independently of the effect.

It should be evident, on reflection, that the principle underlying (1) is the un-exceptionable one that causal connections can ultimately be established only by empirically correlating cause and effect, and not by *a priori* reasoning. For (1) says, in effect, that if we cannot establish a causal connection between two types of events directly, by empirically correlating events of the type in question, then we must at least be able to establish the connection indirectly or by a suitable analogy, i.e. by empirically correlating events of a similar sort. Perhaps the best way to see the correctness of (1), however, is to imagine cases where the requirement that it lays down is not satisfied. For example, suppose that there had been no cases for Boyle to point to, in which the manner of causation was generically similar to the one that he inferred in order to explain the inverse ratio between the pressure and volume of a gas. Then Boyle could not have justifiably inferred that the kinetic hypothesis was the best explanation of that ratio. For how could he possibly have answered a critic who offered some different explanation, if not by pointing out that on the kinetic hypothesis, the variations in pressure are caused in the same manner as that in which similar effects are known to be produced?[44]

If proposition (1) is acceptable, then it explains the requirement that, in an inference to the best explanation, there be in principle an independent way to ascertain the presence of the cause. For there is a logical relationship between that requirement and the requirement laid down in the consequent of (1). This relationship is expressed in the following proposition, which I take to be analytically true:

(2)   If there are cases in which (*a*) the manner of causation is generic-ally similar to the one being inferred, and (*b*) there is in fact an independent way of ascertaining the occurrence of the cause, then there is in principle an independent way of ascertaining the occurrence of the inferred cause.

(To see that this is an analytic proposition, reflect again on the relationship between the case of the bulls colliding against the walls of a bull-pen and the case of the gas molecules colliding against the walls of a gas-container. As we saw, the bull case is generically similar (so far as proximate causation goes) to the molecule case; so that clause (*a*) of (2) is satisfied. But in the bull case (unlike the molecule case, in Boyle's day), there is in fact an independent way of ascertaining the occurrence of the cause; so that clause (*b*) is satisfied as well. What (2) says is that it *follows* from these two points that there must be in principle an independent way of ascertaining the occurrence of the cause in the molecule case. In other words, the difference between the two cases can only be that in the inference case (i.e. the molecule case), there is some practical impediment to ascertaining the occurrence of the cause independently of the effect (e.g. the cause is too small to be observed); as opposed to there being something that makes it in principle impossible to do so. If there were something making it in principle impossible to ascertain the occurrence of the inferred cause independently of the effect, then there could not be other cases in which both (a) and (b) were true. Any other case of causation in which (a) was true would have to be one in which (b) was false, and any other case of causation in which (b) was true would have to be one in which (a) was false.) Now it follows from (1) and (2) that:

(3)   In order for an inference to the best explanation to be justified, there must be in principle an independent way of ascertaining the occurrence of the inferred cause.

Thus (1), in conjunction with (2), provides a rationale for the requirement imposed above upon (causal) inferences to the best explanation.[45]

We are now in a position to see exactly why Locke's defense of the Justification Thesis is a failure. The regress arguments of Chapters One and Three have shown that:

(4)   There is in principle no way of ascertaining that a physical thing is stimulating one's sense-receptors, independently of immediately perceiving certain sense-data.

But from (3) and (4), it certainly follows that Locke's inference to the best explanation is unjustified. Alternatively, to put the matter in a way that highlights the basic reason for the failure of Locke's inference, it follows from (4) and (2) that:

(5)   There are no cases of causation in which (a) the manner of causation is generically similar to the causation of sense-data by physical things stimulating one's sense-receptors, and (b) the occurrence of the cause can in fact be ascertained independently of the effect.

Thus, if the inference from the occurrence of certain sense-data to the existence of certain physical things stimulating our sense-receptors is challenged, we cannot justify it by pointing to any generically similar case in which there is in fact an independent way to establish the existence of the cause. And this means, as indeed follows from (5) and (1), that:

(6)   An inference to the best explanation, from the occurrence of
           sense-data to the existence of physical things stimulating one's
           sense-receptors, is not justified.

Therefore, Locke's thesis that the best explanation of our sense-data is "the
brisk acting of some objects without" upon our sense-organs remains unjustified. This fact is effectively brought out by challenging Locke to rule out
rival hypotheses about the causes of our sense-data, such as Descartes's hypothesis of an evil deceiver and its contemporary variants.

5. THE JUSTIFICATION THESIS. (II)

The foregoing criticism of Locke, I believe, applies *mutatis mutandis* to any
attempt to establish the Justification Thesis by an inference to the best explanation. However, since a broadly Lockean position continues to seem plausible to some contemporary philosophers, it will be useful to consider a more
recent attempt. In *The Analysis of Matter*, Bertrand Russell gives an ingenious
defense of the Justification Thesis along Lockean lines.[46] Russell's argument
is in two stages. In stage I, he argues that each of us has good inductive
grounds for believing that there are sense-data other than our own. In other
words, stage I attempts to show that it is reasonable, on inductive grounds, to
reject solipsism and believe in 'other minds'. In stage II, Russell argues that
the best explanation of the systematic correspondence between different
persons' sense-data is that they are all caused by a world of physical objects.
I shall expound both stages of Russell's argument, but limit my critical remarks to stage II. For, in allowing himself to appeal in stage II to the sense-
data of other people, Russell is obviously using a much broader evidence base
for his inference to the best explanation than do philosophers who attempt to
found such an inference on the sense-data of a single perceiver. So if, as I shall
argue, stage II of Russell's argument is unsuccessful, this will show *a fortiori*
that attempts of the latter, more typical sort are bound to fail as well.

Russell begins stage I by pointing out that we can each correlate certain of
our own sense-data with sense-data associated with our own bodily behavior.
The type of correlation Russell has in mind can be illustrated by the following
examples: when I have tactual sense-data of a certain sort, I have visual sense-
data as of my fingers striking typewriter keys; when I feel very chilly, I have
visual sense-data as of my body shivering; when I have auditory sense-data
as of hearing jazz, I have visual sense-data as of my foot beating time; when
I have visual sense-data as of an acquaintance approaching, I have auditory
sense-data as of my own voice saying 'hello'. Next, Russell points out that

there is a similarity between sense-data associated with one's own bodily behavior and sense-data associated with the bodily behavior of other persons. For example, suppose that at a football game I hear the national anthem played and promptly rise to my feet along with everyone else in the stadium. Then there is a similarity between the visual sense-data associated with my own act of rising to my feet and the visual sense-data associated with other persons' acts of rising to their feet. Russell admits that noting this similarity is partly a result of interpretation, because the sense-data associated with my own behavior do not exactly resemble those associated with the same behavior as performed by the other persons. Even if I pay close attention to the changing position of my limbs as I rise to my feet, this change does not look very much like that which I associate with anyone else's rising to his feet. So noting the similarity between the sense-data associated with my own act of rising and the sense-data associated with other persons' acts of rising is already a complex matter from a psychological point of view, involving the ability to imagine how my own body would appear if I could watch myself rising to my feet from a distance. Waiving this complexity, however, we may say that when I have auditory sense-data as of hearing the national anthem played, I note a similarity between the visual sense-data associated with my own bodily response of rising to my feet and the visual sense-data associated with the other persons' responses of rising to their feet. (In other cases, such as the visual sense-data as of my own foot beating time and those as of my listening-companion's foot beating time, the similarity is more direct.) Therefore, I can legitimately infer that the latter are prompted in the same way as in my own case, i.e. by auditory sense-data akin to those I experience upon hearing the national anthem. This inference is an induction from a case where I observe both members of a pair of correlated items, to cases where I observe only one member of similar pairs and infer the other. In my own case, I observe both members of the pair: I immediately perceive auditory sense-data as of the national anthem being played and visual sense-data as of my rising to my feet. So, upon immediately perceiving visual sense-data similar to the latter except for being as of *other* persons' rising to their feet, I infer that these were produced by auditory sense-data akin to my own.

Russell claims, for stage I of his argument, that it allows us "to infer a proposition of great philosophic importance, namely: there are existents which I do not perceive [i.e. others' sense-data]". He adds that

this proposition . . . if induction is valid at all, must be taken as reasonably certain . . . . The argument, though not demonstrative, is as good as any of the fundamental inductions of science.[47]

This is because

... the argument is the usual causal-inductive type of argument upon which all empirical laws are based. We perceive A and B conjoined in a number of cases, and we then infer A and B [Russell means: A from B] in a case where we do not know by perception whether A is present or not.[48]

No doubt, various objections might be raised against Russell's argument as I have so far expounded it. I propose, however, to grant the plausibility of stage I, at least for the sake of the argument, and to go on directly to stage II. For, as noted above, if the inference to physical things as causes of our sense-data fails even when one appeals to the sense-data of a plurality of perceivers, then surely it must fail also when it is based, as is usually the case, on the sense-data of a single perceiver.

In stage II, Russell argues that the best explanation of the systematic correspondence between different persons' sense-data is the existence of certain physical objects causally related to each other and to our sense-data in accordance with the laws of science. The following example illustrates the gist of Russell's reasoning: (1) at a given time the visual sense-data obtained by the members of the President's cabinet resemble and differ from each other in a certain systematic way, i.e. they constitute an ordered group which might be characterized as "different perspectival views of a rectangular surface from several points surrounding it and roughly equidistant from its edges"; and (2) the best explanation of this fact is that those sense-data are caused, in accordance with scientific laws which include the laws of perspective, by a rectangular conference table around which the cabinet members are all sitting. Let us examine these two points in turn.

How can we know that the cabinet members' sense-data do constitute the ordered group characterized above, and more generally that the sense-data had by other people fall into patterns or groups between whose members there is a systematic correspondence? Well, the inference to the existence of other people's sense-data is at the same time an inference to the qualities of those sense-data: the others' sense-data must resemble the sense-data we ourselves would have if the sense-data we associate with our own bodily behavior and situation were similar to those we now associate with their bodily behavior and situation. For example, suppose a cabinet member A has visual sense-data as of another cabinet member B sitting at the narrow end of the rectangular conference table and looking down its entire length. Then A can infer that the visual sense-data obtained by B are like those A would himself obtain were he to have sense-data as of sitting at that end of the table and looking down its entire length. Furthermore — and this is a very important point — the sense-data from which we can make inferences concerning other persons' sense-data include the auditory sense-data which we associate with their verbal behavior or speech. For example, when I have sense-data as of my companion saying 'there is a police car entering the freeway up ahead', I am justified by Russell's argument in believing that these sense-data are accompanied by visual sense-data similar to those that would accompany sense-data as of *my* saying 'there is a police car entering the freeway up ahead'. As Russell puts it:

In virtue of the above argument, I shall now assume that we may enlarge our own experience by testimony — i.e. that the noises we hear when it seems to us that other people are talking do in fact express something analogous to what we would be expressing if we made similar noises. This is a particular instance of the principle contained in the preceding paragraph. [i.e. in the last-quoted passage] [49]

The admissibility of testimony greatly strengthens our inductive evidence for believing that there is a complex, thoroughgoing, and systematic correspondence between different persons' sense-data.

We may take it as established, then, not only that there exist sense-data other than our own, but that these fall into patterns or groups (such as the sense-data had by the presidential cabinet members) between whose members there is a systematic correspondence. On the basis of such groups of sense-data, Russell says, we can form the conception of a space whose occupants are related to the sense-data in accordance with the laws of perspective.

Confining ourselves, to begin with, to the percepts of various observers, we can form groups of percepts connected approximately, though not exactly, by laws which may be called laws of 'perspective'. By means of these laws, together with the changes in other percepts which are connected with the perception of bodily movement, we can form the conception of a space in which percipients are situated, and we find that in this space all the percepts belonging to one group (i.e. of the same physical object, from the standpoint of common sense) can be ordered about a centre, which we take to be the place where the physical object in question is. (For us, this is a *definition* of the place of a physical object.) The centre is not to be conceived as a point, but as a volume, which may be as small as an electron or as large as a star. [50]

We can thus arrive at the laws of perspective, taken in a generalized sense; that is to say, we can correlate the differences between correlated perceptions with differences in the situations of the percipients. And in the space derived from 'points of view' we can place physical objects. For, let A and B be two observers, *a* and *b* their correlated visual percepts, which being correlated, are described as percepts of one physical object O. If the angular dimensions of *a* are larger than those of *b*, we shall say (as a definition) that A is nearer to O than B is. We can thus construct a number of routes converging on O. We shall construct our geometry so that they intersect, and shall define their intersection as the place where O is. [51]

In these two passages, Russell is describing a purely conceptual construction: we can *conceive* the members of ordered groups of sense-data *as* being related to physical objects in accordance with the laws of perspective. What assures us, however, that this construction corresponds to the facts, i.e. that our sense-data really are related to (caused by) physical objects in accordance with the laws of perceptive? Russell's answer — and this is the crucial final step of stage II of his argument — is that this hypothesis provides the best explanation of the ordered groups of sense-data. In accepting this explanation, we accept the hypothesis that a group of sense-data is altered (acquires members or loses members) by the occurrence of events which are connected to each other and to our sense-data in accordance with scientific laws including the laws of persepctive. In other words, we accept the hypothesis that our sense-data are really caused by objects that affect each other and ourselves in accordance with laws of science, including those laws that pertain to the perceptual process itself, and which presumably (though Russell does not explicitly say this) refer to the objects' causal action upon our sense-receptors. Russell summarizes this as follows:

The essential assumption for what is commonly called the causal theory is that the group of percepts can be enlarged by the addition of other events, ranged in the same space about the same centre, and connected both with each other and with the group of percepts by laws which include the laws of perspective. The essential points are (1) the arrangement about a centre, (2) the continuity between percepts and correlated events in other parts of the space derived from percepts and locomotion. The first is a matter of observation; the second is a hypothesis designed to secure simplicity and continuity in the laws of correlation suggested by the grouping of percepts. It cannot be demonstrated, but its merits are of the same kind as those of any other scientific theory.[52]

Does stage II of Russell's argument succeed in establishing the justification thesis of the causal theory? Reverting for a moment to Grice's formulation of that thesis (since it makes reference to other persons' sense-data), does the argument succeed in showing that

a claim on the part of X to perceive M, if it needs to be justified at all, is justified by showing that the existence of M is required if the circumstances reported by certain true sense-datum statements, some of which may be about persons other than X, are to be causally accounted for?[53]

Unfortunately, the argument does not succeed. For, even if we grant that from our own sense-data we can inductively infer the existence of sense-data obtained by other persons, and falling into ordered groups between whose members there is a systematic 'perspectival' correspondence, we need not therefore grant that the best explanation of these sense-data is that they really are caused by physical objects in accordance with laws of perspective. Other explanations are possible, which would account just as well for the ordered groups of sense-data. Consider for example Leibniz's theory of preestablished harmony. According to this 17th century metaphysical theory, what we call other persons are nothing but monads, i.e. spiritual substances or souls each of which has a continual series of perceptions. The perceptions of the monads always correspond to each other, somewhat in the same way, Leibniz says, "as the same city is variously represented according to the various situations of him who is regarding it".[54] But the explanation of this systematic correspondence between the monads' perceptions is not that these perceptions are caused by material things in accordance with the laws of perspective. For according to Leibniz, matter is unreal; what we call material things are nothing but appearances. Instead, the explanation of the systematic correspondence is that God created the monads in such a way that every monad's perceptions would always reflect to some degree the perceptions of every other monad. Only by instituting this preestablished harmony between the monads' perceptions could God realize his plan, which was to create the best of all possible worlds, defined by Leibniz as "the one which is at the same time the simplest in hypotheses and the richest in phenomena".[55] Now if we assume with Russell that there is in principle no way to justify any explanation of sense-data except in terms of the qualities and relations of sense-data themselves — our own as well as those of other persons — then why isn't Leibniz's explanation of the systematic correspondence between different persons' sense-data just as good as Russell's?

Perhaps it will be suggested that Russell's explanation is better because it is *simpler*. (Russell himself appeals to its simplicity a number of times, and other modern defenders of the causal theory have also invoked the principle of parsimony.) This suggestion might be supported by pointing out that any satisfactory explanation of our sense-data must explain the occurrence of the sense-data *from* which the inference to other persons' sense-data proceeds, i.e. of the sense-data associated with other persons' bodily behavior. And isn't the simplest explanation of these sense-data that they really are caused by the *bodily* behavior of other persons responding to their experiences with the same bodily behavior we ourselves exhibit when we have similar experiences — and so by a certain sort of physical thing (a human organism) affecting our sense-receptors? This is certainly the familiar explanation, and the one we all accept. But is it the simplest possible explanation? It does not appear to be: with a little ingenuity one can think of other explanations that are just as simple. Leibniz, for example, held not only that persons are incorporeal substances, but also that there is never any causal interaction between them: 'monads', as he put it, "have no windows through which anything may come in or go out".[56] Therefore, the sense-data that I associate with another person's bodily behavior cannot possibly really result from his *body causally affecting me*. What then explains the fact that these sense-data are accompanied by sense-data similar to those I myself have when the sense-data I associate with my own bodily behavior are similar to those I now associate with his bodily behavior? Well, this fact is just a particular instance of the preestablished harmony, i.e. of God's having created the monads in such a way that the perceptions of a monad would always reflect the perceptions of every other monad. The sense-data I associate with another person's bodily behavior reflect (are signs of) his sense-data, in that they are similar to the sense-data I associate with my own bodily behavior when I have sense-data similar to his; however the sense-data I associate with his bodily behavior only *appear* to be caused by his body affecting my sense-organs, since neither of us really possesses a body and there is really no causal interaction between us. If what one wants is the *simplest* explanation of the fact that certain sense-data (those we associate with other persons' bodily behavior) are reliable indicators of certain other sense-data (those had by other persons), i.e. of the fact that the former are not accompanied by sense-data totally different from our own or by no sense-data other than our own, then Leibniz's explanation is as satisfactory as Russell's. For the difference between them is that on Russell's account sense-data of a certain kind SD_b, which are associated with bodily behavior of a certain sort (e.g. with wincing), are correlated with bodily behavior of a certain sort B (e.g. wincing) which itself is correlated with sense-data of a certain kind SD_d (e.g. pain), while on Leibniz's account sense-data of kind SD_b are correlated with sense-data of kind SD_d in virtue of a preestablished harmony between the two kinds of sense-data; and plainly Leibniz's account is not *more complicated* than Russell's.[57]

If we presuppose the reasonableness of common-sense and scientific beliefs about the world, then of course Leibniz's theory does introduce unecessary complications into our overall account. For we must then explain the existence of innumerable beliefs that are reasonable but false. But, as I stressed in the previous section, one is not entitled to presuppose the reasonableness of common-sense and scientific beliefs when attempting to establish the Justification Thesis of the Causal Theory. And on the other hand, if we stick scrupulously (as Russell tries to do) to beliefs about the qualities and relations of sense-data — even including those of other persons — then the appeal to simplicity is of no avail. For what reason is there to suppose that of all the logically possible explanations of the systematic and complex correspondence between different persons' sense-data, Russell's explanation in terms of physical objects causing those sense-data in accordance with laws of perspective must be the simplest one? Surely other equally simple explanations could be devised, e.g. by building certain fixed principles no more complicated than the laws of perspective into the design of the preestablished harmony; or by supposing, as Price suggests, that a Berkeleyan God *conceives* of a world of physical objects producing our sense-data in accordance with laws of perspective and thereupon causes our sense-data to occur *as if* they were being so produced though in fact matter does not exist.[58] I submit that no matter how complex the facts about sense-data are, if explanations of those facts other than Russell's are logically possible, then at least some of these explanations will be as simple as Russell's. Of course, it might be suggested that once a certain level of complexity is reached, describing our sense-data as the result of a Leibnizian preestablished harmony or a Berkeleyan God's 'Divine Language of Ideas' differs only verbally from describing them as the result of physical objects that behave in certain lawful ways: these are only misleading ways of redescribing the material world — mere logomachies. However, to say this would be to reject attempts to establish the Justification Thesis by an inference to the best explanation, or any other form of inductive reasoning. For it would be to reject the assumption that such explanations of our sense-data as Leibniz's or Berkeley's are logically possible, in favor of the view that there is a logical or conceptual connection between sufficiently complex sets of sense-data and the existence of physical objects. This view, which is the one maintained by phenomenalists, will be considered in the following chapter.

I want to conclude this chapter by stating the reason for the failure of Russell's argument in a general way, so as to bring out the fact that it applies to *any* attempt to establish the Justification Thesis by an inference to the best explanation, or by any other form of inductive reasoning. In attempting to establish the Justification Thesis in such a manner, the causal theorist implicitly accepts the following two propositions:

(a)   The only way in principle of knowing that any physical thing is perceived is by immediately perceiving certain sense-data.[59]

(b)   There is only a contingent connection between the occurrence of any set of sense-data, no matter how orderly, systematic, and prolonged, and the perception of any physical thing. (No matter how orderly, systematic, and prolonged the set of sense-data is, it remains logically possible that no physical thing was perceived.)

This is relevantly analogous to holding the following two propositions:

(*a'*)   The only way in principle of knowing whether a person feels happy is by knowing whether (s)he is smiling.

(*b'*)   There is only a contingent connection between smiling and feeling happy. (Even if a person smiles all the time, it remains logically possible that (s)he doesn't feel happy.)

If both (*a'*) and (*b'*) were true, then it would be impossible to establish any kind of inductive connection between smiling and feelings of happiness. Establishing such a connection requires that there be some independent way of determining whether a person feels happy, i.e. some way *other* than determining whether (s)he is smiling. Only if there is some such independent test for a person's feeling happy can we identify cases of smiling, identify separately cases of a person's feeling happy, and go on to determine under what circumstances the best explanation of someone's smiling is that he or she feels happy. If there were in principle no way to identify feelings of happiness independently of smiling, then we would not even know how to *look* for a contingent correlation between the two.

I conclude that any attempt to establish the Justification Thesis of the Causal Theory by some form of inductive reasoning must necessarily fail. Any such attempt presupposes (*a*) and (*b*), but (*a*) and (*b*) make it impossible for the occurrence of one's sense-data to provide any inductive support for the belief or claim that one is perceiving some physical thing(s). Accordingly, it is not surprising to find that in attempting to establish the Justification Thesis, causal theorists frequently slip into denying (*a*). For example, when Locke takes for granted, in his first 'concurrent reason', that he knows that people possess sense-organs, he is implicitly denying (*a*).[60] But this is to abandon the purpose of a sense-datum epistemology, which is to show that our knowledge of the physical world can be derived from knowledge about sense-data. Alternatively, were a causal theorist to imply that there is a logical or conceptual absurdity in deceiver hypotheses, he would be implicitly denying (*b*). But this would be to admit that the inference from the occurrence of certain sense-data to the perception of physical things is not an inductive inference. And it would be, as we shall see in the following chapter, to embrace phenomenalism — a theory which attempts to solve the problem of perception by acknowledging (*a*) but denying (*b*).

NOTES

[1] Grice's article originally appeared in *Proceedings of the Aristotelian Society*, Supp. Vol. 35 (1961), pp. 121–168. It is reprinted in G. J. Warnock (ed.), *The Philosophy of Perception* (Oxford University Press, 1967), pp. 85–126. My page references, all of which are to Section V, VI, or VII of the article, will be to the Warnock volume.

[2] Grice's full, final formulation of the theory goes as follows. "(1) It is true that X perceives M if, and only if, some present-tense sense-datum statement is true of X which reports a state of affairs for which M, in a way to be indicated by example, is causally responsible, and (2) a claim on the part of X to perceive M, if it needs to be justified at all, is justified by showing that the existence of M is required if the circumstances reported by certain true sense-datum statements, some of which may be about persons other than X, are to be causally accounted for." (p. 112) In discussing the analytic thesis I shall explain (and indeed adopt in my own final formulation) Grice's phrase, 'in a way to be indicated by example'. My reason for not including a reference to other persons' experiences in the justification thesis is that, though such a claim might indeed help to justify X's claim to perceive M, it would itself have to be justified by showing that the circumstances it reports are causally required to account for some of X's *own* perceptual experiences.

[3] 'The Causal Theory of Perception', p. 109.

[4] 'The Causal Theory of Perception', p. 103.

[5] See Sir Russell Brain, 'Hallucinations', p. 58 and *passim*. In R. J. Hirst (ed.), *Perception and the External World* (Macmillan, New York, 1965), pp. 51–60.

[6] Cf. p. 92, above.

[7] 'The Causal Theory of Perception', pp. 103–104.

[8] 'The Causal Theory of Perception', p. 105.

[9] R. M. Chisholm, *Perceiving*, p. 149. Cf. pp. 142–151.

[10] See Frederick I. Dretske, *Seeing and Knowing* (The University of Chicago Press, Chicago, 1969), pp. 51–52; J. L. Pollock, *Knowledge and Justification* (Princeton University Press, Princeton, 1974), pp. 121–122. For a critique of Chisholm's definitions that does *not* turn on simply rejecting the type of analysis Chisholm gives, see Roderick Firth, 'The Men Themselves; Or the Role of Causation in Our Concept of Seeing', in Hector-Neri Castañeda (ed.), *Intentionality, Minds, and Perception* (Wayne State University Press, Detroit, 1967), pp. 357–382.

[11] 'The Causal Theory of Perception', p. 105.

[12] *Perceiving*, p. 150.

[13] *Perceiving*, p. 151.

[14] *Perceiving*, p. 150–151.

[15] 'The Causal Theory of Perception', p. 105.

[16] 'The Causal Theory of Perception', p. 105.

[17] 'The Causal Theory of Perception', p. 105.

[18] For a good account of this kind of overlapping, see C. I. Lewis, *Mind and the World Order* (Dover Publications, New York, 1956, [1929]), pp. 84–85. Lewis there discusses the relation between his own and a chemist's conceptions of helium gas.

[19] George Berkeley, *Principles of Human Knowledge*, Section 8; *Three Dialogues Between Hylas and Philonous*, p. 147. The page reference to the *Dialogues* is, again, to C. M. Turbayne (ed.), *Principles, Dialogues, and Correspondence*.

[20] Compare, for example, *Essay Concerning Human Understanding*, Book IV, Chapter IV, Section 3 with Book IV, Chapter XI, Section 1 and Section 3.

[21] 'The Causal Theory of Perception', p. 107.

[22] These points were discussed more fully in Chapter Three, Section 1. For helpful critical discussions of the 'scientific' argument, see also G. J. Warnock, *English Philosophy Since 1900*, Second Edition (Oxford University, New York, 1969), pp. 79–83, and George Pitcher, *A Theory of Perception* (Princeton University Press, Princeton, 1971), pp. 43–59.

[23] 'Immediately perceived' should of course here be taken to mean 'immediately perceived$_e$'.

[24] See Chapter Three, Section 1.

[25] More precisely, premiss (6) is a verbally different version of what logically follows from our final formulation of the analytic thesis, AT_3, conjoined with (P): in premiss (6) the passive voice has been substituted for the active voice and the words 'by the senses' have been added.

[26] See Chapter Three, Section 3.

[27] See Georges Dicker, 'The Concept of Immediate Perception in Berkeley's Immaterialism', forthcoming in C. M. Turbayne (ed.), *Berkeley: Critical and Interpretative Essays* (University of Minnesota Press, Minneapolis).

[28] This is not to deny that some causal theorists have made the mistake of holding what R. J. Hirst calls the 'Actual Inference' as opposed to the 'Justificatory Inference' view. (R. J. Hirst, *The Problems of Perception* (George Allen and Unwin, Ltd., London 1959), pp. 148–149.) My point is that a causal theorist *need not* (and should not) hold the 'Actual Inference' view.

[29] In my exposition of this argument as well as my division of the question, I am following H. H. Price, *Perception*, pp. 72–74.

[30] H. H. Price, *Perception*, p. 73.

[31] The force of the words 'in principle' here is this: (1) The reasons why the presence of physical things stimulating the sense-receptors cannot be known independently of the occurrence of sense-data are not merely practical limitations of our perceptual powers, which could be overcome e.g. by building a very powerful microscope or by any other technological advance. Rather, these reasons are provided by the vicious-regress arguments of Chapters One and Three and so are matters of principle. (2) While it would be logically possible for there to be some way of knowing the presence of physical things that would not be subject to the regress arguments (e.g. intuition, clairvoyance or whatnot) – so that 'in principle no independent way' does not mean anything quite so strong as 'no logically possible independent way' – it is a very general contingent truth, and in that sense a matter of principle, that sense-perception is our only way of knowing the presence of physical things.

[32] David Hume, *A Treatise of Human Nature* (Oxford, Oxford University Press, 1965 [1739]), p. 212.

[33] David Hume, *An Inquiry Concerning Human Understanding*, Section 12, Part I, Paragraph 12.

[34] Book Four, Chapter XI ('Of Our Knowledge of the Existence of Other Things'.) The next several quotations are taken from subsections 4–7 of this chapter.

[35] *Essay*, Book IV, Chapter XI, Section 5.

[36] *Essay*, Book IV, Chapter XI, Section 4.

[37] Descartes, *The Philosophical Works of Descartes*, trans. by Haldane and Ross,

Volume I (Dover Publications, New York, 1955 [1641]), p. 161. (*Meditation III*)
References to this work will hereafter be abbreviated as '*HR I*'.
38 *HR I*, pp. 160–161, 191.
39 *HR I*, p. 189.
40 *HR I*, pp. 147–148.
41 George Berkeley, *The Principles of Human Knowledge*, Section 20.
42 John L. Pollock, *Knowledge and Justification* (Princeton University Press, Princeton, New Jersey, 1974), pp. 3–4.
43 For an explanation of 'in principle no way of knowing', see Note 31 of the present chapter.
44 It might be claimed that Boyle's explanation was the best because it was the *simplest*. But such a claim would rest squarely on the point I am making: Boyle's explanation was the simplest precisely because it did not unecessarily multiply types of causal connections. More will be said about simplicity below.
45 Some such requirement as is laid down by (3) is recognized, explicitly or implicitly, by many philosophers. See for example Jonathan Bennett, *Locke, Berkeley, Hume* (Oxford University Press, Oxford, 1971), p. 70; A. J. Ayer, 'The Causal Theory of Perception', *The Aristotelian Society*, Supplementary Volume LI (1977), pp. 112–113; R. M. Chisholm, *Theory of Knowledge*, 2nd ed. (Prentice-Hall, Englewood Cliffs, N. J., 1977), p. 67.
46 The relevant portion of *The Analysis of Matter* is reprinted in R. J. Hirst (ed.), *Perception and the External World* (Macmillan, New York, 1956), pp. 209–223. Page references will be to this anthology.
47 Russell, p. 214.
48 Russell, p. 213.
49 Russell, p. 214.
50 Russell, p. 223.
51 Russell, p. 216. I think that by "laws of perspective taken in a generalized sense", Russell means laws that cover sense-data of all sense-modalities (not only vision), though the illustration he goes on to offer applies only to visual sense-data.
52 Russell, p. 223.
53 See Note 2 of this chapter.
54 Leibniz, *Discourse on Metaphysics*, Proposition IX.
55 Leibniz, *Discourse on Metaphysics*, Proposition VI.
56 Leibniz, *Monadology*, Section 7.
57 It might be thought that on Leibniz's theory there is an asymmetry between the sense-data associated with my own behavior and those associated with others' behavior, because the former are prompted by certain sense-data of mine while the latter conform to the preestablished harmony. But this would be a misunderstanding of Leibniz's theory, according to which the sense-data associated with my and with others' bodily behavior both conform to the preestablished harmony, and can both be accompanied by felt volitions.
58 H. H. Price, *Perception*, p. 93.
59 The meaning of 'in principle' here is the one explained in Note 31 in the present chapter.
60 See page 102, above. Sometimes the denial of (*a*) takes subtler forms. For example, A. O. Lovejoy argues that if I leave a fire burning in my fireplace and return

later to find a heap of ashes, I can infer inductively that the fire continued to burn during my absence, just as I have observed fires doing on occasions when I remained before my fireplace watching them burn down. This is a straightforward application of the principle that, roughly put, what is true of observed cases is true of unobserved cases — the principle of induction. Lovejoy infers that it is reasonable to believe that such processes as fires continue to exist while no one is perceiving them, which he takes to be the defining mark of the physically existent. But Lovejoy's argument assumes that on past occasions he knew he was before a fireplace and was seeing a fire; rather than, say, experiencing an elaborate hallucination concocted by some Cartesian deceiver. Without this question-begging assumption, he could not inductively infer that what *continued* to exist unperceived was a fire: perhaps the only thing that continued to exist was the deceiver's intention to deceive him again by presenting him with ash sense-data after a suitable interval of time and in a suitable context of other sense-data. (A. O. Lovejoy, 'The Justification of Realism', pp. 226–227 in R. J. Hirst (ed.), *Perception and the External World*, pp. 224–234. Reprinted from Lovejoy's *The Revolt Against Dualism*, Open Court Publishing Company, 1929.)

CHAPTER SIX

PHENOMENALISM

The traditional alternative to the causal theory of perception is phenomenalism. Phenomenalism and the causal theory are generally regarded as competing theories of perception. In the following chapter, I shall propose a strictly epistemological form of phenomenalism which is compatible with the causal theory and can be combined with it so as to yield a plausible, unified theory of perception. First, however, we must examine the two standard forms of phenomenalism: ontological phenomenalism and analytical phenomenalism. This is the task of the present chapter. Sections 1 and 2 will be devoted to ontological phenomenalism, and Section 3 to analytical phenomenalism. Since analytical phenomenalism overlaps to a certain extent with our own strictly epistemological phenomenalism, the discussion of analytical phenomenalism will be carried over into the following chapter as well.

1. ONTOLOGICAL PHENOMENALISM: ITS ADVANTAGES

The fundamental thesis of ontological phenomenalism can be put as follows:

OP: A physical thing is nothing but the group or family of sense-data which are obtained or could be obtained by perceiving that thing.

The disjunctive phrase 'are obtained or could be obtained' is included in order to make OP sufficiently broad to cover two versions of ontological phenomenalism: the earliest version proposed by Berkeley, according to which physical things are composed of actual sense-data ('collections of ideas'), and the more recent version stemming from J. S. Mill, according to which physical things are composed mainly of possible sense-data ('permanent possibilities of sensation'). The difference between these two versions will be explained more fully in the next section, where it will be seen that the appeal to possible sense-data is an attempt to overcome a difficulty that arises from the view that physical things are composed only of actual sense-data.

Initially it might seem that OP cannot possibly be true. For the argument from perceptual relativity showed that sense-data are not identical with the physical things or surfaces to which they belong. But does not OP directly contradict this conclusion? No, it does not. For OP does not

123

entail that any sense-datum, such as one of the colored patches immediately perceived upon looking at Moore's envelope, is identical with the physical thing or surface to which it belongs. Rather, *OP* entails that a physical thing is identical with an entire group or family of sense-data. Consider for example the sense-data obtained by looking at the envelope from various distances and angles, by touching various portions of it, by smelling it, etc. Consider, in other words, all the sense-data that could be obtained by perceiving the envelope under various conditions. These sense-data constitute a family or an orderly group, in that they are related to each other in certain systematic ways. Now according to ontological phenomenalism, the envelope is nothing over and above this entire orderly group of visual, tactual, and perhaps also olfactory, auditory, and gustatory sense-data; it is nothing but a complex family of sense-data. Though this view needs to be spelled out in more detail (exactly what principles of order characterize such a 'family' of sense-data?), it does not imply that any sense-datum in the family is identical with the envelope or its surface.

Although ontological phenomenalism does not falsely imply that any sense-datum is identical with the physical thing to which it belongs, it does imply a novel conception of physical things. To say that an envelope or a piano is nothing but the totality of sense-data that could be obtained by perceiving it seems like a considerable departure from common sense (though a phenomenalist would be quick to challenge us to say what *more* these objects consist in). What reasons are there, then, in favor of ontological phenomenalism? What are the advantages of this theory?

The basic reason for adopting phenomenalism is to avoid scepticism.[1] Scepticism with regard to the senses — the view that we cannot justify any perceptual claim or belief concerning physical things — seems to be the unwanted consequence of the classical causal theory. For that theory, as we have seen, is committed to the following two propositions:

(*a*)   The only way in principle of knowing that any physical thing is perceived is by immediately perceiving a certain set of sense-data.

(*b*)   There is only a contingent connection between the occurrence of any set of sense-data, no matter how orderly, systematic, and prolonged, and the perception of any physical thing.

As I argued in the previous chapter, given both (*a*) and (*b*) it is impossible to give any sort of inductive argument from premises about sense-data to the conclusion that some physical thing(s) is perceived. For (*b*) means that it is always a logical possibility that any sequence of sense-data — no matter how orderly, systematic, and prolonged — constitutes only a dream or a hallucination. But since according to (a) there is in principle no way of knowing that we perceive any physical thing *other* than by immediately perceiving sense-data, this logical possibility cannot even be shown to be improbable. Furthermore, if it is logically possible for any set of sense-data to constitute only a dream or hallucination — if (b) is true — then obviously it is impossible to give any valid *deductive* argument from premises about sense-data to the conclusion that some physical thing is perceived. The upshot is that perceptual claims or beliefs concerning physical things can be justified neither by induction nor by deduction. Therefore they cannot be justified at all, and we are accordingly left with scepticism.[2]

Phenomenalism attempts to avoid this impasse by acknowledging (a) but denying (b). If a physical thing *is* nothing but a family of sense-data, then the connection between the occurrence of all those sense-data and the perception of the physical thing is not contingent but necessary. Thus, perceptual claims or beliefs concerning physical things can be justified deductively from premises about sense-data. This is not to say that induction does not enter into the justification for believing that we perceive a physical thing. On the contrary, it plays an important role: from the occurrence of certain members of a given family of sense-data, we can infer inductively that other members are obtainable. For example, suppose a person is immediately perceiving certain visual sense-data which he takes to belong to a table. These sense-data alone are only a small subset of the family of sense-data that constitutes the table. But, provided the person has past experience of tables, he can infer inductively from their occurrence that many other members of the family — including other visual sense-data, tactual sense-data, and perhaps other kinds of sense-data as well — are obtainable. Thus, the connection between the sense-data immediately perceived at a particular time and all those further sense-data whose occurrence would confirm that one is seeing a table is a contingent one learned by experience. However, the connection between the former sense-data plus the latter sense-data on the one hand, and the perception of a (real) table on the other hand, is necessary.

We can deepen our understanding of phenomenalism by contrasting one aspect of this theory with its counterpart in the classical causal theory. I am referring to the way in which, according to each theory, one would tell the difference between 'appearance' and 'reality' in particular cases. For example, consider really seeing a puddle of water on the pavement ahead, versus having an illusion of a puddle of water on the pavement ahead (as sometimes happens when driving on a hot day). The classical causal theory analyzes the difference in the following way. If one is really seeing a puddle of water ahead, then one immediately perceives a shimmery visual sense-datum which is caused by a puddle of water that itself is not immediately perceived.[3] But if one is experiencing an illusion, then one immediately perceives a (perhaps exactly similar) shimmery sense-datum which is not caused by any puddle of water ahead. Now suppose the perceiver wants to know whether he is really seeing a puddle of water ahead or only experiencing an illusion: how can he tell the difference between the two? Well, he can undertake to drive closer to the place where the puddle seems to be. If the shimmery sense-datum continues to exist and grows continuously larger as he seems to approach the place where the puddle is, this ought to confirm the judgment that he is really seeing a puddle of water; while if the shimmery sense-datum vanishes or remains unaltered as he seems to approach the place where the puddle is, this ought to disconfirm that judgment. If for some reason this test does not settle the matter, the perceiver might undertake to check the pavement tactually for wetness: obtaining tactual sense-data of wetness upon obtaining sense-data as of touching the pavement where the puddle seems to be should strongly confirm the judgment that he was really seeing a puddle of water there. However — and this is the crucial point — neither these nor any other perceptual tests can really help to settle the matter if (a) and (b) are both true. For if (b) is true, a question must arise concerning any new sense-data obtained as a result of performing various tests intended to confirm the judgment that one is seeing a puddle of water; namely, the question whether these sense-data are really caused by such physical circumstances as would confirm that judgment. For example, the question arises whether the expanding, shimmery sense-datum is really caused by a wet surface to which the perceiver is drawing closer or by some physiological or atmospheric quirk, and whether the sense-data of wetness are really caused by contact with wet pavement or by some sudden abnormality in one's fingertips. Thus, with respect to each of the sense-data obtained as a result of performing various tests intended to establish (or disestablish) the 'authenticity' of the original, shimmery sense-datum, the same question must recur: are these sense-data the effects of physical circumstances whose presence confirms the judgment that one is seeing a puddle of water, or are they just further segments of a systematic illusion, hallucination, or dream in which one only seems to perceive such circumstances? Yet if (a) is also true, then these further sense-data are in principle the only way that a perceiver has of telling whether he is really seeing a puddle of water or experiencing an illusion. The upshot is that if (a) and (b) are both true, then the difference between really seeing a puddle of water ahead and having the illusion of seeing a puddle of water ahead — and more generally between 'reality' and 'appearance' — cannot be perceptually made out at all.

Let us now consider how, according to phenomenalism, one would tell the difference between seeing a puddle of water ahead and experiencing an illusion of one. First, it must be conceded that the original, shimmery sense-datum might be seen whether or not there was a puddle of water ahead, and that accordingly the perceiver cannot tell just by inspecting *this* sense-datum whether he is really seeing a puddle of water or experiencing an illusion. However, it does not follow that he has no perceptual way of distinguishing between the two. For a (real) puddle of water is nothing but a certain orderly group or family of sense-data. Therefore, if one is really seeing a puddle of water, then the shimmery sense-datum can be followed in time by the other members of this family of sense-data. On the other hand, if the shimmery sense-datum is an illusion, then it cannot be followed in time by the other sense-data that together with it would constitute a (real) puddle of water. It may of course be followed by *some* of these sense-data. For example, the shimmery sense-datum might, because of certain atmospheric conditions, gradually shrink and ultimately vanish just as if it had belonged to a puddle of evaporating water. But if the shimmery sense-datum is an illusion, then not *all* the sense-data that would be obtainable if it really belonged to a puddle of water will be obtainable. Exactly what sense-data will not be obtainable depends on what principles of order — what relations among sense-data — are definitive of the family of sense-data that constitutes a puddle of water. But the crucial point is that whatever these principles turn out to be, it *follows* from the thesis of ontological phenomenalism — physical things are nothing but orderly groups or families of sense-data — that there must be some difference between the sense-data that are obtainable if one is really seeing a puddle of water and those that are obtainable if one is not really seeing a puddle of water. For if a puddle of water is nothing but a certain family of sense-data, then one is perceiving a puddle of water if and only if all the members of this family are obtainable. Thus, it follows as an immediate corollary of *OP* that there is a perceptual criterion for distinguishing between seeing a puddle of water and having an illusion of one, and more generally between perceiving a physical thing of a certain sort and having an illusion, hallucination, or dream in which one only seems to perceive a thing of that sort. This criterion is further perceptual experience (i.e. further sense-data), where 'further' has an essentially temporal meaning, i.e. means subsequent or future experience. It is important to note, moreover, that this criterion does not serve merely for distinguishing between 'appearance' and 'reality'. Further perceptual experience is also the criterion for distinguishing one sort of (real) thing from another. Seeing a music-box, for example, can be followed in time by sense-data very different from seeing a jack-in-the-box; even if intially the two were visually indistinguishable.

The best way to appreciate the advantages of phenomenalism is to see how the theory fares against the radical sceptical hypothesis first proposed by Descartes. This hypothesis, it will be remembered, is that perhaps there is no physical world at all; instead there is a powerful arch-deceiver who causes us to have all the very same sense-data that we would have if there were one. He presents us with orderly groups of sense-data that occur in certain lawful ways. Fire sense-data are obtainable whenever smoke sense-data occur, sense-data as of objects falling to earth are obtainable whenever sense-data as of objects being released in mid-air occur, sense-data as of water boiling are obtainable whenever sense-data as of water being heated to a certain temperature occur, and so forth. Nevertheless, there are no such things as smoke, fire, falling objects, or boiling water. All of these are only parts of a perpetual, systematic hallucination generated by the arch-deceiver. As I argued in sections 4 and 5 of the preceding chapter, the classical causal theory is incapable of showing that this 'deceiver hypothesis' is any less reasonable than the hypothesis that we perceive physical things. Phenomenalism, however, can rebut the deceiver hypothesis as follows. The deceiver hypothesis grants that our sense-data fall into orderly groups or families, that they are coherent and law-like, that we can make reliable predictions concerning future sense-data on the basis of present and past sense-data, etc. Indeed, all of this must be granted in order for the hypothesis to have any force. It must be impossible for us to detect the hallucination, so it has to be a perfect hallucination — one which is in every way just like perceiving a physical world. In other words, the arch-deceiver can perpetually fool us only by exactly duplicating the orderliness and lawlikeness of a world of physical things behaving in accordance with the laws of science. But this means that the deceiver hypothesis is *self-contradictory*. For physical things are nothing but orderly groups or patterns of sense-data. Therefore, to admit that our sense-data fall into such patterns is *already* to admit that they do *not* constitute a hallucination. In general terms, order, lawlikeness, and predictability are precisely the defining marks of reality, those which set it off from mere appearance.[4] So to grant that our sense-data exhibit order, lawlikeness, and predictability is to grant that they constitute a physical world. One cannot then go on to suggest that they constitute only a prolonged hallucination, without contradicting oneself. The deceiver hypothesis both grants that our sense-data possess the defining marks of reality, and then asserts that our sense-data may constitute only a hallucination. Therefore it is a self-contradictory hypothesis. This argument can also be put as a dilemma: either the truth of the deceiver hypothesis would make some difference to our sense-data, or it would not. If it would, then the hallucination could be detected and so the hypothesis has no force. If it would not — if our sense-data would be just as orderly and lawlike as if we were perceiving a physical world — then the hypothesis is self-contradictory. Therefore, either the deceiver hypothesis is without force or it is self-contradictory.

To summarize: ontological phenomenalism purports, by reducing physical objects to families of sense-data, to provide (*a*) a perceptual criterion for distinguishing between 'appearance' and 'reality', and (*b*) a refutation of deceiver hypotheses. The theory's basic strategy, then, is to attempt to solve an epistemological problem by means of a metaphysical (ontological) reductionism. Accordingly, we must now consider whether this reductionism is acceptable, or whether it has consequences whose undesirability outweighs the value of the epistemological gold derivable from it. This is the task of the following section.

2. ONTOLOGICAL PHENOMENALISM: ITS PARADOXES

In this section, I shall argue that ontological phenomenalism leads to three difficulties which outweigh the theory's epistemological advantages. The first difficulty, which has not been widely noted by either phenomenalists or their critics, is that if we accept ontological phenomenalism, then we cannot possibly accept a causal analysis of perceiving. We must reject the idea that perceiving is to be analyzed in terms of the object's causing the perceiver to have a perceptual experience — a highly damaging implication since, as I have argued, this idea is fundamentally correct. The second and third difficulties are well-known ones. They are, respectively, that ontological phenomenalism implies paradoxical accounts of the status of physical objects at times when they are not being perceived, and implies that physical objects or their constituents are not publicly observable. In the literature, the two latter difficulties arise partly from a metaphysical assumption about sense-data that has been neither made nor denied in this book; namely that sense-data are 'mental' entities whose *esse* is *percipi*. I shall show, however, that even if we assume only that sense-data are the immediate objects of perception, both difficulties still arise for phenomenalism, albeit in a somewhat different form.

Let us turn to the first difficulty. Intuitively, it may seem obvious that the fundamental thesis of ontological phenomenalism — physical things are composed of the sense-data that are or could be obtained by perceiving them — is incompatible with a causal analysis of perceiving. For such an analysis evidently implies that the sense-data obtained by perceiving a physical thing are *effects* of the thing; and clearly those sense-data cannot be *both* constituents of the thing and effects of it. In order to confirm this intuition, however, we must demonstrate that ontological phenomenalsim, if conjoined with a causal analysis of perceiving, does entail the absurdity that the sense-data obtained by perceiving a physical thing are effects which are identical with (constituents of) their own causes.

In order to demonstrate this, we need first to define the notion of 'a sense-datum *obtained by* perceiving a physical thing'. This notion may be defined in the following way:

> s is a sense-datum obtained by perceiving M = $_{df}$ s is a sense-datum of such a kind that M is perceived if and only if a sense-datum of that kind is immediately perceived.

This definition is intended to reflect the idea, common to both the classical causal theory and ontological phenomenalism, that a particular physical thing is perceived if and only if any of the sense-data falling within a certain, circumscribed class are immediately perceived. How this class is to be circumscribed — whether e.g. in terms of a causal relation of its members to the thing as in the causal theory, or in terms of certain relations among the members of the class as in phenomenalism, or in some other way — is left open by the definition. The definition tells us only that a sense-datum which bears this intimate relationship to the perception of M, i.e. which is of such a kind that immediately perceiving some sense-datum of that kind is necessary and sufficient for perceiving M, is a sense-datum obtained by perceiving M.

It might be thought that the notion of a 'sense-datum obtained by perceiving M' should be defined more broadly, to include certain sense-data only occasionally connected with perceiving M. For example, suppose that while seeing the envelope Moore held upraised before them, the members of his audience obtained visual sense-data as of Moore's forearm and as of a blackboard in the background. Why, it might be asked, aren't these sense-data 'obtained by seeing the envelope?' Well, in a sense they are; inasmuch as they are obtained as a result of seeing the envelope in a particular set of circumstances. But there is a stricter though intuitive sense in which those sense-data are not sense-data obtained by seeing the envelope, but rather sense-data obtained by seeing Moore's forearm and the blackboard, respectively. It is this intuitive notion of 'obtained by perceiving M' that the above definition is intended to capture.[5]

It might now be objected, however, that the definition is too broad to capture this notion. For suppose that, as it happens, people see a certain sort of cactus when and only when they obtain visual sense-data as of a particular kind of rock, because this sort of cactus grows only on rocks of that kind and rocks of that kind are always embellished by cacti of this sort. Then, according to the above definition, it seems that a visual sense-datum as of a rock is a sense-datum obtained by seeing a cactus; and this is counterintuitive. But the reply to this objection is that the 'if and only if' of the definition must not be interpreted as expressing merely a material equivalence, but as expressing a logical equivalence. Therefore, only sense-data of such a kind that, as a matter of logical necessity, M is perceived if and only if a sense-datum of that kind is immediately perceived, are sense-data 'obtained by perceiving M'. Although this point does not enlighten us as to how the kind of sense-datum involved is to be characterized, it does preclude many sense-data from being sense-data 'obtained by perceiving' various physical objects (e.g. visual sense-data as of a rock from being sense-data obtained by seeing a cactus).

Having defined the notion of a sense-datum obtained by perceiving M, we can now demonstrate that ontological phenomenalism is incompatible with a causal analysis of perceiving. As our first premiss, let us take the thesis of ontological phenomenalism:

(1)   A physical thing is composed of the sense-data that are or could be obtained by perceiving that thing.

Letting 'S' stand for any perceiver and 'M' for any physical thing, it follows from (1) that:

(2)   All sense-data that S obtains by perceiving M are constituents of M.[6]

We may now substitute the *definiens* of 'sense-datum obtained by perceiving M' into (2). This yields our third premiss:

(3)   All sense-data of such a kind that S perceives M if and only if S immediately perceives sense-data of that kind are constituents of M.

Since our aim is to show that ontological phenomenalism, when conjoined with a causal analysis of perceiving, entails an absurdity, let us take, as our

next premiss, a causal analysis of perceiving. Any such analysis, when formulated in terms of the sense-datum analysis of perceptual experience pre-
supposed by ontological phenomenalism, will conform to the general schema:
'S perceives M if and only if S immediately perceives sense-data caused by M
in manner R'. (On the particular analysis of perceiving that we have adopted,
'manner R' would be spelled out as 'by stimulating S's sense-receptors in a
way to be indicated by examples'.)[7] Accordingly, since the argument being
developed is intended to show that ontological phenomenalism leads to an
absurdity when conjoined with any causal analysis of perceiving, let us take
this schema as our next premiss:

    (4)   S perceives M if and only if S immediately perceives sense-data
                caused by M in manner R.

The next two premisses are both analytic truths:

    (5)   If S perceives M if and only if S immediately perceives sense-data
                caused by M in manner R, then all sense-data of such a kind that
                S perceives M if and only if S immediately perceives sense-data
                of that kind are sense-data of the kind: caused by M in manner
                R.[8]
    (6)   If all sense-data of such a kind that S perceives M if and only if
                S immediately perceives sense-data of that kind are sense-data of
                the kind: caused by M in manner R, then all sense-data of such a
                kind that S perceives M if and only if S immediately perceives
                sense-data of that kind are effects of M.

It follows from (4), (5), and (6) that:

    (7)   All sense-data of such a kind that S perceives M if and only if S
                immediately perceives sense-data of that kind are effects of M.

We can now deduce syllogistically from (3) and (7) that:

    (8)   Some effects of M are constituents of M.

But (8) is absurdly false. An effect cannot possibly be identical with its
own cause or part-cause. Yet, (8) implies the truth of such statements as:
'sense-datum d is an effect of physical object M, whose constituents are A, B,
C, . . . ; and d is identical with B.' (Compare: 'smoke-cloud s is an effect of a
fire composed of flames F_1, F_2, F_3, . . . ; and s is identical with F_2'.) Thus
ontological phenomenalism, when conjoined with a causal analysis of perceiving, entails an absurdity. So if we were to accept ontological phenomenalism,

then we would have to deny what we have seen to be a conceptual truth about perceiving.

The incompatability of ontological phenomenalism with a causal analysis of perceiving has two further unpalatable consequences. First, phenomenalism's account of the difference between 'appearance' and 'reality' is curiously incomplete. One consequence of phenomenalism, as we saw in the previous section, is that this difference can be determined perceptually, in terms of further experience. From an epistemological point of view, this is of course an extremely desirable result. Moreover, it is a result that harmonizes well with common sense, since in doubtful cases it is indeed in terms of further experience that we make out the difference between genuine cases of perceiving and cases of hallucination or illusion. However, it must *also* be insisted, from a conceptual or metaphysical point of view, that the difference between 'appearance' and 'reality' turns on the *causes* of our perceptual experiences. For example, a hallucination of a dagger is a perceptual experience that has some cause other than a dagger stimulating the perceiver's eyes, such as a disturbance in his nervous system or his brain; while the perceptual experience had by really seeing a dagger is one that has as one of its causes a dagger stimulating the perceiver's eyes in a certain way. But since ontological phenomenalism maintains that the perceptual experience had by seeing a dagger partly constitutes the dagger, it cannot hold that this experience is caused by the dagger; and so this way of analyzing the difference between the two cases is not available to the theory.

Second, ontological phenomenalism is forced into an implausible position with respect to the explanation of our perceptual experiences or sense-data. Suppose I ask why I am now having visual sense-data of a desk rather than, say, visual sense-data of a door or an elephant. According to ontological phenomenalism, the answer cannot be the obvious one that my present visual sense-data are being caused by a desk and not by a door or an elephant. For these sense-data, being sense-data I obtain by perceiving a desk, are constituents of the desk and so cannot be effects of it. Thus, ontological phenomenalism must hold either that my sense-data have some cause *other* than the desk, which is implausible, or that they occur without any causal explanation whatsoever, which is extraordinary.

The foregoing objections to ontological phenomenalism are very damaging: sufficiently damaging, I believe, to outweigh the theory's advantages. At the very least, they show that if, as I shall argue in the following chapter, a form of phenomenalism can be devised which is compatible with a causal analysis of perceiving, it will be preferable to ontological phenomenalism.

However, there are other objections to the theory; and in the remainder of
this section I wish to consider two of them.

The best-known objection to ontological phenomenalism is that it implies
that physical things have a discontinuous existence, i.e. that they are perpetually 'jumping into and out of existence'. The reason which is given for
this is that sense-data, being entities akin to Locke and Berkeley's 'sensations
or ideas', can exist only while they are being perceived; their *esse* is *percipi*.
Thus, for example, my present visual sense-data of a desk cease to exist when
I shut my eyes or turn around, my tactual sense-data of the desk cease to
exist when I remove my hand from it, and so forth. It follows that the desk
itself, since it is composed only of visual, tactual, and perhaps auditory,
gustatory and olfactory sense-data, ceases to exist when I cease to perceive it;
and begins to exist anew when I perceive it again at a later time. But this, the
objection concludes, is absurd: physical objects continue to exist while they
are not being perceived by anyone, and do not perpetually jump into and out
of existence. Berkeley, who anticipated this objection to his phenomenalism,
put it as follows:

It will be objected that from the foregoing principles it follows that things are at every
moment annihilated and created anew. The objects of sense exist only when they are
perceived; the trees, therefore, are in the garden, or the chairs in the parlor, no longer
than while there is somebody by to perceive them. Upon shutting my eyes all the furni-
ture in the room is reduced to nothing, and barely upon opening them it is again created.[9]

Berkeley's considered reply to this objection (though, as we shall see, he
also hinted at a different reply, which was developed in different ways by
J. S. Mill and by the analytical phenomenalists) is aptly encapsulated in the
following limerick attributed to one Ronald Knox:

> There was a young man who said
> God must think it exceedingly odd
> If he finds that this tree
> Continues to be
> When there's no one about in the quad.

> Dear sir, your astonishment's odd.
> I'm always about in the quad
> And that's why the tree
> Will continue to be
> Since observed by yours faithfully, God.

In other words, Berkeley's reply was that the collections of ideas that constitute a tree, a stone or any other physical thing do *not* cease to exist when you or I are not perceiving them; because an eternal and omisentient Mind — God — perceives them at all times. I shall not belabor the objections to this reply, e.g. that it implies that we are justified in believing that physical things continue to exist when we do not perceive them only if we are justified in believing in the existence of God, and that if atheism happens to be true then physical things are indeed 'at every moment annihilated and created anew'. Berkeley himself argued that since physical things do continue to exist when no finite minds are perceiving them, an infinite mind must exist, thereby turning his phenomenalism into an argument for theism; but this begs the question, since what needs to be shown is that the collections of ideas which supposedly constitute physical things *do* continue to exist unperceived by any finite minds.[10]

Before considering an alternative reply to the objection, let us look more closely at the objection itself. It turns on the assumption that sense-data exist only when they are being (immediately) perceived, i.e. that sense-data do not continue to exist unperceived. Historically, sense-data have generally been assumed to be subjective entities akin to sensations, which do not exist unfelt; or after-images, which do not exist unseen; or lively mental images, which exist 'only in mind'. No doubt this is the most natural assumption to make concerning sense-data: it is one which is suggested by the various methods for introducing them (e.g. by appeals to perceptual relativity), and which is unavoidable if sense-data are regarded as the last members of the causal chains involved in perceiving physical objects (though, as we have just seen, ontological phenomenalists are not entitled to regard sense-data in this way). However, in this book I have made no such assumption. Rather, in elucidating the nature of sense-data, I have adopted a narrowly epistemological interpretation involving (*i*) a special kind of ostensive definition, given in connection with Moore's argument from perceptual relativity; and (*ii*) a verbal definition of the kind of objects thereby picked out as those 'whose existence and nature can be known solely on the basis of a present perceptual experience' (i.e. those which are immediately perceived$_e$), elicited from the arguments from causation and hallucination. It would be a questionable procedure to introduce at this point further assumptions about the nature of sense-data, merely in order to fuel objections to ontological phenomenalism. That is one reason why I attach considerable weight to the previous objection that the theory is incompatible with a causal analysis of perceiving: this objection holds independently of any metaphysical assumptions concerning the status of sense-data. Nevertheless, the traditional objection concerning the continued existence of unperceived objects can be developed on the narrow basis provided by (*i*) and (*ii*), as I shall now show.

The key point is that we cannot *know* of any object, *solely on the basis of a present perceptual experience*, that it will continue to exist when we are no longer perceiving it. It might be thought that we can directly conclude from this that sense-data do *not* continue to exist when they are not being perceived; since sense-data are by definition objects whose nature *can* be known solely on the basis of a present perceptual experience. But this would be a mistake. For we cannot know of any object, solely on the basis of a present perceptual experience, that it will *not* continue to exist unperceived. Yet it would be invalid to conclude from this that sense-data *do* continue to exist unperceived.

We seem, then, to have run into a serious difficulty. For surely either sense-data do or they do not continue to exist unperceived: to deny this would be to violate the law of excluded middle. Furthermore, their continuing to exist unperceived or their failure to do so is certainly part of their nature. But, as we have just seen, whether an object does or does not continue to exist unperceived cannot be known solely on the basis of a present perceptual experience. Therefore, it appears that our definition of sense-data, as objects whose existence and nature can be known solely on the basis of a present perceptual experience, is mistaken; or in any case that there are no objects answering to it.

To resolve this difficulty, it is necessary to distinguish between two possible meanings of 'object whose *nature* can be known solely on the basis of a present perceptual experience'. This phrase could mean either (*a*) 'object *all* of whose properties can be known solely on the basis of a present perceptual experience' or (*b*) 'object *some* of whose properties can be known solely on the basis of a present perceptual experience'. Which meaning must we give to this phrase when it is used in the *definiens* of 'immediate object of perception?'. The answer is obvious: we must give it meaning (*b*). For since sense-data either do or do not have the property of continuing to exist unperceived, yet cannot be known to have either of these properties solely on the basis of a present perceptual experience, it follows that not all their properties can be known solely on the basis of a present perceptual experience, i.e. that only some can be. This is consistent with the epistemological purpose for which sense-data were introduced, which requires only that *something* be knowable in every case of perception, i.e. that there be objects whose existence and at least some of whose properties are knowable solely on the basis of a present perceptual experience.

The implication for ontological phenomenalism of the fact that immediately perceiving sense-data does not enable us to know whether they continue to exist unperceived is this: the theory must not *require* that sense-data continue to exist unperceived; it must be *consistent* with the possibility that sense-data exist only when they are being perceived. To see better what ontological phenomenalsim must not require, it will be useful to consider briefly a suggestion made by Bertrand Russell early in his career. Russell's suggestion was that there exist '*sensibilia*', which he defined as "objects which have the same metaphysical and physical status as sense-data, without necessarily being data to any mind".[11] Intuitively, Russell's idea was that the appearances a thing presents from various places continue to be presented when no one is occupying those places:

. . . continuity makes it not unreasonable to suppose that [things] present *some* appearance at such places. Any such appearance would be included among *sensibilia*. If — *per impossibile* — there were a complete human body with no mind inside it, all those *sensibilia* would exist, in relation to that body, which would be sense-data if there were a mind in the body. What the mind adds to *sensibilia*, in fact, is *merely* awareness . . .[12]

Although for terminological reasons Russell reserved the term 'sense-data' for those *sensibilia* which are present objects of awareness (i.e. which are now immediately perceived), the substance of his suggestion was that sense-data continue to exist unperceived: it is the very same entity which is now immediately perceived and later continues to exist though it is no longer an object of awareness. Russell then went on to propose, in accordance with his principle that "wherever possible, logical constructions are to be substituted for inferred entities", a version of ontological phenomenalism according to which a physical thing is nothing but 'the class of its appearances', i.e. nothing but a group of *sensibilia*.[13] However, granting that it is *possible* that sense-data continue to exist unperceived as 'unsensed *sensibilia*', how can we know that they do? This cannot be known by immediately perceiving the sense-data, as we have just seen. Nor can it be known by deduction; for the property of continuing to exist unperceived is not entailed by any property which a sense-datum can be known to have by immediately perceiving the sense-datum. Nor, finally, can it be known by induction. For induction allows us, roughly speaking, to infer from the fact that things of a certain kind are always observed to have a given property, that unobserved things of that kind have this property as well. But it is logically impossible to observe anything to have the property of continuing to exist unperceived, since in observing a thing we are ourselves perceiving it. The upshot is that we cannot know that there are Russellian *sensibilia*. Thus, ontological phenomenalism must not presuppose that there are such entities; it must allow for the possibility that sense-data cease to exist when they are not being perceived.[14]

This means that the traditional objection to the theory can still be made, though in a somewhat altered form: 'According to Ontological Phenomenalism, physical objects are nothing but families of sense-data'. Now it is possible that sense-data do not continue to exist when no one is (immediately) perceiving them. Therefore, Ontological Phenomenalism is compatible with the supposition that physical things "are at every moment annihilated and created anew". But this is an absurd consequence; for physical things enjoy a continuous, stable mode of existence. Therefore, Ontological Phenomenalism is false.'

The only way to answer this objection would be to show that even if sense-data exist only when they are perceived, Ontological Phenomenalism disallows that physical objects may cease to exist when they are not being perceived. But how can this possibly be shown? How can the existence of physical objects during times when they are not being perceived be guaranteed (or be even possible), if the sense-data which constitute them do not exist at those times? John Stuart Mill, following a hint of Berkeley's, proposed an ingenious answer to this question. Berkeley had said early in his *Principles of Human Knowledge*:

The table I write on I say exists, that is, I see and feel it; and if I were out of my study I should say it existed – meaning thereby that if I was in my study I might perceive it, or that some other spirit actually does perceive it.[15]

As we have seen, Berkeley himself tried to define the continued existence of physical objects in terms of the *second* possibility he here suggests, the 'other spirit' being God. Mill, however, took up Berkeley's first suggestion: 'if I were out of my study I should say it existed – meaning thereby that if I was in my study I might perceive it . . . ''. What Mill did was to introduce the concept of a *permanently possible sense-datum* or, in his own language, a 'permanent possibility of sensation'. Suppose, for example, that you were to visit President's Square in Washington, D. C. and were to look toward the center of the Square. Assuming that there was sufficient light and that your vision was normal, you would then obtain visual sense-data as of a large, White House. Although these sense-data, we can suppose, do not exist now since you are not perceiving them now, they are *possible* sense-data because you *could* obtain them in the circumstances just described. A possible sense-datum is simply one that could be obtained in certain circumstances. Furthermore, the sense-data of the White House are *permanently* possible, because you would always obtain them in the circumstances described. By contrast, another sense-datum you could obtain upon visiting President's Square is a visual sense-datum of a white-wigged statesman. You could obtain such a sense-datum if, say, you were to form a mental image of George Washington while visiting President's Square. So the sense-datum of the wigged statesman, like the sense-datum of the White House, is a possible sense-datum: both are sense-data that could be obtained in the circumstances described. However, the sense-datum of the white-wigged statesman, unlike the sense-data of the White House, is not a *permanently* possible sense-datum, because it would not always be obtained in those circumstances. Now, says Mill, there is a name which we use to distinguish permanently possible sense-data like those of the White House from barely possible ones like the one of the wigged statesman: "These [permanent] possibilities, which are conditional certainties, need a special name to distinguish them from mere vague possibilities, which experience gives no warrant for reckoning upon".[16] This name is: 'MATTER'. 'Matter' is simply the name that we apply to those sense-data which we always obtain under a given set of circumstances, i.e. to permanently possible sense-data; while we use such terms as 'mental image', 'imaginary object', 'fiction of the mind', *etc.* to designate certain sense-data which we may sometimes obtain under those same circumstances. Thus, Mill warns, we must not let the name, 'matter', mislead us into thinking that it denotes something other than sense-data. It denotes only sense-data of a particular, pervasive sort: permanently possible sense-data. "Matter, then, may be defined, a Permanent Possibility of Sensation".[17]

Given this definition of matter, even if we assume that sense-data exist only when they are being perceived, we can safely maintain that physical things continue to exist unperceived. For even if, for example, no sense-data of the White House exist when no one is perceiving such sense-data, it remains true at those times that if anyone *were* to look towards the center of President's Square, he *would* perceive sense-data as of a white house (assuming there was sufficient light and his vision was normal); thus these sense-data are permanently possible ones. But the White House, at times when no one is perceiving it, *consists* of permanently possible sense-data and *nothing more*: it is nothing but a complex family of permanently possible sense-data. To say that the White House continues to exist during intervals of time when no one is perceiving it is to say that even during those times, White-House sense-data *would* be obtained by anyone who placed himself in the appropriate circum-stances. Mill gives the following examples:

I see a piece of white paper on a table. I go into another room, and though I have ceased to see it, I am persuaded that the paper is still there. I no longer have the sensations which it gave me; but I believe that when I place myself in the circumstances in which I had those sensations, that is, when I go again into the room, I shall again have them; and further, that there has been no intervening moment at which this would not have been the case.[18]

I believe that Calcutta exists, though I do not perceive it, and that it would still exist if every percipient inhabitant were suddenly to leave the place, or be struck dead. But when I analyze this belief, all I find is, that were these events to take place, the per-manent possibility of sensation which I call Calcutta would still remain; that if I were suddenly transported to the banks of the Hoogly, I would still have the sensations which, if now present, would lead me to affirm that Calcutta exists here and now.[19]

By generalizing from these examples, we can arrive at Mill's view of the physical world in general. Except for those portions of it that are now being perceived, which presumably consist of actual sense-data, the physical world is merely a great set of permanently possible sense-data. Since at any given time only a tiny portion (relatively speaking) of the physical world is being perceived, it follows that most of what we call physical reality consists of nothing more than 'permanent possibilities of sensation'. Think, for example, of the uninhabited portions of the earth's surface, such as arid deserts, high mountains, etc., and of the matter underground that constitutes most of the earth's bulk. All of these, on Mill's view, are merely possible sense-data: their existence consists solely in the fact that under suitable circumstances certain sense-data would be perceived. And this applies, of course, to the unlimited stretches of the universe. Distant planets, stars and constellations are nothing but permanently possible sense-data which may *never* become actual since no one may ever perceive them. As Mill puts it,

The conception I form of the world existing at any moment, comprises, along with the sensations I am feeling, a countless variety of possibilities of sensation; namely, the whole of those which past observation tells me that I could, under any supposable cir-cumstances, experience at this moment, together with an indefinite and illimitable multi-tude of others which though I do not know that I could, yet it is possible that I might, experience in circumstances not known to me. These various possibilities are the impor-tant thing to me in the world. My present sensations are generally of little importance, and are moreover fugitive: the possibilities, on the other hand, are permanent, which is the character that mainly distinguishes our idea of Substance or Matter from our notion of sensation.[20]

What of this theory? Does it provide a satisfactory account of what it would be for a physical thing to continue in existence even though none of the sense-data which constitute the thing existed? Well, the least that can be said is that the theory is rather strange: unperceived objects certainly *seem* to be something more than possible sense-data. The oddity of Mill's theory is brought out, in an indirect way, by the following objection to it. Suppose that you see heavy black smoke pouring from an oil tanker. The flames are contained deep inside the tanker's hold, where no one can see them. Thus the fire is merely a set of possible sense-data. Its existence reduces to such facts as these: if someone were looking into the hold, he would obtain bright, orange-red sense-data; if someone had the misfortune to be down there, he would obtain sense-data of great heat and pain, etc. On the other hand, the smoke, since you are seeing it, consists at least partly of actual sense-data. Now the cause of the smoke you perceive is of course the fire, which no one is perceiving. Therefore, in this case an actual effect is produced by a mere possibility! Obviously, cases of this sort could be multiplied indefinitely: mere possibilities of sensation can support the upper stories of a building, can exert a gravitational pull on the earth, etc. Thus, Mill's theory has the paradoxical consequence that actual effects can be caused by mere possibilities.

Even apart from this (standard) objection, Mill's theory is a paradoxical one. There is something inescapably queer about the idea that a substantial entity such as the White House — not to mention most of the rest of physical reality — is really only a group of possible sense-data, i.e. sense-data that do not actually exist but would exist under certain specifiable circumstances. Of course it is true that if there is a white house in the middle of President's Square, then we can obtain certain visual sense-data by looking into the Square, tactual sense-data by walking to its center and stretching out our hands, and so forth. But common sense balks at the suggestion that the White House *is* or might be nothing but these obtainable or possible sense-data. Such a suggestion seems to reduce a categorically existing entity to a mere possibility, to give it a purely hypothetical mode of being, and in the end to deprive it of its existence. For it must be emphasized that possible sense-data, unlike Russellian *sensibilia*, do not actually exist: possible existence, far from being a mode of existence, is a mode of nonexistence. But how can an existent thing be composed of nonexistent constituents? Mill's theory would seem to trade on a confusion about the status of a merely possible sense-datum — to treat it as one that really exists after all. But the truth of the matter is that talk about possible sense-data is elliptical for talk about truths of the form, 'under such-and-such circumstances, such-and-such sense-data would exist'. And the idea that physical things are literally *composed* partly of actual sense-data, but mainly of *truths* of that form, borders on incoherence. The upshot is that on reflection, Mill's view that unperceived physical things are 'permanent possibilities of sensation' is no less paradoxical, and is somewhat more mysterious, than the view that physical things cease to exist when we do not perceive them, or that they continue to exist only as ideas in the mind of God.[21]

I shall conclude this section by considering briefly a final objection to ontological phenomenalism. This is that the theory implies that physical things are not publicly observable. The reason given for this is that sense-data are essentially *private* objects: no two persons can possibly perceive numerically the same sense-datum. Thus, since according to phenomenalism physical things are composed of nothing but sense-data, it seems to follow from the theory that no two persons can perceive the same physical thing. And this, of course, is an intolerable paradox.

This objection, like the previous one, is commonly based on the assumption that sense-data are 'mental' entities akin to sensations. However, also like the previous objection, it can be made to turn solely on the definition of sense-data as *immediate* objects of perception. For we cannot know of any object, solely on the basis of a present perceptual experience, that it can be perceived by other persons. For all we can tell solely on the basis of a present perceptual experience, a sense-datum may indeed be a private, subjective entity akin to a sensation or to a mental image. On the other hand, we cannot tell, solely on the basis of a present perceptual experience, that the sense-datum is *not* perceivable by other persons. But the law of excluded middle dictates that sense-data either are or are not publicly observable. So it must be concluded that the properties of being publicly observable or not publicly observable, though every sense-datum must possess one of the pair and none can possess both, are not among the properties of a sense-datum that we can know it to have by immediately perceiving the sense-datum. Hence, as before, ontological phenomenalism must be *compatible* with the possibility that no sense-datum can be perceived by two or more persons. But then the theory seems to imply the absurdity that quite possibly no physical object can be perceived by two or more persons.

It has been suggested that this paradox can be avoided by supposing that the families of sense-data which constitute physical things include the sense-data of many different persons.[22] In other words, we can suppose that a physical thing is composed partly of my sense-data, partly of yours, partly of a third person's, and so forth. Accordingly, the thing is publicly observable or intersubjectively perceivable. But this suggestion does not really dispose of the objection. For it still follows from ontological phenomenalism that the constituent elements of physical things − sense-data − may be of such a nature that no two persons can perceive them. And it is exceedingly paradoxical to suppose that physical reality could be composed of such 'private' elements.

The conclusions to be drawn from our discussion of the advantages and the paradoxes of ontological phenomenalism are as follows. From a strictly epistemological point of view, ontological phenomenalism is superior to the classical causal theory of perception. In particular, the derivability of a perceptual criterion for distinguishing between 'appearance' and 'reality', and from this of a refutation of deceiver hypotheses, are assets of the theory. However, this epistemological superiority is purchased at the cost of intolerable metaphysical paradoxes. The implications of ontological phenomenalism − that a causal analysis of perceiving must be flatly rejected, that unperceived objects may be nothing but possible sense-data, that actual effects may be caused by mere possibilities, and that physical things or their constituents may not be publicly observable − are no easier to accept than the epistemological scepticism which we have seen to be the unwanted consequence of the classical causal theory.

The historical development of phenomenalism from Berkeley to modern times may be viewed as a series of attempts to maintain the theory's epistemological advantages without incurring its metaphysical liabilities. Mill attempted to take the first step in this direction, by freeing Berkeleyan phenomenalism from its reliance on postulating an eternal and omnisentient Mind to account for the continuous existence of unperceived objects. And the analytical phenomenalists of the present century, as we shall see in the next section, attempted to eliminate the paradoxes of phenomenalism at one stroke, by radically reinterpreting the sense-datum theory.

3. THE LINGUISTIC VERSION OF THE SENSE-DATUM THEORY AND ANALYTICAL PHENOMENALISM

In the contemporary version of phenomenalism to be considered in this section, there is an attempt to root out the source of the paradoxes of ontological phenomenalism. These paradoxes, as we have seen, follow from the view that physical things are literally *composed* of the sense-data obtained or obtainable by perceiving them. But that view is also the source of the theory's epistemological advantages, inasmuch as it allows phenomenalism to maintain *contra* the classical causal theory that the relation between certain sets of sense-data and the perception of physical things is not contingent but necessary. So at this point the problem for phenomenalism can be put as follows: how can the thesis that there is a noncontingent, conceptual connection between certain sets of sense-data and the perception of physical things be maintained, *without* literally identifying the things with families of sense-data?

The only way in which this can be done is by radically reinterpreting the sense-datum theory. Specifically, the sense-datum theory must be de-ontologized: sense-data must not be considered as *objects* or *entities* of a special kind. For given the traditional view of sense-data as objects of immediate perception, the only way to construe a necessary relation between sets of sense-data and the perception of physical things is as a relation of identity between the sets of sense-data and the things. This is because, as we have seen, a consistent sense-datum epistemology (whether it be a phenomenalistic theory or a causal one) is committed to the proposition that the only way in principle of knowing that any physical thing is perceived is by immediately perceiving certain sense-data. Thus, the necessary relation between immediately perceiving certain sense-data and perceiving physical things cannot stem from certain supposedly self-evident or *a priori* principles (such as e.g. Descartes's principle that there is a perfect God who would not allow us to be deceived about the causes of our sense-data); for these principles would be an additional, independent source of our knowledge that we perceive physical things. Accordingly, the necessary relation can only stem from there being an identity between certain sets of sense-data and certain physical things; unless sense-data are not objects or entities of any kind, in which case it would make no sense to assert such an identity. In other words, if we assume that (*a*) there is a necessary relation between immediately perceiving certain sets of sense-data and perceiving certain physical things, (*b*) the only way in principle of knowing that any physical thing is perceived is by immediately perceiving certain sense-data, and (*c*) sense-data are objects or entities, then it follows that (*d*) physical things are identical with certain sets of sense-data and, hence, are literally composed of sense-data. Therefore, the only way to reject (*d*) while retaining (*a*) and (*b*) is to deny (*c*): it is (*c*), at bottom, which is the source of the paradoxes that follow from (*d*). But is there any alternative to conceiving of sense-data as objects or entities of a special kind, as we have done ever since introducing sense-data in connection with Moore's envelope?

In an important book entitled *The Foundations of Empirical Knowledge*, A. J. Ayer attempted to supply such an alternative.[23] In that book Ayer introduced what has come to be known as the linguistic version of the sense-datum theory. He then went on to formulate a corresponding version of phenomenalism, now known as analytical phenomenalism, according to which physical things are not literally composed of sense-data but are 'logical constructions' of sense-data.[24]

J. L. Austin has argued, influentially, that Ayer did not really de-ontologize the sense-datum theory.[25] It is true that many passages in Ayer's book suggest, as Austin points out, that despite his disclaimers Ayer still conceives of sense-data in the traditional way. And in expounding analytical phenomenalism, Ayer often seems to imply that physical things are literally constructed out of sense-data, despite his official position that the construction is merely a 'logical' one. Nevertheless, I would assess Ayer's achievement in the *Foundations* differently from Austin. For none of the theses Ayer defends in that book require that sense-data be objects or entities; and the statements which seem to imply an ontological construal of phenomenalism could be paraphrased so as no longer to do so. My criticism of Ayer, rather, is that instead of replacing the traditional sense-datum theory with a better analysis of perceptual experience — instead of replacing bad metaphysics with good metaphysics — he tried to avoid metaphysics altogether in favor of pure linguistic analysis. As a result, Ayer suppressed or at least abstracted from metaphysical questions concerning the nature of perceptual experience. Ultimately, however, phenomenalism cannot avoid the question of what Chisholm calls 'the status of appearances', for unless this question is faced squarely, it will not be clear whether the theory can really avoid the paradoxes of ontological phenomenalism. In particular, in order to show that phenomenalism need not be incompatible with a causal analysis of perceiving, and especially in order to exhibit perspicuously how the two can be combined, it is essential to give an explicit, positive account of the nature of perceptual experience. I believe that the 'adverbial theory', pioneered by Reid and Ducasse and recently defended by Chisholm, provides the needed account; and in the following chapter I shall argue in favor of this theory. Nevertheless, the linguistic version of the sense-datum theory is an instructive step in the right direction: by attempting to deprive sense-data of their object-status without providing an alternative analysis of perceptual experience, it both suggests the possibility of and shows the need for such an alternative. As for analytical phenomenalism, it is closely related to the purely epistemological phenomenalism that I shall propose in the following chapter. Accordingly, as the last stage in preparing the way for putting forward a constructive hypothesis, I want to consider the linguistic version of the sense-datum theory and the analytical phenomenalism that Ayer introduced in *The Foundations of Empirical Knowledge*.

Ayer's most novel contention in the *Foundations* was that it is a mistake to suppose that when one introduces sense-data one is calling attention to a special kind of object.[26] Instead, one is introducing a new terminology, the 'sense-datum terminology'. The function of the sense-datum terminology is to pick out and describe the common element in a normal perceptual experience and a phenomenologically indistinguishable experience had while hallucinating, suffering from an illusion, or dreaming. Suppose for example that Hamlet really sees a dagger. A few minutes later, he hallucinates an exactly similar dagger. Now these two experiences have something in common. The purpose of the sense-datum terminology is to pick out and describe this common element. The common element, itself, Ayer calls a sense-datum. But he maintains that this can be done without implying that the sense-datum is a special kind of object, entity, or existent — one concerning which we can ask whether it exists only while it is being perceived, whether it is publicly observable, and so forth. A sense-datum is simply the common element in phenomenologically indistinguishable normal and abnormal perceptual experiences; this does not commit us to *any* view about the metaphysical status of sense-data. Thus, if we like we can suppose that when Hamlet sees the dagger, the only object that he sees is a physical object — a metal-and-wood one, to be exact. On the other hand, when he hallucinates the dagger, what he sees is a mere mental image. Thus, we can admit that what Hamlet sees in the two cases is ontologically very different. However, we must also admit that the two experiences — seeing a dagger and hallucinating a dagger — may be qualitatively or phenomenologically indistinguishable. Therefore, it is in our interest to have a terminology that can be used to pick out and to describe just what is common to the two experiences. It is in our interest because statements couched in this terminology will (provided the perceiver is attentive and has the relevant concepts) always express *knowledge*: they can never be false just because the experience they refer to turns out to have been a hallucination, illusion or dream rather than a normal perceptual experience. Thus, suppose that Hamlet were to describe his experience with the statement, 'I see a dagger-like sense-datum'. This statement would be true whether Hamlet had been really seeing a dagger or only hallucinating a dagger. For the statement is noncommittal, *neutral*, as to whether one is really seeing a dagger or only hallucinating one; it refers solely to what is *common* to seeing a dagger and hallucinating a dagger. As Ayer puts it:

If we accept this recommendation [to use the sense-datum terminology] it will not be because our ordinary language is defective, in the sense that it does not furnish us with the means of describing all the facts, or in the sense that it obliges us to misdescribe some of them; but simply because it is not so good an instrument as the sense-datum language for our special purposes. For since in philosophizing about perception our main object is to analyze the relationship of our sense-experiences to the propositions we put forward concerning material things, it is useful for us to have a terminology that enables us to refer to the contents of our experiences independently of the material things that they are taken to present.[27]

Thus what we obtain by introducing the term 'sense-datum' is a means of referring to appearances without prejudging the questions what it is, if anything, that they are appearances *of*, and what it is, if anything, that they are appearances *to*.[28]

The linguistic version of the sense-datum theory can be expressed concisely in terms of the logical relation between statements of the form 'some physical thing M is perceived' and 'some sense-datum d is sensed'.[29] Given that a sense-datum is simply the common element in an experience in which a physical thing is really perceived and a hallucination, illusion, or dream in which it only seems to be perceived, the logical relation between such statements must be as follows. Whenever a physical thing is perceived, a sense-datum is sensed: 'some physical thing M is perceived' entails 'some sense-datum d is sensed'. On the other hand, it is not the case that whenever a sense-datum is sensed, a physical thing is perceived: 'some sense-datum d is sensed' does *not* entail 'some physical thing M is perceived'. For since sense-data are the common element in phenomenologically indistinguishable normal perceptual experiences and hallucinations, illusions and dreams, they are also sensed when one is *merely* hallucinating, having an illusion, or dreaming.

Now if the word 'sense-datum' is understood in this way, then if it is ever true that a physical object is being perceived, it must also be true that some sense-datum is sensed . . . . But the converse entailment does not hold. I believe that I am now perceiving a match-box and this belief is directly based on the evidence of my senses. But from the fact that I am sensing the sense-data I am now sensing it does not *follow* that I am perceiving a match-box. For . . . my having the sense-experiences I am now having is compatible with there being no such match-box there; it is compatible with my being the victim of an illusion.[30]

Although the statement that a sense-datum is sensed does not entail that any physical thing is being perceived, any statement that some physical thing is being perceived must be justified by statements referring solely to sense-data. Furthermore, if scepticism is to be avoided, this justification cannot be merely an inductive one, as we have seen. The main question before us, accordingly, is this: Given that no statement of the form 'sense-datum d is being sensed' entails any statement of the form 'physical thing M is being perceived', how can statements of the latter form nevertheless be non-inductively justified by statements referring exclusively to sense-data? Ayer's answer is that although *by itself* the statement that a given sense-datum is being sensed does not entail that any physical thing is being perceived, *in conjunction with other statements referring to sense-data that would be sensed* under certain conditions, it does provide the desired justification.[31]

In giving this answer, Ayer is invoking his analytical version of phenomenalism. This can be seen by noting the similarity between Ayer's position and ontological phenomenalism: just as ontological phenomenalsim holds that a particular sense-datum is not a constituent of a physical thing unless it belongs to family of sense-data most of which are possible rather than actual, so Ayer holds that a particular sense-datum statement does not justify a physical-thing statement except in conjunction with other sense-datum statements most of which are hypothetical statements asserting that certain sense-data would be sensed under certain conditions. As he puts it:

. . . when I say, truly as it happens, that I am now perceiving a match-box, part of what I am saying is that I am sensing sense-data of a certain kind; but only part. I am saying that and something more. But what more? That is our problem. And the phenomenalist's answer to it is that the more that I am saying is that further sense-data of the appropriate sort would, in the appropriate conditions, be obtainable.[32]

Implicit in this brief passage is the fundamental thesis of analytical phenomenalism. This thesis is that any statement referring to a physical thing can be reformulated as, reduced to, or 'translated' into a conjunction of statements referring exclusively to sense-data. Thus, the difference between ontological and analytical phenomenalism is this: Ontological phenomenalism maintains that physical things are literally composed of actual or possible sense-data, while analytical phenomenalism denies that physical things are literally composed of sense-data. Instead, analytical phenomenalism maintains that physical things are 'logical constructions' out of sense-data. And what this puzzling and perhaps misleading claim means is only this: *statements* referring to physical things can be reformulated as *statements* referring exclusively to sense-data. As Ayer put it in the passage where he first distinguished his phenomenalism from ontological phenomenalism:

A common way of expressing this conclusion [that 'any proposition that refers to a material thing must somehow be expressible in terms of sense-data'] is to say that material things are nothing but collections of actual and possible sense-data. But this is a misleading formula and one that provokes objections which a more accurate way of speaking might avoid. Thus, it is sometimes argued, by those who reject this 'pheno-menalistic' analysis of the nature of material things, that to conceive of such things as houses or trees or stones as mere collections of actual and possible sense-data is to ignore their 'unity' and 'substantiality', and that, in any case, it is hard to see how any-thing can be composed of so shadowy a being as a possible sense-datum. But these objections are founded upon the mistaken assumption that a material thing is supposed to consist of sense-data, as a patchwork quilt consists of different coloured patches of silk. To remove this misconception, it must be made clear that what the statement that material things consist of sense-data must be understood to designate is not a factual but a linguistic relationship. What is being claimed is that the propositions which are or-dinarily expressed by sentences which refer to material things could also be expressed by sentences which referred exclusively to sense-data; and the inclusion of possible as well as actual sense-data among the elements of the material things must be taken only to imply a recognition of the fact that some of these statements about sense-data will have to be hypothetical. As for the belief in the 'unity' and 'substantiality' of material things, I shall show that it may be correctly represented as involving no more than the attribution to visual and tactual sense-data of certain relations which do, in fact, obtain in our experience.[33]

What is meant by the assertion that statements referring to physical things can be reformulated as, reduced to, translated into statements referring exclu-sively to sense-data; or that they 'must somehow be expressible in terms of sense-data?' Such terms as 'reformulated', 'reduced', 'translated', etc. are here obviously vague. Can the fundamental thesis of analytical phenome-nalism be formulated in a more precise way? The standard answer to this question is that the relationship between sense-data statements and physical-thing statements is one of *logical equivalence*.[34] In other words, any state-ment referring to a physical thing is logically equivalent to a conjunction of statements referring only to sense-data. Thus, let P stand for a physical-thing statement, e.g. 'there is a white house in President's Square'; and let S_1 & . . . S_n stand for a certain conjunction of sense-data statements. Then analytical phenomenalism, on the standard construal, maintains that:

$$P \text{ is logically equivalent to } S_1 \& \ldots \& S_n,$$

which is to say that:

(1) P entails S_1 & . . . S_n, i.e. $\dfrac{P}{\therefore S_1 \& \ldots \& S_n}$ is valid,

and

(2) S_1 & . . . & S_n entails P, i.e. $\dfrac{S_1 \& \ldots \& S_n}{\therefore P}$ is valid.

Strictly speaking, only one of these two entailments is needed in order to refute scepticism. This is entailment (2), from the set of sense-datum statements to the physical-thing statement. If this entailment holds, then the epistemological sceptic is refuted. For the sceptic maintains that there is no legitimate way of inferring any statement referring to physical things from statements referring only to sense-data; he claims that there is an unbridgeable inferential gap between our sensory evidence and our beliefs concerning physical things. But if (2) is true, then there is the strongest possible inferential connection between them; namely, a deductive connection.

In light of the fact that only entailment (2) is required to solve the epistemological problem of perception, why does analytical phenomenalism also maintain entailment (1), from physical-thing statements to sense-datum statements? In other words, what is the point of holding that there is a mutual entailment or logical equivalence between sense-datum statements and physical-thing statements, rather than merely a one-way entailment from sense-datum statements to physical-thing statements? The answer is that asserting a logical equivalence between the statements allows phenomenalism to maintain that a physical-thing statement and its corresponding set of sense-datum statements are identical in *meaning*. For statements that are logically equivalent have the same meaning (in one important meaning of 'meaning'). For example, 'this is a triangle' and 'this is a closed, three-sided, rectilinear figure' mutually entail each other — are logically equivalent — and so have the same meaning. On the other hand, statements between which there is only a one-way entailment do not have the same meaning. For example, 'this is a tiger' entails 'this is an animal' but not conversely, so these two statements do not have the same meaning. The most that can be said is that their meanings overlap: 'this is an animal' is *part* of the meaning of 'this is a tiger'.

The thesis that there is a logical equivalence rather than only a one-way entailment between conjunctions of sense-datum statements and physical-thing statements, then, implies that a physical-thing statement and its corresponding set of sense-datum statements are identical in meaning (and enables the analytical phenomenalist to hold that the latter provides an *analysis* of the former's meaning). Although the truth of this doctrine is not essential for epistemological purposes, it would significantly strengthen the phenomenalist's answer to scepticism. For suppose first that entailment (2) holds. This means that if S_1 & ... & S_n is known to be true, then sceptical doubts about the truth of P are completely unwarranted; since P follows logically from S_1 & ... & S_n. But now suppose that entailment (1) also holds; so that

P and S_1 & ... & S_n mean the same thing. Then the phenomenalist can add the following point to his refutation of scepticism. Not only are sceptical doubts about P totally unjustified; they are also meaningless, nonsensical. For S_1 & ... & S_n is *all that is meant* by P. Thus, to admit that S_1 & ... & S_n is true but to doubt whether P is true is doubly absurd. It is not just like admitting that 'this is a tiger' is true and doubting whether 'this is an animal' is true, which is bad enough. Rather, it is like admitting that 'this is a closed, three-sided, rectilinear figure' is true and doubting whether 'this is a triangle' is true.

The thesis that statements referring to physical things are logically equivalent to conjunctions of statements referring solely to sense-data — the equivalence thesis, as I shall call it — is the contemporary version of the Berkeley-Mill doctrine that physical things are nothing but families of sense-data. Analytical phenomenalists contend that their view provides a refutation of scepticism and at the same time avoids the metaphysical paradoxes of ontological phenomenalism. *If* the equivalence thesis is true, and *if* analytical phenomenalism really avoids the absurdities of ontological phenomenalism, then the theory does indeed provide a powerful refutation of scepticism. However, both of these 'ifs' are large ones. It is not clear that analytical phenomenalism really avoids the paradoxes of ontological phenomenalism, because despite Ayer's disclaimers, the sense-datum terminology certainly seems to imply that sense-data are objects or entities after all: those that we 'sense' in normal and hallucinatory experiences alike and to which sense-datum statements 'refer'. Only if we give a positive account of the status of appearances that does not reify them into sense-data will it be clear that phenomenalism need not imply any metaphysical absurdities. Furthermore, establishing the equivalence thesis is no easy task; and many contemporary philosophers would say that it cannot be done. For in recent years, philosophers have argued that neither of the two entailments claimed by analytical phenomenalism holds. One of the most influential critics is Chisholm, who has argued that no physical-thing statement entails any sense-datum statement whatever.[35] But Chisholm is only one of many critics: 'refutations' of phenomenalism are a staple of recent works on perception. Even Ayer, the champion of analytical phenomenalism, has never endorsed the equivalence thesis. In *The Foundations of Empirical Knowledge* (1940) he argued that neither entailment can be maintained; in his essay 'Phenomenalism' (1947) he defended the epistemologically crucial entailment of thing-statements by sense-datum statements but rejected the converse entailment; in subsequent works, e.g. in *The Problem of Knowledge* (1956), he again rejects both entailments.[36]

My own view is that the arguments against the equivalence thesis are inconclusive; and that the crucial entailment of physical-thing statements by sense-datum statements can be successfully defended. However, since analytical phenomenalism is clearly unacceptable unless it can really avoid the paradoxes of ontological phenomenalism, I propose to postpone my defense of the equivalence thesis until after it has been established, in Section 1–3 of the following chapter, that phenomenalism can be construed as a strictly epistemological view which does not imply any metaphysical absurdities and which is fully compatible with a causal analysis of perceiving. Thus, I shall return to the equivalence thesis in the second half of the following chapter.

NOTES

[1] Although throughout this section and the next I shall be discussing ontological phenomenalism, for brevity's sake I shall frequently speak simply of 'phenomenalism'.

[2] For an excellent account of the general pattern of sceptical argument involved here, and of the types of possible responses to it, see A. J. Ayer, *The Problem of Knowledge*, pp. 75–81. Some philosophers, notably R. M. Chisholm, would accept the proposition that perceptual claims can be justified neither inductively nor deductively but deny that scepticism follows from this. Chisholm's position will be discussed in the following chapter, Section 4.

[3] Strictly speaking it is not necessary that the visual sense-datum be a shimmery one, but only that it be caused by a puddle of water (stimulating the perceiver's eyes in the appropriate way). I am supposing that the sense-datum is a shimmery one for the sake of the example, in order to insure the sense-datum's qualitative likeness to sense-data obtained during a certain, familiar type of illusion.

[4] Historically this point comes from Berkeley, who writes in *The Principles of Human Knowledge* that "the ideas of sense . . . have . . . a steadiness, order, and coherence, and are not excited at random . . . but in a regular train or series . . . . The ideas of sense are allowed to have more reality in them, that is, to be more strong, orderly, and coherent than the creatures of the mind." (*Principles* 30 and 33) Berkeley went on to add, however, that the ideas of sense exhibit such order because they are produced in us by God. See *Principles* 30–33.

[5] The notion of a 'sense-datum obtained by perceiving M' would seem to be essentially the same as the notion of a 'sense-datum belonging to M' employed by Price, Moore, and others.

[6] Sometimes, ontological phenomenalism is represented as holding only that all *visual* and *tactual* sense-data obtained by perceiving a thing are constituents of it, while auditory, gustatory, and olfactory sense-data are regarded as external effects of the thing. The argument being developed could be easily modified to accomodate this refinement, by prefixing 'sense-data' with 'visual and tactual' throughout. It would then show that ontological phenomenalism (so construed) is incompatible with a causal analysis of visual and tactual perception.

⁷ See Chapter Five, Section 2.

⁸ It might be objected that (5) is not an analytic truth, because sense-data of some other kind K (e.g. sense-data resembling M) might be such that S perceives M if and only if S immediately perceives sense-data of that kind. If this objection were correct, then (5) would have to be replaced by (5′): 'If S perceives M if and only if S immediately perceives sense-data caused by M in manner R, then *some* sense-data of such a kind that S perceives M if and only if S immediately perceives sense-data of that kind are sense-data of the kind: caused by M in manner R '; and the rest of the argument would proceed, *mutatis mutandis*, in the same way as the one being developed. However, the objection is mistaken. For although it is true that sense-data of some other kind K might be such that S perceives M if and only if S immediately perceives sense-data of that kind, those sense-data would also have to be sense-data of the kind: caused by M in manner R (they would have to be of *both* this kind *and* kind K). For otherwise, S could perceive M even if S did not immediately perceive any sense-data of the kind: caused by M in manner R, which would contradict the antecedent of (5). To put the point differently, the denial of (5)'s consequent, obtained by changing that consequent from an A proposition to an O proposition, contradicts (5)'s antecedent. Hence (5) is a logical truth as it stands, and need not be replaced by (5′) for the argument being developed to be sound.

⁹ George Berkeley, *The Principles of Human Knowledge*, Principle 45.

¹⁰ In fairness to the historical Berkeley, it should be remembered that Berkeley thought he had *demonstrated* beyond any doubt that physical objects must be composed of 'sensations or ideas'; thus he could claim that his theological hypothesis was the *only* reasonable way of accomodating the common-sense conviction that physical objects continue to exist when we do not perceive them. I discuss some of Berkeley's arguments critically in the two papers on Berkeley listed in the Bibliography, on p. 217

¹¹ Bertrand Russell, 'The Relation of Sense-Data to Physics' (1914), p. 143, in *Mysticism and Logic* (Doubleday, Garden City, New York), pp. 140–173.

¹² 'The Relation of Sense-Data to Physics', pp. 144–145.

¹³ 'The Relation of Sense-Data to Physics', pp. 149–150. Russell subsequently gave up this theory in favor of the causal theory.

¹⁴ In his book *Bertrand Russell* (Viking Press, New York, 1972), A. J. Ayer interprets Russell as distinguishing between two sorts of inferences: 'horizontal' ones in which the entities inferred are of the same kind as those from which they are inferred, and 'vertical' ones in which the former are of a different kind from the latter. He then explicates Russell's principle that logical constructions are wherever possible to be substituted for inferred entities as meaning that "the resources of the horizontal type of inference should be exhausted before we have recourse to the vertical". (pp. 34–35.) Russell evidently supposed, then, that the inference from the present existence of a sense-datum to its continued existence as an unsensed *sensibile* is a horizontal one, *sensibilia* being entities of the same kind as sense-data. However, sense-data are entities of the same kind as *sensibilia* only if sense-data *do* continue to exist unperceived, which is the very point in question. Russell could have known that the inference was a horizontal one only if he already knew that sense-data continue to exist unperceived as unsensed *sensibilia*.

¹⁵ George Berkeley, *Principles of Human Knowledge*, Principle 3. Cf. also Principles 58–59.

¹⁶ John Stuart Mill, *An Examination of Sir William Hamilton's Philosophy* (William V. Spencer, Boston, 1865), Vol. I, p. 238. Chapter XI of this work, which contains

the exposition of phenomenalism in full, is widely anthologized, e.g. in R. J. Hirst
(ed.), *Perception and the External World* (Macmillan, New York, 1965), pp. 274–282.
[17] *An Examination of Sir William Hamilton's Philosophy*, p. 243.
[18] *An Examination of Sir William Hamilton's Philosophy*, p. 237.
[19] *An Examination of Sir William Hamilton's Philosophy*, p. 246. As this passage suggests, Mill's view might be formulated as one about the analysis or meaning of statements about physical things. Mill could be taken as suggesting that 'Calcutta exists' means something like 'under certain circumstances, Calcutta-sensations would be obtained'. This suggestion, which was first explicitly made by Berkeley in the last-cited passage from his *Principles of Human Knowledge* and was developed in the twentieth century by the analytical phenomenalists, will be discussed in the following section and in Chapter Seven.
[20] *An Examination of Sir William Hamilton's Philosophy*, pp. 237–238.
[21] Some of the points made in this paragraph are nicely put by Price in *Perception*, pp. 284–285.
[22] James W. Cornman, *Perception, Common Sense, and Science* (Yale University Press, New Haven and London, 1975), p. 208.
[23] Alfred Jules Ayer, *The Foundations of Empirical Knowledge* (St. Martin's Press, New York, 1963 [1940]).
[24] The meaning of the term 'logical construction', will be explained later in this section.
[25] J. L. Austin, *Sense and Sensibilia* (Oxford University Press, New York, 1962), pp. 59–61.
[26] As Ayer notes on p. 25, his point had been anticipated by G. A. Paul in 'Is There a Problem about Sense-Data?' (*Aristotelian Society Supplementary Proceedings*, 1936). Reprinted in Robert J. Swartz, *Perceiving, Sensing, and Knowing* (University of California Press, Berkeley, 1976), pp. 271–287.
[27] *The Foundation of Empirical Knowledge*, pp. 25–26.
[28] A. J. Ayer, *Philosophical Essays* (Macmillan, New York, 1954), p. 131.
[29] Rather than saying that sense-data are 'immediately perceived', Ayer usually says that they are 'sensed'; possibly because the former term suggests too strongly that sense-data are objects. I shall adopt Ayer's usage in this section.
[30] A. J. Ayer, *Philosophical Essays*, p. 132. Cf. *Foundations of Empirical Knowledge*, p. 230, p. 235.
[31] I speak here of 'the desired justification' rather than simply of an entailment because, as we shall see, Ayer himself does not hold (except in the 1947 essay, 'Phenomenalism', reprinted in his *Philosophical Essays*) that the conjunction of sense-datum statements formally entails that a physical thing is perceived. But he does hold that the justification is based on the meanings of the statements involved, from which it follows that it is not merely an inductive one.
[32] *Philosophical Essays*, p. 132. Cf. *Foundations of Empirical Knowledge*, pp. 237–238.
[33] *The Foundations of Empirical Knowledge*, pp. 231–232. Cf. *Philosophical Essays*, pp. 132–133.
[34] Ayer himself, however, has never endorsed this answer, as we shall see below.
[35] R. M. Chisholm, *Perceiving: A Philosophical Study*, pp. 189–197.
[36] In light of Ayer's rejection of the equivalence thesis in *The Foundations of Empirical Knowledge*, it may seem incongruous that this book is commonly regarded as the classi-

cal *defense* of analytical phenomenalism. But there is no incongruity, because the phenomenalism Ayer defends in the *Foundations* does not require that the equivalence thesis be true. Ayer's phenomenalism in that work can be summarized in three theses: (1) no finite set of sense-datum statements either entails or is entailed by any physical-thing statement, (2) sense-data nevertheless exhibit certain principles of order that make it both possible and very convenient to apply physical-object concepts or terminology (Ayer's very instructive discussion of these principles is in Chapter V, Section 23 of the *Foundations*), and (3) discourse about physical things, *insofar as it is meaningful*, is reducible to discourse about sense-data. Ayer can consistently hold both (1) and (3) because his defense of (3) does not rest on the equivalence thesis. Instead, it rests on his verification theory of meaning, according to which the meaning of a statement is exhausted by whatever evidence would verify or confirm it. Since the only evidence that would verify or confirm a statement referring to a physical thing is the sensing of certain sense-data, it follows that the meaning of statements referring to physical things is exhausted by the sense-datum statements that would verify them even if the two kinds of statements are not logically equivalent. So it does matter whether physical-thing statements are logically equivalent to conjunctions of sense-datum statements: discourse about physical things, insofar as it is meaningful, must be reducible to discourse about sense-data, as must appearance/reality talk.

This interpretation of Ayer's phenomenalism as resting on the verification theory of meaning is supported by passages in the *Foundations*, e.g. " . . . even though the term 'material thing' is not synonymous with any set of terms that stand for species of sense-data, any proposition that refers to a material thing must somehow be expressible in terms of sense-data, if it is to be empirically significant". (p. 231) Here Ayer is saying that despite the truth of thesis (1) above, thesis (3) is true. Later he also says: " . . . a reference to sense-data will provide a general elucidation of the meaning of statements about material things by showing what is the kind of evidence by which they may be verified. And this may be regarded as the purpose of the phenomenalist analysis". (p. 235)

In light of the objections to the verification theory of meaning (e.g. that it entails a criterion of meaningfulness on which that criterion itself is meaningless, and which has never been formulated in a way that does not either rule out as nonsense perfectly meaningful statements or countenance as meaningful supposedly nonsensical ones), it is doubtful that phenomenalism can be successfully defended by such a wholesale appeal to verificationism.

CHAPTER SEVEN

PHENOMENALISM AND THE CAUSAL THEORY OF PERCEPTION: A COMBINED THEORY

We have seen that neither the classical causal theory of perception nor onto-logical phenomenalism provides an adequate epistemology of perception. The classical causal theory implies a causal analysis of perceiving and a realist metaphysic that cannot be denied without doing violence to both the concept of perceiving and common-sense, but it fails on epistemological grounds. Ontological phenomenalism is very attractive from a purely epistemological point of view, but fails because it is incompatible with a causal analysis of perceiving and implies other metaphysical absurdities as well. Analytical phenomenalism is an attempt to secure the epistemological advantages of ontological phenomenalism without incurring its metaphysical paradoxes. Whether analytical phenomenalism succeeds in providing an adequate episte-mology of perception, then, depends (as I said in the previous chapter) on two questions. First, is analytical phenomenalism compatible with the causal analysis of perceiving and the realist metaphysic implied by the causal theory; i.e. can one consistently be both a phenomenalist and a (causal) realist? Second, does analytical phenomenalism provide an adequate account of the justification of perceptual beliefs concerning physical things? In this chapter, I shall argue that affirmative answers may be given to both of these questions. Sections 1–3 will be concerned primarily with the first question, and Sec-tions 4–6 primarily with the second. For reasons that will emerge in the course of my discussion, however, I shall call the phenomenalist element of the combined theory 'epistemological phenomenalism' rather than 'analytical phenomenalism'.

1. PRELIMINARY CONSIDERATIONS IN FAVOR OF A COMBINED THEORY

In order to give some initial plausibility to the idea that phenomenalism and the causal theory can be combined into a unified theory, let us consider an example. Suppose that at this moment you are perceiving a dagger. There is a dagger before you, reflecting light into your eyes and causing you to have a visual experience you call 'seeing a dagger'. Suppose, however, that for some reason — perhaps because you have lately been having realistic visual hallucinations – you doubt whether you are really seeing a dagger. Finally, suppose that you want to know whether you are or are not now seeing a dagger. How, if such a situation actually occurred, would you attempt to settle the matter? The answer seems quite obvious. You would perform various tests to see what other perceptual experiences you could obtain. For example, you might try to obtain experiences of grasping a solid handle, or of pressing the dagger into something, or of hearing someone say to you, 'yes, there really is a dagger in front of you'. Notice, however, that *what* these further experiences are supposed to determine is the true *cause* of your present visual experience. The purpose of seeing whether you can obtain tactual experiences as of grasping the dagger, kinesthetic experiences as of pressing it into something, or auditory experiences as of hearing someone say, 'yes, there really is a dagger in front of you', is to determine whether your present visual experience is being partly caused by a dagger. And this is just another way of saying that the purpose of trying to obtain these further experiences is to determine whether you are really seeing a dagger. Thus, the example suggests that a causal analysis of perceiving may be combined with a phenomenalist epistemology. It suggests, in other words, that instances of perceptual knowledge can be understood in terms of a combined theory, roughly as follows. The causal theory correctly holds that a person perceives a physical object just in case that object is causing him to have a perceptual experience by stimulating his sense-receptors in the appropriate way. However, this can happen without the person's *knowing* that he is perceiving the object. Something *more* is required, in addition to the fact that the person's present perceptual experience is being caused by a physical object stimulating his sense-receptors in the appropriate way, for him to *know* that he is perceiving the object. What is additionally required is, as phenomenalism maintains, that the person have correct, justified expectations about what other experiences he could obtain. Thus, a perceiver may assign the correct *cause* to his *present* perceptual experience by correctly anticipating what *future* experiences he could obtain. This is not to say that these expectations must always be tested or even consciously entertained. But the perceiver must have them, at least in the sense that he would be prepared to revise or retract his perceptual judgment if they turned out to be incorrect.

Although the epistemology of phenomenalism is *prima facie* compatible with a causal analysis of perceiving, this fact has not been widely seen, and has certainly not been emphasized, by analytical phenomenalists.[1] For example, in *The Foundations of Empirical Knowledge* Ayer gives the standard reason for rejecting the causal theory – i.e. that causal reasoning cannot be used to establish the existence of something which is in principle unperceivable — and sharply contrasts his phenomenalism with the causal theory; and in his more recent *The Problem of Knowledge* he suggests in passing that the causal theory is compatible with phenomenalism but does not develop this point at all.[2] The failure of analytical phenomenalists to see more clearly that their theory is compatible with a causal analysis of perceiving is unfortunate. For the purpose of analytical phenomenalism is to free phenomenalism from the paradoxes of ontological phenomenalism, and one of these paradoxes is precisely the incompatability of the latter with such an analysis of perceiving. Nevertheless, the analytical phenomenalists' failure to appreciate the implications of their own position is not difficult to explain. In their desire to avoid metaphysics completely in favor of linguistic analysis, they did not seek to develop an alternative view of the 'status of appearances' to replace the traditional sense-datum theory. So despite their disclaimers, they continued to conceive of sense-data as objects or entities that literally constitute physical things. But such a view, as we have seen, is incompatible with a causal analysis of perceiving: the sense-data obtained by perceiving a physical thing cannot be both constituents of the thing and effects of it. In this way, the analytical phenomenalists' lack of interest in developing an alternative to the traditional sense-datum theory helped to prevent them from seeing the possibility of combining the epistemology of phenomenalism with a causal analysis of perceiving and the realist metaphysic implied by such an analysis.[3] Accordingly, I shall now present an alternative to the traditional sense-datum theory: the 'adverbial theory'. After this theory has been explained, it will be possible to use it in formulating our combined phenomenalistic and causal theory of perception.

2. THE ADVERBIAL THEORY OF APPEARING

Suppose that you are having a perceptual experience in which it looks to you exactly as if there is a dagger before your eyes — an experience that you might have whether you were really seeing a dagger or only having a completely realistic visual hallucination of a dagger. What can you *know* solely on the basis of this experience? Well, you cannot know 'I am seeing a dagger', since your present visual experience would be exactly the same if you were hallucinating a dagger. But neither can you know 'I am hallucinating (dreaming of) a dagger', since your present visual experience would be exactly the same if you were really seeing a dagger. What then *can* you know on the basis of your present visual experience alone? Surely there must be something that you can so know. For the experience can serve as a basis or cue for anticipating further experiences. Suppose, for example, that you anticipate (correctly or incorrectly) that if you try a certain grasping action, you will have tactual experiences as of grasping a solid handle. On what basis do you make this prediction? Evidently, you make it on the basis of your present visual experience, together with a general belief, based on past experience, that this sort of visual experience will, at least when it occurs within a suitable context of other experiences, be followed by such tactual experiences if you initiate a certain grasping action. So your present visual experience does yield some sort of knowledge: it isn't merely a surd, for if it were it could not serve as a basis for anticipating other experiences. Our question is: what is this knowledge, since it is neither 'I see a dagger' nor 'I am hallucinating (having an illusion of, dreaming of) a dagger?'.

The traditional candidate for such knowledge is, of course, 'I see a daggerlike sense-datum' (more strictly: 'I immediately perceive a daggerlike visual sense-datum').[4] However, we have now reached the stage of our inquiry where we are justified in rejecting the sense-datum theory. Let me summarize the case against the theory, beginning with the traditional version on which sense-data are taken to be special objects or entities.

Such objects, as I have argued, should be countenanced only if they can serve their epistemological function of explaining how perception can be a source of knowledge about the physical world. Now if we hold with the classical causal theory that the relation between the occurrence of any set of sense-data and the perception of any physical thing(s) is a contingent one, then, far from being able to explain this, we are driven to scepticism. On the other hand, if we hold with phenomenalism that the relation between certain sets of sense-data and the perception of physical things is a necessary one, then we are led into the paradoxes of ontological phenomenalism. Therefore, the traditional sense-datum theory cannot perform its epistemological function and should accordingly be rejected.

As for the linguistic sense-datum theory, the first point to bear in mind is that it is *not* an alternative metaphysical analysis of perceptual experience. Rather, it deliberately abstains from taking any position regarding 'the status of appearances'. It is compatible with any view of the nature of perceptual experience, *including* the traditional sense-datum theory. Therefore, it would be a mistake to regard it as a substitute for an analysis of perceptual experience. Rather, the linguistic sense-datum theory is *at best* provisional or incomplete: it needs to be complemented or 'filled in' by a positive account of the nature of perceptual experience.

But even this appraisal of the theory puts it in too favorable a light. The truth is that the sense-datum terminology should be avoided altogether. For although it is not *supposed* to have any metaphysical implications, it inevitably suggests that sense-data are objects or entities of a special kind — those that we 'sense' or 'immediately perceive' and that are presented to us in both normal and hallucinatory experiences. By continuing to employ the sense-datum terminology, Ayer and others invite us to continue thinking of perceptual experience as being analyzable into the sensing (or immediate perception) of special objects. One unfortunate consequence of this is that when the linguistic sense-datum theory is linked with a phenomenalistic epistemology to form modern analytical phenomenalism, it also invites us to continue thinking of phenomenalism as being essentially a paradoxical theory about the nature of physical reality. So long as phenomenalism is formulated, in the sense-datum terminology, as the view that statements referring to physical things are reducible to hypothetical statements referring solely to sense-data, the feeling persists that the physical things themselves are being reduced to something far less substantial. In particular, Mill's picture of the physical world as being nothing but a vast collection of possible sense-data remains firmly tied to phenomenalism. It does not help for analytical phenomenalists to insist that no such ontological reduction is intended. What is needed is an explicit, positive account of the nature of perceptual experience, formulated in a perspicuous and non-misleading terminology, in virtue of which it can be made clear that there need be nothing paradoxical or reductionistic about phenomenalism. Unless phenomenalism can be linked with such an account rather than with the sense-datum theory (whether in its traditional or its linguistic formulation), the idea is likely to persist that the phenomenalist is wittingly or unwittingly depriving physical objects of their categorical status and granting them a merely hypothetical status instead.[5]

The required account of perceptual experience is, I believe, provided by the adverbial theory of appearing. Though this view of appearing was pioneered by Thomas Reid in the 18th century and defended in modern times by C. J. Ducasse, it has been recently formulated with exceptional clarity by R. M. Chisholm.[6] I shall follow Chisholm closely in presenting the theory, though the central use to which I intend to put it is certainly not Chisholm's (he rejects phenomenalism).

How, to return to our example, can the knowledge expressed in the statement

        I see a daggerlike sense-datum

be expressed without using the notion of a sense-datum? As a first approximation, Chisholm would reformulate the statement as

> Something appears (looks) daggerlike to me.[7]

Notice that, as we saw in Chapter Two, Section 2, it would be a mistake to suppose that we can deduce the former statement from the latter. For such an inference would be an instance of the 'Sense-Datum Fallacy' (i.e. the fallacy of inferring 'S perceives an appearance or sense-datum which is F' from 'something appears F to S').[8] However, the statement 'something appears or looks daggerlike to me', as it stands, does not express the knowledge represented in 'I see a daggerlike sense-datum'. For the word 'something', as it would ordinarily be understood, implies that there is some physical object which is appearing daggerlike to me.[9] But then the statement does not express what can be known *solely* on the basis of one's present perceptual experience, since it implies that I am really perceiving a physical object rather than hallucinating or dreaming. The solution Chisholm proposes is to introduce, by means of two further transformations, a special locution. First, the previous statement is transformed into

> I am appeared to daggerly by something.

Second, the words 'by something' are dropped so that all that remains is

> I am appeared to daggerly.

The corresponding general formula is

> I am appeared to F-ly.

In these statements, the terms 'daggerly' and 'F-ly' are not adjectives used in order to attribute a property to a thing. Rather, they are *adverbs* used to describe the *way* one is appeared to (thus the name 'adverbial theory'). They function much like 'gently' in 'I am pushed gently', which does not attribute a property to a substance but rather describes the way I am pushed; or like 'slowly' in 'I am walking slowly', which again does not attribute a property to a thing but characterizes the way I am walking.[10] Now since 'daggerly' does not attribute a property to a thing or substance, the statement 'I am appeared to daggerly' does not imply that there *is* some physical thing which is doing the appearing, and can therefore be used to express what can be known solely on the basis of one's present perceptual experience. But neither, for the same reason, does the statement imply that there is some *other* type of thing, such as a sense-datum or an appearance, of which 'daggerly' is being predicated. Therefore, 'I am appeared to daggerly' expresses the knowledge represented in 'I see a daggerlike sense-datum' without employing the substantival notion of a sense-datum; 'I am appeared to F-ly' performs the epistemological function of 'I immediately perceive a sense-datum which is F' without introducing any special objects of perception. No doubt the locution 'appeared to F-ly' sounds odd, being a technical one introduced for a special purpose. But since the locution does serve the purpose of enabling us to express what is knowable solely on the basis of a given perceptual experience without reifying appearances, its oddity does not constitute any objection to it. Moreover, it can be paraphrased in ordinary English: 'I am appeared to daggerly', for example, can be paraphrased as 'it looks as if I am seeing a dagger', or 'it looks to me as if I am seeing a dagger', or 'it looks (to me) exactly as if I am seeing a dagger'.[11] Finally, notice that if we wanted to assert, in the adverbial terminology, that the perceiver was really perceiving an object and not hallucinating, we could do so by simply re-introducing the words 'by something' or more specific words, so as to obtain e.g.

I am appeared to daggerly by a dagger.

But in order to formulate what can be known solely on the basis of one's present perceptual experience, this prepositional phrase must be omitted.

The adverbial theory, as I have so far presented it, may seem to be only a linguistic stratagem, rather than a metaphysical view about the nature of perceptual experience. But although the theory may be inspired by linguistic considerations, it is no mere linguistic recommendation. This may be seen by contrasting the way it would characterize what takes place in genuine cases of perception (i.e. in cases where adding 'by something' as just indicated yields a true statement), and what takes place in cases of hallucination (i.e. in cases where adding 'by something' yields a false statement), with the way the traditional sense-datum theory would characterize the same things.

Consider first normal perception. In normal perception there is a causal process involving the stimulus-object, sense-receptors, nervous system, and brain. Philosophers have been puzzled by the question: how should the outcome of this process — the conscious event or perceptual experience — be characterized? According to the sense-datum theory, it consists in the occurrence of a sense-datum which is immediately perceived or sensed. Thus, the sense-datum theory introduces an extra object of perception distinct from the stimulus object.

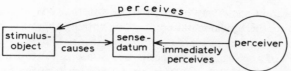

If there were something to gain by this, i.e. if countenancing sense-data could help to explain how perception yields knowledge of the physical world, then their introduction might be justified. But we have seen that a sense-datum based epistemology (whether of the causal or phenomenalistic variety) cannot succeed: we have provided a purely 'internal' refutation of the sense-datum theory, by showing that even apart from any special difficulties attaching to sense-data, they cannot serve the only purpose that could justify their introduction. So we need not go any further than we have already done into the puzzling questions about the nature of sense-data that philosophers have raised by way of objection to the sense-datum theory, but may reject the theory in favor of a simpler analysis of perceptual experience.[12] (Of course, if in this way we can successfully explain how perception yields knowledge of the physical world, then our case against the sense-datum theory will be even stronger.) And the adverbial theory is a simpler analysis. For on the adverbial theory, the outcome of the perceptual process is simply that the stimulus-object appears some way to the perceiver.

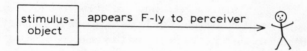

Thus, the *only* object perceived is the stimulus-object itself: no extra object of perception is introduced. For it is only the stimulus-object itself, and not also a sense-datum belonging to it, that appears some way to the perceiver or that does the appearing.

In order to spell out more fully the metaphysical aspects of the adverbial theory (as it applies to non-hallucinatory perception), let us consider the following question. What *are* a thing's ways of appearing? Do they belong to the thing that appears or to the perceiver to whom it appears: are they 'objective' or 'subjective'? The answer is that a thing's ways of appearing are *relational properties* of it.[13] A relational property is one that a thing has by virtue of being related to another thing. For example, 'being a brother' and 'being to the left' are relational properties, since a person cannot be a brother unless he is a brother of another person and a thing cannot be to the left unless it is to the left of another thing (if only the observer). Likewise, a thing cannot appear in some way unless it appears in that way *to* a perceiver. As Chisholm puts the fundamental point: ". . . nothing appears — in any way at all — unless it appears in some way *to* some living thing."[14] Accordingly, a thing's ways of appearing are properly categorized as relational properties of it.[15] Of course, a thing's ways of appearing (or its 'appearings') are also effects of it, for they are caused by the thing when it affects a perceiver's sense-receptors in a certain way. Thus a thing's ways of appearing are both relational properties of it and effects of it.

Before turning to the adverbial theory's account of hallucination, it should be pointed out that one could accept the foregoing 'adverbial' analysis of genuine perception and also subscribe to a 'substantival' analysis of hallucinatory perception. In other words, one *could* hold that while in genuine perception the only object that appears is the stimulus-object, whose ways of appearing are then relational properties of it and effects of it, in hallucinatory perception what appears is a special, purely sensory object. Furthermore, it is important to realize that we cannot show that such a view is mistaken merely by describing hallucinations in the adverbial terminology: if hallucinatory entities really exist, they cannot be caused to cease to exist merely by our adopting a certain terminology. Rather, the adverbial terminology can at most show that we are not *committed* to the existence of hallucinatory entities by our language, by showing that we can describe hallucinations without referring to such objects. But that there are no purely sensory objects can only be established on extra-linguistic grounds, such as the general, theoretical grounds that led us in the end to reject sense-data. Finally, it should be noted that the central reason we have given for rejecting sense-data — that they cannot serve their epistemological function — does not show that we should also reject hallucinatory objects. For, as we saw in Chapter Four, Section 1, a hallucinatory entity, since its existence cannot be known solely on the basis of a given perceptual experience, is not the same thing as a sense-datum; so that in rejecting the latter we do not necessarily reject the former. Furthermore, if we were to countenance hallucinatory entities, the epistemological problem raised by hallucinations could still be formulated (the formulation would go, roughly: "since the way a physical thing appears can be indistinguishable from the way a purely sensory object appears, how can we know whether we are being appeared to by a physical thing or by a purely sensory object?"), and it could still be solved in the manner to be proposed in this chapter. Accordingly, for our purposes it is not necessary to argue that such objects should not be countenanced.

Nevertheless, we are justified in rejecting hallucinatory objects, if we can

give a plausible analysis of hallucinatory experience without appealing to
them. For such objects are extremely puzzling: they are not locatable in
physical space, they are generally inaccessible to all but one sense-modality,
they seem not to have rear surfaces, and so forth. Therefore, it is significant
that the adverbial theory does provide a plausible analysis of hallucinatory
experiences (as well as after-images, mental images, mirages, dream imagery,
and the like) that dispenses with purely sensory objects.

To see that this is so, consider a case of hallucination. Suppose that a man
is hallucinating a pink rat. Then his being appeared to pink-ratly is neither a
relational property of a physical thing, nor an effect of a physical thing
stimulating his sense-receptors in the manner appropriate to perceiving. It
might seem, therefore, that in cases of this sort we must grant that the person
is appeared to by a special, purely sensory entity. However, the adverbial
terminology shows that we need not countenance such objects even in
describing hallucinations and other experiences in which no physical thing
is appearing to the subject. For in the phrase 'appeared to pink-ratly', the
term 'pink-ratly' is not an adjective attributing a property to a thing or
substance. Rather, it is again an adverb describing the *way* the person is
appeared to. Thus, we can deny that in a hallucination there is *any* object or
entity which is appearing to the person. We can maintain, instead, that being
appeared to pink-ratly in a hallucination is merely a non-relational, psychological state of the person, and an effect of certain occurrences in his
brain or nervous system. Of course, it is true that there *seems* to be a pink rat
in the person's field of vision; his consciousness can be said to be 'of' a pink
rat, to be directed upon a pink rat. But this 'intentionality' of consciousness
is a phenomenological fact which should not be converted into a metaphysical doctrine.

In order to show more clearly that no such reification of appearances is
called for here, it is useful to introduce the active locution 'sensing F-ly' as
a synonym for the passive locution 'appeared to F-ly'.[16] We can then say
that a person who is hallucinating a pink rat is 'sensing pink-ratly', or that
he 'senses pink-ratly'. And we can make use of an instructive analogy originally
given by C. J. Ducasse.[17] We say that a person who is waltzing is 'dancing
a waltz'. But a waltz is not an object that a person dances, as an apple is an
object that a person eats; rather the waltz is just a way of dancing. It would
be more perspicuous, therefore, to say that the person is 'dancing waltzily',
using the adverb 'waltzily' rather than the noun phrase 'a waltz' to describe
the way the person is dancing. Of course, this linguistic maneuver is here
quite unnecessary, because no one is actually misled by the noun phrase into

thinking that a waltz is an object that a person dances. On the other hand, when we say that a person who is hallucinating is 'sensing a pink rat' or that he 'senses a pink rat', it is easy to be misled into thinking that a hallucinatory pink rat is really an object that the person senses. Therefore, it is worth pointing out that we can more perspicuously say that the person is 'sensing pink-ratly' or that he 'senses pink-ratly', using the adverb 'pink-ratly' rather than the noun phrase 'a pink rat' to describe the way in which the person is sensing. The adverbial locution brings out the fact that what we call a hallucinatory pink rat is not really an object that a person senses, anymore than a waltz is an object that a person dances; rather it is a way of sensing, just as waltzing is a way of dancing. For sensing pink-ratly is not related to sensing as an object to an act (as is an apple to the act of eating it), but rather as a species of sensing to the genus (as is waltzing to dancing). Thus, to sense pink-ratly is simply to sense in a particular manner, rather than to sense a particular object; it is to be in a non-relational sensory state, rather than to be related to a sensory object. The upshot is that whether we use the passive locution 'appeared to F-ly' or the active locution 'sensing F-ly', the adverbial theory enables us to dispel the notion that a hallucination is the awareness of a special, purely sensory object, in favor of the simpler, less puzzling view that a hallucination is merely a psychological state of the perceiver.

Let us conclude the present section by relating the adverbial theory's analysis of perceptual experience to the epistemological issues still before us. As we have seen, the way in which we are appeared to during a hallucination may be indistinguishable from the way we are appeared to by a physical object. In either kind of case we may, for example, be appeared to daggerly, or sense daggerly. Yet our being appeared to daggerly by a physical object is a relational property of the object, while our being appeared to daggerly in a hallucination is a nonrelational conscious state. It follows that a relational property of an object can be indistinguishable from a mere state of a conscious object.[18] There is nothing odd about this; anymore than it should be odd that a real, botantical apple can be visually indistinguishable from a wax apple. Of course the fact that a real apple can be visually indistinguishable from a wax apple does mean that one cannot tell, just by looking, whether one is seeing a real apple or a well-executed wax replica. The test is further experience. Likewise, the fact that a relational property of a physical object can be indistinguishable from a non-relational state of a conscious subject brings us back to the epistemological question raised by the arguments from hallucination and from causation: how can one know whether one's being appeared to F-ly on a given occasion is a relational property of an object (in which case one is perceiving an object) or merely a non-relational, conscious state of oneself (in which case one is hallucinating, dreaming, or the like)? This question can also be put as follows. By knowing what is expressed by 'I am appeared to F-ly', one can know only that *either* one's being appeared to F-ly is a relational property of a physical object, *or* that one's being appeared to F-ly is a non-relational conscious state.[19] How, then, can one know which of these disjuncts is true? The answer proposed by epistemological phenomenalism is that such a case is no different in principle from the case of the apple: one can know whether one is really perceiving an object or only having an experience in which one seems to perceive an object by seeing what further experiences (further ways of being appeared to or ways of sensing) are obtainable. Our task in the ensuing sections will be to show that this answer is adequate.

3. A COMBINED THEORY

The combined theory that I shall defend can be formulated concisely as the conjunction of two propositions:

> *Epistemological Phenomenalism* (*EP*): Knowledge of physical things is exhaustively knowledge of their ways of appearing, i.e. of the ways they do and would appear to us under various conditions.

> &

> *Causal Thesis* (*CT*): Perceptual knowledge of physical things is knowledge of certain causes of the ways we are appeared to.

In order to provide a successful defense of this combined theory, it must be established that *EP* and *CT* are (*a*) compatible with each other and (*b*) both true. I shall begin by making a number of explanatory remarks about each of them separately.

The intent of *EP* is to provide a purely epistemological version of phenomenalism. One of the principal objections to phenomenalism has been and continues to be that it is reductionistic, i.e. that it reduces physical things to families of appearances or sense-data. *If* phenomenalism must lead to this reduction, then it should indeed be rejected; for it is from the reduction of physical things to sense-data that all the paradoxes of ontological phenomenalism follow. However, phenomenalism does not necessarily lead to such a reduction. Phenomenalism is (should be) essentially an epistemological view; namely, the view that our *knowledge* about physical things is exhaustively, or nothing but, knowledge of their various ways of appearing. The idea that this view is necessarily reductionistic stems from the erroneous view about the status of appearances that we have now rejected. Once the ways things appear to perceivers are reified into sense-data, a purely epistemological interpretation of phenomenalism becomes impossible. For the fundamental insight of the theory — that knowledge of physical things is exhaustively knowledge of the ways they do and would appear — is transformed into the view that knowledge of physical things is exhaustively knowledge of actual and possible *appearances* (sense-data). But this is impossible if physical things and appearances are separate classes of entities. The solution is to identify or collapse the two by reducing physical things to appearances.

It may be objected, however, that even if physical things' ways of appearing are not reified into sense-data or appearances, *EP* is still reductionistic: for does it not reduce the things to their ways of appearing? This objection turns on the following principle:

>   Principle *P*: If knowledge of *X*'s is exhaustively knowledge of *Y*'s, then *X*'s *are Y*'s.

It is true that *EP*, in conjunction with Principle *P*, entails that physical things are (nothing but) their ways of appearing. However, Principle *P* is not unqualifiedly true; it holds only under certain conditions. I shall now show that in virtue of these conditions, *EP* would be reductionistic if it were formulated in terms of the sense-datum theory, but is not reductionistic when formulated, as above, in terms of the adverbial theory of appearing.

One set of conditions which is sufficient for the *truth* of Principle *P* is the following: (1) *X*'s and *Y*'s are both objects or entities of any kind, and (2) 'knowledge of *X*'s' means *adequate* knowledge of *X*'s, as opposed to any knowledge of *X*'s, no matter how partial or incomplete, that someone happens to possess. Therefore, if *EP* were formulated, in terms of the sense-datum theory, as:

>   knowledge of physical things is exhaustively knowledge of actual and possible sense-data

then it would imply that physical things are nothing but actual and possible sense-data. For both conditions for the truth of Principle *P* would be satisfied, since [condition (1)] physical things and sense-data are both objects or entities of a certain kind, and [condition (2)] the phenomenalist certainly intends to characterize *adequate* knowledge of physical things. I shall not attempt to define the notion of 'adequate knowledge', for the following point (which is all that my argument requires) is clear on any intuitive understanding of that notion: adequate knowledge of some object or kind of object cannot be exhaustively, or nothing but, knowledge of some *other* object or kind of object. This is why it would be impossible, as noted above, for knowledge (i.e. adequate knowledge) of physical things to be exhaustively knowledge of sense-data if these were two separate classes of objects. The upshot is that if *EP* were formulated in terms of the sense-datum theory, it would imply that physical things are reducible to sense-data.

On the other hand, when *EP* is formulated in terms of the adverbial theory, it does not imply that physical things are reducible to their ways of appearing. For one condition which is sufficient for the *falsity* of Principle *P* is the following: *X*'s are objects of some kind but *Y*'s are relational properties of those objects. Suppose, for example, that our knowledge of some very remote celestial objects were exhaustively knowledge of their distances from various stars and planets. It would not follow that those objects were nothing but their distances from these stars and planets. This is not merely because such knowledge would be inadequate, though no doubt it would be. It is also because the remote objects' distances from various stars and planets are relational properties of the objects, and a thing cannot be identical with its relational properties. Otherwise, its nonexistence would follow logically from the fact that certain other objects − i.e. those by virtue of being related to which it had possessed its relational properties − had ceased to exist; which is absurd. But, as we saw in the previous section, a thing's ways of appearing are relational properties of it, which it has by virtue of appearing some way *to* a living being. Therefore, the proposition that (adequate) knowledge of physical things is exhaustively knowledge of their ways of appearing does not imply that physical things are identical with or reducible to their ways of appearing. I conclude that *EP*, provided it is formulated in terms of the adverbial theory, is not reductionistic.

More needs to be said about *EP*, of course, in order to establish its truth. We shall complete our defense of it after showing more fully how it can be combined with *CT*. Let us now turn our attention to *CT*. Unlike the foregoing remarks about *EP*, the following considerations are intended both to clarify the meaning of *CT* and to establish its truth.

As I have stated it, *CT* is ambiguous. It may be understood as being equivalent to

CT_a: Perceptual knowledge of physical things is knowledge of what the perceiver knows to be certain causes of the ways (s)he is appeared to.

Alternatively, it may be understood as being equivalent to

> CT_b: Perceptual knowledge of physical things is knowledge of what are
> in fact certain causes of the ways the perceiver is appeared to.

The difference, of course, is that CT_a requires, while CT_b does not require, that the perceiver *know* that the object perceived is a cause of his or her perceptual experience.

It might be held that *CT* should be understood in the sense of CT_b rather than CT_a, on the grounds that a person can have perceptual knowledge of physical things without having any conception of causality, or of the distinction between perceptual experience and the objects of perception. Cannot a young child, for example, know that his mother is approaching by hearing her footsteps or her voice, even though he lacks the conceptual sophistication requisite for him to realize that his mother is a cause of his auditory experience? It seems indisputable that he can. So it must be conceded that if what is meant by saying that the child has perceptual knowledge of his mother's presence is that he knows she is present *because* he hears her or *by* hearing her, then he can have perceptual knowledge of his mother's presence without knowing that she is a cause of the way he is being ('auditorily') appeared to.

However, from the fact that the child knows that his mother is present by hearing her or because he hears her, it does not follow that he knows *that he hears* his mother. In other words, from the fact that the child has acquired, by his sense of hearing, the knowledge that might be expressed as 'mother is coming' or 'mother is here', it does not follow that he has the knowledge that might be expressed as 'I hear mother' or 'I hear mother coming'. Unlike the former, the latter does require that the child know that his mother is the source, origin, or cause of his auditory experience. To put the point generally, there is an important distinction to be made between such perceptual knowledge as is expressible in statements of the form 'this is X' or 'X is F', and such perceptual knowledge as is expressible in statements of the form 'I perceive X' or 'I perceive X to be F'.[20] The former is simply knowledge acquired by perception; the latter, in addition to being knowledge acquired by perception, is also knowledge of the perceptual nature of one's knowledge. And while the former does not require that the perceiver know that his perceptual experience is being caused by the object perceived, the latter does.

This claim should not be surprising, in light of our discussion of the causal theory of perception. For according to the analytic thesis of the causal theory, formulated in terms of the adverbial analysis of perceptual experience, 'S perceives X' may be analyzed as 'X, by stimulating S's sense-receptors in a way to be indicated by examples, is a part-cause of the ways S is being appeared to'. It follows that first-person perceptual judgments of the form 'I perceive X' may be analyzed as 'X, by stimulating my sense-receptors in a way to be indicated by examples, is a part-cause of the ways I am being appeared to'. But if the analysis of such perceptual judgments includes a causal claim, then surely the knowledge that they express is causal knowledge.

This may be confirmed by reflecting on examples involving various sense-modalities. Suppose, to take a case of gustatory perception, that S knows that he is tasting a potato chip; S has the knowledge expressible in the perceptual judgment, 'I taste a potato chip'. Surely this implies that S knows that the potato chip is the source of, is responsible for, is 'giving him' the gustatory experiences he is enjoying. It would be inconsistent for S to say, 'I know that I am now tasting a potato chip, but I do not know whether my present gustatory experiences are being produced by a potato chip'.[21] Nor does saying for purposes of analysis, as I shall do below, that S's perceptual judgment assigns to the potato chip the role of causing him to be appeared to in certain ways, imply more than the rudimentary understanding on S's part of the potato chip's causal role suggested by such terms as 'source of', 'responsible for', and the like. Of course, S might enjoy the same gustatory experiences without such understanding. But this would not amount to S's knowing that he is tasting a potato chip, or knowing that he perceives something to be a potato chip. It would be easy to give examples confirming that perceptual judgments of the form 'I hear X', 'I smell X', and 'I feel (touch) X', too, represent the perceiver as knowing that X is causally responsible for his perceptual experience.

With respect to judgments of the form 'I see X', however, some hesitation may be felt. As Roderick Firth says:

It is not implausible . . . to hold that in smelling a skunk as we drive along a country road, we normally judge, among other things, that our olfactory experience is caused by a skunk. An analogous judgment may occur in hearing the sound of a distant bell. In the case of vision, however, which is felt to be characterized by a special 'immediacy', this causal analysis of perceptual judgment is less convincing; and some philosophers have argued that in our natural unphilosophical states of visual perception we are 'naive realists' in our perceptual judgments, implying by this that we fail to distinguish our perceptual experience from the perceived object in a way that would even allow us, at the moment, to judge that the latter is the cause of the former.[22]

Perhaps the philosophers Firth mentions are thinking primarily of visually-based judgments of the form 'this is (an) X', 'here's X', and the like, rather than judgments of the form 'I see (an) X'; in which case we need not dispute their claim. But it is possible that they would extend their remarks to the latter kind of perceptual judgments as well, in which case we may question whether the phenomenological facts they appeal to warrant their position. These facts themselves are genuine enough. Seeing does seem to have a special 'immediacy' that sets it off from other modes of perception. Perhaps this is because in gustatory and tactual perception, the fact that physical *contact* with the perceived object is required impresses the causal aspect of perception on us; and it is not unnatural to think of odors and sounds as being *transmitted* from the perceived object. (This may be because the sound and odor of an object often fades and eventually disappears as we move away from it though we can still see it, and this suggests that the sound and smell must 'travel' from the object to us, and can only travel a limited distance from it.) In visual perception, by contrast, no contact occurs; nor is it so natural to think of transmission (though of course it does occur). There is also the fact that seeing is more continual than other modes of perception: so long as we are conscious and do not shut our eyes or go into the dark, we continue to have visual experience. On the other hand, other modes of perception are generally episodic: we are not continually conscious of hearing, smelling, tasting or touching objects (though of course this varies with the environment and other factors). Thus, we do not readily think of visual experience, as we do of other modes of perceptual experience, as being broken up into episodes to which we can assign particular objects as causes.

Although these phenomenological facts are interesting and could be further elaborated, they do not show that the knowledge expressed in judgments of the form 'I see X', unlike that expressed in their counterparts for other sense-modalities, is non-causal knowledge. For these facts are relevant primarily to (i.e. influence primarily the character of) the unreflective frame of mind in which we generally make judgments of the form 'here's (an) X' or 'this is (an) X' and the like, rather than the more reflective one in which we make judgments of the form 'I see (an) X', or ask ourselves, 'Do I really see (an) X?'. Furthermore, the causal analysis of perceiving we have defended is not *less* plausible for seeing than for other modes of perception, even as it applies to first-person perceptual judgments. But if the analysis of 'I see X' contains a causal claim, then, again, the knowledge it expresses is (at least in part) causal knowledge. Finally, when the question is raised, whether one's visual experience is really being caused by an object one seems to see or in some other manner, e.g. whether the reader's present visual experience is really being caused by a printed page or by an expert stimulating his or her brain with delicate electrodes, the question is immediately felt as a challenge (whether reasonable or not) to one's belief that one sees the object. This shows that even if it does not normally occur to us that the objects we see are causes of our visual experience, this is certainly part of what we believe in believing that we see them. I conclude that, phenomenological niceties apart, there is no fundamental difference between the kind of knowledge expressed in judgments of the form 'I see (an) X' and that expressed in their counterparts for other sense-modalities.

Let me summarize what has been established concerning CT. First, provided that perceptual knowledge is taken to be the kind of knowledge expressible in judgments of the form 'I perceive X', CT in the sense of CT_a is true. In other words, the proposition: 'knowledge expressible in judgments of the form "I perceive X" is knowledge of what the perceiver knows to be certain causes of the ways (s)he is appeared to', is true. For this proposition follows from the analytic thesis of the causal theory as applied to first-person perceptual judgments, and is confirmed by reflecting directly on examples of such judgments. As for CT understood in the sense of CT_b, it is true whether 'perceptual knowledge' is taken to mean knowledge expressible in judgments of the form 'I perceive X', or to merely mean knowledge acquired by perception. For on the former interpretation of 'perceptual knowledge', CT_b follows logically from CT_a and the principle that what are known to be F's are in fact F's (i.e. the truth-condition for knowledge). And on the latter interpretation of 'perceptual knowledge', CT_b means: 'knowledge of physical things acquired by perceiving those things is knowledge of what are in fact certain causes of the ways the perceiver is appeared to', which obviously follows from the analytic thesis of the causal theory of perception.[23]

It follows from these results that whether CT should be understood as being equivalent to CT_a or CT_b depends upon which meaning we give to 'perceptual knowledge'. If CT is taken to mean CT_a, then perceptual knowledge must be taken to imply knowledge of the perceptual nature of one's knowledge, i.e. to be the kind of knowledge expressible in judgments of the form 'I perceive (an) X'. If CT is taken to mean CT_b, then perceptual knowledge may be taken to imply no more than that one's knowledge is acquired by perception, i.e. to be the kind of knowledge expressible in perception-based judgments of the form 'this is (an) X' (though it may also be taken to be the former kind of knowledge). So there is no need to say that one interpretation of CT is 'correct' and the other 'incorrect'; the two interpretations simply pertain to different kinds of perceptual knowledge.

However, in what follows I shall be interested primarily in the 'self-reflec-

tive' kind of perceptual knowledge characterized by CT_a. For it is the fundamental kind of perceptual knowledge from an epistemological point of view.
This is not to say that a person must have this kind of knowledge before
having the other, non-reflective kind. On the contrary, as we have seen, a
child can perceptually know what is expressible as 'mother is here' without
knowing what is expressible as 'I perceive mother'; he can know by his senses
that his mother is present without knowing that he perceives her to be present. From a psycho-genetic point of view, then, knowing perceptually that
(an) X is present is prior to – i.e. comes before – knowing that one perceives
(an) X. However, if it were impossible for anyone ever to know that (s)he perceives X, then it is very doubtful that anyone could ever know that X is
present. For no one, upon being asked, '*how* do you know that X is present?'
would ever be in a position to answer: 'because I *perceive X*'. But since we
have no way of acquiring knowledge of physical things that does not ultimately depend upon acquiring such knowledge by perception, this means that
no one would ever be able to justify any (non-analytic) knowledge-claim
concerning any physical thing. From an epistemological point of view, therefore, knowing that one perceives (an) X is prior to knowing by perception
that (an) X is present. Thus, there is a sense in which the young child's
knowledge that X is present is parasitic on the *possibility*, realized in the case
of more mature knowers, of knowing that one perceives X. In light of our
own ability to justify 'this is X' or 'here is an X' by reference to 'I perceive
(an) X', we grant that the child can know the former before becoming able
to justify it by reference to the latter. Whether this amounts to allowing that
the child is justified in his perceptual beliefs though he cannot yet justify
them, or to allowing that he can have knowledge without justification, is not
important for our purposes.[24] What we must do is to explain the possibility
of the epistemologically fundamental kind of perceptual knowledge characterized by CT_a. And this we hope to accomplish by combining CT_a with EP.

The next question before us, accordingly, is whether EP and CT (understood in the sense of CT_a) are compatible, as they must be if our combined
theory is to be coherent. Since EP is a universal claim about knowledge of
physical things, it entails that *perceptual* knowledge of physical things is
exhaustively knowledge of their ways of appearing. Accordingly, our question reduces to this: can we consistently maintain that perceptual knowledge of physical things is both (*a*) knowledge of certain causes of ways of
appearing, and (*b*) exhaustively knowledge of ways of appearing themselves?

To show that this question may be answered affirmatively, let us exhibit
the analysis of perceptual judgments that results from combining EP and CT_a.

A perceptual judgment of the form 'I perceive (an) X' assigns a cause C to certain ways of appearing A by predicting that certain further ways of appearing E would occur under certain conditions. For example, the judgment 'I see a cube of sugar' assigns a cause (the cube of sugar) to certain ways of appearing (e.g. appearing cubical, white, and gritty) by predicting that certain further ways of appearing (e.g. feeling hard, then tasting sweet, and others) would occur if I should seem to place the cube in my mouth.[25] Accordingly, there are two important distinctions to be made: (*i*) between the actual ways of appearing to which a cause is assigned and the possible ways of appearing the expecting of which constitutes assigning the cause, and (*ii*) between both these sets of ways of appearing and the cause itself. These distinctions show that the combined theory altogether avoids the causal paradoxes of ontological versions of phenomenalism. For they show that the present analysis implies neither (*a*) that E is the cause of A (so that 'the possible is the cause of the actual', as in Mill's phenomenalism), nor (*b*) that A is identical with some constituent of C (so that an effect is identical with some constituent of its own part-cause, as follows from attempting to combine any version of ontological phenomenalism with a causal analysis of perceiving), nor (*c*) that E is identical with some constituent of C (so that a potential effect is identical with some constituent of its own part-cause, as would follow from attempting to combine Mill's phenomenalism with a causal analysis of perceiving). Of course, if one goes on to verify a perceptual judgment, then some of the expected ways of appearing become actual and are caused by the thing whose existence is affirmed by the judgment. But at no point is any effect treated as being identical with any constituent of its own cause or part-cause. Rather, the theory implies only that our *knowledge* of a certain kind of cause (a physical thing) is exhausted by knowledge of certain of its effects (its ways of appearing).

It may be objected, however, that even if the above analysis is correct, it only shows that we have perceptual knowledge of physical things *by means* of our knowledge of their ways of appearing. It does not show that our perceptual knowledge of physical things could *be* exhaustively knowledge of their ways of appearing. Moreover, the objection would continue, no knowledge about the causes of ways of appearing can possibly be exhaustively knowledge of ways of appearing themselves. For consider a simple analogy. Suppose that a certain virus were known by the symptoms it causes but could not itself be observed even through the most powerful microscope. It would be false to say that our knowledge of the virus was exhaustively knowledge of its symptoms, because the virus is something distinct from the symptoms that it causes. Likewise, it must be false to say that our perceptual knowledge of physical things is exhaustively knowledge of their ways of appearing, because the things are distinct from the ways of appearing that they cause.

But the two cases are disanalogous in a crucial respect. We can readily conceive of what it would be to observe the virus itself rather than its symptoms. For example, we might see the virus through a new, more powerful kind of microscope. And since we have actually observed other viruses, even now we can make inductive inferences about what we would see through such a microscope. This is why we can say that our knowledge of the virus is not exhausted by our knowledge of its symptoms. On the other hand, we cannot conceive of what it would be to perceive a physical thing itself as distinct from its appearing some way to us. There is no conceivable perceptual access to a thing more direct or intimate than its appearing some way to us, or causing us to be appeared to. No inductive inference based on some of a thing's ways of appearing can suggest any perceptual knowledge of the thing which is *not* knowledge of other ways in which it would appear to us. Thus there is no more direct or intimate way in which our perceptual knowledge could be about a thing than by being about its ways of appearing. This is why we can say that our perceptual knowledge of physical things is exhaustively knowledge of their ways of appearing, even though the things are distinct from the ways of appearing that they cause.

A better analogy is this. Suppose that there were *in principle* no way of knowing about a certain virus except by the symptoms it produced; just as there is in principle no way of perceptually knowing a physical thing except by knowing its ways of appearing. We could then say that our knowledge of this virus was exhausted by knowledge of its symptoms. We would be holding both (*a*) that our knowledge of the virus is exhaustively knowledge of its symptoms, and (*b*) that the virus causally produces those symptoms. Moreover, there would be a conceptual connection between the presence of all the symptoms and the presence of the virus. Given the occurrence of all the symptoms, it would be nonsensical to ask whether their cause might be something other than the virus in question. This does not mean that it could never be a genuine empirical question whether the virus was present. For if we observed the presence of some but not all the symptoms, we could inquire whether the other symptoms were present too. This might require experimentation as well as simple observation, and would certainly be an empirical way of finding out whether the virus was present.

This analogy is still imperfect and even misleading if taken the wrong way. For example, it suggests that like the virus physical things are unobservable;

whereas I have maintained that being appeared to by a physical thing *is* observing it in the most direct conceivable way. Furthermore, the assumption that a virus could be unobservable in principle is contrary-to-fact; I am not suggesting that any physical thing could really be unobservable *in principle*. Finally, unlike a thing's ways of appearing, the virus's symptoms are not relational properties of it but seem rather to be entities in their own right, in which case the suppositions I have made imply, because of Principle *P*, that either the virus is reducible to its symptoms (in which case it cannot be a cause of those symptoms) or that our knowledge of the virus is not adequate knowledge.

Nevertheless, if we abstract from the respects in which the analogy is misleading, then it illustrates nicely the way in which epistemological phenomenalism and the causal theory of perception can be combined. Physical things cause us to be appeared to in various ways. These ways of appearing are the only conceivable perceptual access we can have to the things. There is, according to epistemological phenomenalism, a conceptual connection between certain sets of ways of being appeared to and the perception (and therefore the existence) of certain physical things. Given the occurrence of some members of one of these sets, we can investigate whether other members of the set are obtainable, thereby making empirical inquiries about the physical things that cause them. But given the occurrence of a complete set, it is nonsensical to ask whether it might have been produced by some cause other than a particular physical thing.

I shall conclude the present section by addressing a question which is suggested by the example of the virus. How should epistemological phenomenalism deal with theoretical entities, such as subatomic particles that can be observed only by the traces they make in cloud chambers? One possible answer is that although theoretical entities have no actual ways of appearing, they have observable effects (e.g. the traces) from which we can infer how they *would* appear under certain nonactual conditions; and that our knowledge of them is exhaustively knowledge of such merely possible ways of appearing. This is also a possible way of characterizing knowledge of past events that have no actual ways of appearing. Fossils, historical documents, etc. are observable effects from which we can infer inductively how certain past events would have appeared to us had we been able to observe them.

However, this suggestion does not seem to be the best way to deal with theoretical entities. This is because for physical reasons such entities can *never* be observed except by their observable effects on special instruments. Hence we would have to say that our knowledge of theoretical entities is exhaustively knowledge of how they would appear under certain conditions that never obtain (e.g. 'if our eyesight were a million times more powerful'). Perhaps such idealization of the observation conditions is unavoidable with respect to certain events in the remote past: nothing at the origin of the solar system could have appeared any way at all to us unless we assume counter-factually that our sense-receptors could have functioned despite the extreme heat, lack of oxygen, etc. But such assumptions are unnecessary with respect to theoretical entities. For we can say that certain of their observable effects are ways in which those entities themselves appear to us; e.g. that the ways in which traces in cloud chambers appear are ways in which subatomic particles themselves appear.

If we do say this, however, it becomes necessary to provide a criterion for distinguishing between ways of appearing which are, and ways of appearing which are not, ways in which the thing causing them itself appears to us. For not all ways of appearing caused by a given thing are ways in which that thing itself appears to us: the way in which the headlines of the *New York Times* appeared on the day Oswald assassinated President Kennedy was an effect of Oswald's act, but not a way in which Oswald himself or his act appeared.[26] What is needed is a nonarbitrary way of allowing that the ways traces in cloud chambers appear are ways in which subatomic particles themselves appear, without allowing that the way in which the headlines appeared was a way in which Oswald appeared. I suggest that the following criterion is acceptable: a way of appearing W caused by an object or event X is a way in which X itself appears just in case the intermediate causal factors whereby W results from X belong to a disjunctive set some member of which is physically necessary to yield observations of X. Thus, a cloud chamber or some other special instrument is physically necessary to yield observations of subatomic particles — such an instrument, like a microscope or a telescope, can be regarded virtually as an extension of the sense-receptors — whereas the various causes (reporters' stories, printing presses, etc.) whereby the appalling headlines ultimately resulted from Oswald's act did not belong to a disjunctive set some member of which was physically necessary to yield observations of Oswald or his act.

Finally, it should be noted that our strictly epistemological phenomenalism is in a better position with respect to theoretical entities than ontological phenomenalism. For while the latter must adopt an Instrumentalist view of such entities according to which they are nothing but conceptual tools for predicting the course of our sense-data, the former is compatible with a Realist interpretation of science.

4. EPISTEMOLOGICAL PHENOMENALISM AND 'CRITICAL COGNITIVISM'

As previously noted, a successful defense of our combined theory must show (*a*) that *CT* and *EP* are compatible, and (*b*) that *CT* and *EP* are both true. Part of this task has now been accomplished. We have shown that *CT* is true (on the relevant interpretations of 'perceptual knowledge') and that it is fully compatible with *EP*. We have also answered some possible objections to *EP*, viz. that it is reductionistic and that it cannot account for our knowledge of theoretical entities. But it remains to be shown that *EP* — the phenomenalist element of the combined theory — is true.

We shall proceed by returning to a question that we left unanswered at the end of the previous chapter, namely, whether the equivalence thesis of analytical phenomenalism is true. This thesis, it will be remembered, is that statements referring to physical things are logically equivalent to conjunctions of statements referring to sense-data that are or would be sensed under various conditions. However, since we have rejected the sense-datum theory in favor of the adverbial theory, let us reformulate the thesis to be evaluated as follows:

ET: Statements referring to physical things are logically equivalent to conjunctions of statements referring to the ways we are or would be appeared to under various conditions.

If we can establish that *ET* is true, then we shall have shown that *EP* is true; for *ET* is surely a sufficient condition for the truth of *EP*.

In defending *ET*, we shall be parting company with the majority of contemporary philosophers. For as we noted at the end of the previous chapter, in recent years philosophers have advanced persuasive arguments against the possibility of an equivalence between statements referring to physical things (hereafter called 'thing-statements') and statements referring to ways of appearing (hereafter called 'appear-statements'). Thus, while many contemporary philosophers would accept a causal analysis of perceiving, and would (I suspect) be prepared to grant that such an analysis is compatible with a strictly epistemological phenomenalism, they would reject *ET* and so be sceptical about the truth of *EP*.

R. M. Chisholm, for example, characterizes what he calls 'taking' in a manner that closely resembles our own analysis of perceptual judgment.

If our perceiver takes something to be a cat, then he believes that a cat is one of the causes of the way he is appeared to. And he believes further that by 'varying' the cat in suitable ways – for example, by moving it – he could produce concomitant variations in the way he is appeared to.[27]

. . . whenever a man perceives something to have some characteristic and thus takes it to have some characteristic, he accepts – or assumes – certain propositions about sensing, or 'being appeared to'. If he takes something to be a row of trees, then . . . he is sensing in a certain way; he assumes, with respect to one of the ways he is sensing, that, if he were not sensing in that way, he would not be perceiving a tree. Moreover, he assumes that, if he were to *act* in certain ways, he would sense in still other ways – ways in which he would not sense if he were not now perceiving a tree. In saying that he assumes or accepts these propositions, I do not mean that they are the object of deliberate or conscious inference . . . I merely mean that, if he were to learn that they are false, he would be surprised and would then set out, deliberately and consciously, to revise his store of beliefs.[28]

If a man now takes something to be a tree, he believes that, under the conditions now obtaining, he would *not* be appeared to in just the way he is appeared to unless the thing were a tree. And he believes that if he were now to act in certain ways – if he were to approach the thing he takes to be a tree, or if he were to reach out and touch it – he would be appeared to in still other ways characteristic of a tree. It is accurate to say, I think, that phenomenalism is based upon an interpretation of such facts as these.[29]

However, for reasons that we shall examine presently, Chisholm rejects phenomenalism. Instead, he holds a position which he calls 'Critical Cognitivism'.[30] According to this position, beliefs about physical objects cannot be justified either inductively or deductively from premises referring solely to ways of appearing. Nevertheless, we need not embrace scepticism. Instead, Critical Cognitivism holds that we may accept certain epistemic rules or principles according to which being appeared to in certain ways justifies (or, in Chisholm's terminology, 'makes evident') certain propositions about physical objects. According to one of these rules, for example,

. . . if S takes something to be red, or blue, or green, or yellow, then it is evident to S that there is something [i.e. some physical thing] that *is* red, or blue, or green, or yellow. This would also hold true for other sensible characteristics and relations.[31]

And if it then also happens to be true that S is seeing a red, or blue, or green, or yellow physical object, then it follows from Chisholm's definition of knowledge as (roughly) true, evident belief that S knows that he is seeing such an object.

The drawback of this position is that the Critical Cognitivist's epistemic rules or principles, being neither inductive nor deductive, are put forward as ultimate, *sui generis* principles of epistemic justification. (In *Perceiving*, Chisholm suggests that they are synthetic *a priori*.[32] Chisholm's defense of such principles is, essentially, that since neither an inductive nor a deductive justification of thing-statements from appear-statements is possible, accepting the principles is the only alternative to scepticism. And since scepticism is plainly false, the principles ought to be accepted.[33]

This way of defending Critical Cognitivism reflects a conception of epistemology that differs significantly from the traditional one stemming largely from Descartes. On the Cartesian conception, the main task of epistemology is to defend the possibility of knowledge against scepticism. As Ayer puts it in the Preface of *The Problem of Knowledge*:

Having maintained that to say that one knows a fact is to claim the right to be sure of it, I show how such claims may be disputed on philosophical grounds. Though their targets vary, these sceptical challenges follow a consistent pattern; the same line of reasoning is used to impugn our knowledge of the external world, or of the past, or of the experiences of others. *The attempt to meet these objections supplies the main subject-matter of what is called the theory of knowledge* . . . [my empahsis] [34]

By contrast, Chisholm and those epistemologists who follow him do not accept this conception of the theory of knowledge. Instead, they maintain, the epistemologist should assume from the outset that we know pretty much those things that we think we know. His task is then to formulate, in a rigorous and precise manner, the epistemic rules or principles needed in order to justify all and only those kinds of beliefs which he has assumed to be instances of knowledge.[35] And if it turns out that (as the sceptics Ayer has in mind would argue) neither inductive nor deductive principles are sufficient for this purpose, this is no reason to suppose that scepticism is correct. Rather, it just means that the epistemologist must seek to formulate whatever non-inductive and non-deductive principles or rules are required to justify the beliefs in question. As Chisholm puts it in the Introduction of *Theory of Knowledge*:

. . . if we take as our premises the whole of what is directly evident at any time [the 'directly evident' prominently includes appear-statements and excludes thing-statements], we cannot formulate a good deductive argument, and we cannot formulate a good inductive argument, in which any of the things we ordinarily say we know appears as a conclusion. It may be, therefore, that in addition to the 'rules of deduction' and the 'rules of induction', there are also certain basic 'rules of evidence'. The deductive logician tries to formulate the first type of rule; the inductive logician tries to formulate the second; and the epistemologist tries to formulate the third.[36]

This conception of epistemology has given rise within the past ten years to a specialization called 'epistemic logic', which is the enterprise of defining and interrelating the concepts used within epistemic rules and systematizing the rules.

We can agree with Chisholm that the outcome of an inquiry into the epistemology of perception ought not to be the denial that we have any knowledge of the physical world. The problem of perception and knowledge, as we have already emphasized, is the intellectual one of understanding *how* perception can provide such knowledge despite the perplexities that arise when one reflects on this question. Failure to solve the problem would not show that we lack such knowledge, but rather that we lack an adequate understanding of how it is possible to have it. Nevertheless, the Chisholmian solution — adopting a set of ultimate principles that allow us to say that we know just those things which we *want* to say that we know — is unconvincing. The perplexity concerning how perceptual knowledge of the physical world is possible just gets transferred from one place to another, i.e. from the puzzles generated by the regress arguments of Chapters One and Three to the status of the epistemic principles. To the extent that those puzzles are genuine, compelling ones, they are not resolved by invoking the principles; while if perchance the puzzles are not genuine but rest on confusions, the principles are unnecessary. Possibly Chisholm would deny the second horn of this dilemma. For he presents the problem of perception and knowledge in a way that makes it seem to be independent of puzzles about abnormal conditions of observation, abnormal causes of perceptual experience, hallucinations, and the like. Roughly speaking, Chisholm maintains that if one were asked to justify a perceptual judgment such as 'I see a book', it would be appropriate to appeal to some more cautious claim such as 'I see something that looks like a book', and then to justify that claim by appealing to some still more cautious one and so on, until in the end one comes to something like 'I seem to see a book' or 'I am appeared to bookly'. The problem is then to exhibit the (non-inductive and non-deductive) principles in virtue of which the original perceptual judgment can be justified by such a maximally cautious, 'directly evident' claim or set of such claims. Chisholm contends that this problem arises quite apart from any doubt or attitude of scepticism concerning the original judgment; indeed he says that "one of the unfortunate consequences of the work of Descartes and, in the present century, the work of Bertrand Russell and Edmund Husserl, is the widely accepted supposition that questions about . . . justification . . . must be *challenges* or expressions of *doubts*.[37] However, the fact that it is possible to make a sequence of increasingly cautious claims such as those listed above does not *by itself* show that such a procedure is needed or appropriate for justifying perceptual judgments. There must be independent grounds for thinking that perceptual judgments stand in need of justification (as opposed to being 'self-justifying', as some philosophers would hold). And it is precisely the puzzles generated by cases of misperception, illusion, hallucination, etc. that constitute these independent grounds. So *pace* Chisholm, the chain of justification sketched above has no rationale independently of the sceptical doubts associated with these puzzles. But, to return to the first horn of our dilemma, if these puzzles are genuine ones, then they are not resolved by introducing a set of ultimate epistemic principles.

Can we do any better than to adopt such a set of principles? I shall now try to show that we can, by defending the phenomenalist thesis that there is a deductive connection between appear-statements and thing-statements against the most persuasive arguments that have been raised against it. I shall examine first the arguments against the entailment of appear-statements by thing-statements, and finally the epistemologically crucial entailment of thing-statements by appear-statements.

5. EPISTEMOLOGICAL PHENOMENALISM (I): THE ENTAILMENT OF APPEAR-STATEMENTS BY THING-STATEMENTS

In a widely-anthologized section of *Perceiving*, R. M. Chisholm argues that no thing-statement entails *any*, not even a single, appear-statement.[38] Chisholm presents his argument in a somewhat formal way. But the idea on which the argument turns is a simple one. The way in which a physical thing appears to a perceiver is always a function of three factors:

(1)   the properties of the thing,
(2)   the conditions of observation (e.g. light, distance),
(3)   the perceiver's physiological state.

For example, suppose that the thing perceived is white. From this alone we cannot know what color it will appear to a perceiver. In order to determine that, we must also know what sort of light the thing is seen under and whether the perceiver's color-vision is normal. In general, it is impossible to determine, just from the fact that a physical thing has a certain property, how it will appear to a perceiver. For the way it will appear always depends also upon the conditions of observation and the perceiver's physiological state. Therefore, no statement to the effect that a physical thing has a certain property can possibly entail any statement describing how it does or would appear to a perceiver.

Chisholm's formal argument is as follows. It is a principle of logic that P entails R only if it is not the case that P, in conjunction with any statement

S which is compatible with *P*, entails not-*R*. But this principle is *never* satisfied when *P* is a thing-statement and *R* is an appear-statement. For it is always possible to formulate a statement *S*, describing the conditions of observation or the perceiver's physiological state, such that *S* is compatible with *P* but the conjunction of *P* and *S* entails not-*R*. Chisholm gives the following example. Suppose that *P* stands for 'This is red' and *R* stands for 'Redness will be sensed' (i.e. *S* will be appeared to redly). Then it is possible to find a statement *Q* referring to observation conditions such that *P* and *Q* do entail *R*, namely:

This is perceived under normal conditions; and if this is red and is perceived under normal conditions, then redness will be sensed. (*Q*)[39]

However, it is also possible to find a statement *S* referring to observation conditions such that *P* and *S* entail not-*R*, for instance:

This is perceived under conditions which are normal except for the presence of blue lights; and if this is red and is perceived under conditions which are normal except for the presence of blue lights, redness will not be sensed. (*S*)[40]

Clearly *S* is not incompatible with *P*; there is no contradiction in asserting both *S* and *P*. But *P*, in conjunction with *S*, entails not-*R*. Therefore, by the logical principle cited above, *P* does not entail *R*.

This example, of course, hardly refutes phenomenalism. For the appear-statement *R* is a categorical statement. Hence it should be obvious without Chisholm's argument that *P* cannot entail *R*. For suppose, as is logically possible, that no one ever looks at the red object *P* refers to or any other red object, and that no one ever misperceives some object to be red or has a dream or hallucination in which he seems to perceive a red object. Then *P* will be true but *R* will remain eternally false. So of course *P* does not entail *R*. This is why the phenomenalist's appear-statements must be hypothetical ones — statements to the effect that *if* one is appeared to in certain ways, then one will be appeared to in certain other ways. Furthermore, these hypothetical statements must not be construed as material implications but as subjunctive conditionals. For since a material conditional is true whenever its antecedent is false, if the appear-statements were construed as material conditionals, phenomenalism would imply the absurdity that any statement whatever about any unperceived object is true.[41]

Chisholm shows, however, that his argument applies to hypothetical appear-statements no less than to categorical ones. Suppose, for example, that the thing-statement is:

There is a cube of sugar before me (*P*)

and that the appear-statement is:

> If I should seem to see something white, cubical and gritty and to perform a certain reaching, grasping and biting action, a sweet taste would follow. (R)[42]

Typically, a phenomenalist would hold that P entails R as well as a large number of other appear-statements having the same form as R (and conversely that these appear-statements entail P); and at first sight this may look like a plausible doctrine. But though it may seem that P entails R, it does not do so. For as Chisholm points out, there are many statements S, compatible with P and describing observation conditions or the perceiver's physiological state, such that P and S entail not-R. Two such statements are:

> I am in a laboratory where all sugar cubes are chemically treated to make them tasteless, such that if there is a cube of sugar before me, then it is not the case that if I should seem to see something white, cubical and gritty and to perform a certain reaching, grasping and biting action, a sweet taste would follow. (S)

> I have a deficiency of the taste buds which prevents me from tasting sweetness, such that if there is a cube of sugar before me, then it is not the case that if I should seem to see something white, cubical and gritty and to perform a certain reaching, grasping and biting action, a sweet taste would follow. (S_1)

This is an incisive argument. But how damaging is it to phenomenalism? In introducing the argument Chisholm says

. . . every form of phenomenalism involves the thesis that anything we know about material things may be expressed in statements referring solely to appearances. Since many of the problems discussed in this book would require a very different treatment if this thesis were true, I shall now state my reasons for believing it to be false.[43]

Thus, what Chisholm takes to be common to all forms of phenomenalism, and also believes he has shown to be false, is "the thesis that anything we know about material things may be expressed in statements referring solely to appearances". Notice that this thesis (assuming 'appearances' is taken to mean 'ways of being appeared to' and not 'sense-data') is virtually identical to what I have called 'Epistemological Phenomenalism'. Chisholm sees that phenomenalism is fundamentally an epistemological thesis, not necessarily a thesis about language and certainly not one about the constitution of material things. Indeed, in the article in which he first put forward his argument against phenomenalism, Chisholm says:

The problem is an epistemological one, concerning our beliefs or judgements about
material things, and could be discussed without reference to statements at all. The present issues, however, may be brought into clearer light if we . . . discuss the relations
between statements.[44]

Our question, then, is as follows. Chisholm's argument does show quite conclusively that no simple thing-statement such as 'this is red' or 'there is a cube
of sugar before me' entails even a single appear-statement. Must we conclude
from this that it is false that 'anything we know about material things can be
expressed in statements referring solely to appearances', and so that *EP* is
false?

I do not think that we should draw this conclusion. For what do we know
about material things that could *not* be expressed in statements referring
solely to their ways of appearing? Is it our knowledge of observation conditions (of such things as light, atmospheric conditions, and the like), or of our
own physiological states (of such matters as being drugged, numb, chilled,
and the like) that could not be so expressed? What then does such knowledge consist in, over and above the knowledge of certain ways of appearing?
The component of our knowledge of physical things that cannot be expressed
in terms of ways in which we are or would be appeared to seems utterly
mysterious — so much so that there is something paradoxical about an
argument purporting to *prove* that our knowledge of physical things is not
exhausted by knowledge of their various ways of appearing.

Accordingly, I shall now try to show that Chisholm's argument does not
disprove *EP*. Recall the basic point on which the argument turns. This is that
the thing perceived is never the only cause of the way it appears to a perceiver. Two other causal factors — the conditions of observation and the
perceiver's physiological state — also help to determine the way the thing
appears. This is why no simple thing-statement such as 'this is red' or 'there is
a cube of sugar before me' can entail any appear-statement. Chisholm himself
explains this point very clearly:

The difficulties [of phenomenalism] may be traced to the 'perceptual relativity' which
the Critical Realists had stressed — the the fact that the ways in which things appear
depend, not only upon the objective properties of the thing, but also upon the conditions under which the thing is perceived and upon the state of the person who perceives
it. To translate or paraphrase a simple thing statement into a collection of appearance
statements, or even to find a single appearance statement which is implied by the thing
statement, we must find some appearance or appearances which can be uniquely correlated with the physical fact described by the thing statement. But we are not able to
correlate any group of appearances with any particular fact unless we specify those

appearances by reference to some *other* physical fact — by reference to some set of observation conditions and to the state of the particular person who is to sense the appearances. For it is the joint operation of the things we perceive and of the conditions under which we perceive them that determines the ways in which things are going to appear to us. And this constitutes a difficulty in principle for the attempt to translate thing statements into appearance statements . . . .[45]

However, the fact of perceptual relativity does not really constitute a 'difficulty in principle' for the attempt to derive appear-statements from thing-statements; for it does not show that 'we are not able to correlate any group of appearances with any particular fact unless we specify those appearances by reference to some *other* physical fact'. Rather, it shows that instead of starting from simple thing-statements such as 'this is red' or 'there is a cube of sugar before me', the phenomenalist must start from complex thing-statements such as:

> There is an unadulterated sugar cube before me, the present lighting is direct sunlight, and my vision, coordination, and taste receptors are completely normal. (P_1)

From this statement is it possible to determine how the cube of sugar will appear to me. For the way it will appear depends upon its properties, the conditions of observation, my physiological state, *and nothing else*. Thus, from (P_1) we can derive the appear-statement:

> If I should seem to see something white, cubical and gritty before me and to perform a certain reaching, grasping and biting action, a sweet taste would follow. (R)

Of course, P_1 logically implies R only if P_1 is taken in conjunction with an additional premiss, such as: 'If there is an unadulterated sugar cube before me, the present lighting is direct sunlight, and my vision, coordination, and taste receptors are completely normal, then if I should seem to see something white, cubical and gritty before me and to perform a certain reaching, grasping and biting action, a sweet taste would follow'. This premiss, however, is analytically true. Thus the claim that P_1 entails R means that P_1, in conjunction with an analytic statement, logically implies R; just as 'John is a husband' entails 'John is married' because the former, in conjunction with 'if John is a husband, then John is married', logically implies the latter. It follows that there is no statement compatible with P_1 which, in conjunction with P_1, entails not-R; just as there is no statement compatible with 'John is a husband' which in conjunction with it, entails 'it is not the case that John is married'.

It might be objected, however, that there are statements compatible with P_1 and which, conjoined with P_1, entail not-R; e.g. 'there is a piece of chalk before me'. But this objection is mistaken. Of course if there is a sugar cube *and* a piece of chalk before me, and I pick up and bite the chalk instead of the sugar, then I do not experience a sweet taste. But this is perfectly compatible with its being the case that P_1 entails R. For so long as it is true that there is an unadulterated cube of sugar before me, illuminated by direct sunlight, and that my vision, coordination, and taste receptors are completely normal, it cannot possibly be false that *if* I should seem to see something white, cubical and gritty before me and to perform a *certain* reaching, grasping and biting action, a sweet taste would follow. What may be confusing here is that P_1, in conjunction with 'there is a piece of chalk before me', *also* entails:

> It is not the case that if I should seem to see something white, cubical and gritty before me and to perform a certain reaching, grasping and biting action, a sweet taste would follow. (R_1)

So it may seem that there is a statement compatible with P_1 (namely, 'there is a piece of chalk before me') which, in conjunction with P_1, entails the negation of R. But this is not the case. For in R_1, the phrase 'seem . . . to perform a certain reaching, grasping and biting action' describes a *different* anticipated passage of experience from the one described by the same phrase in R. Therefore, R_1 is not the negation (contradictory) of R; and so there is no difficulty in holding both that P_1 alone entails R and that P_1, in conjunction with 'there is a piece of chalk before me', entails R_1. The logic of the situation is analogous to the following case. The statement

> The light switch in my room is operational (p)

entails the statement

> If the light switch in my room is pressed in a certain direction, the light will go on. (q)

Yet p also entails the statement

> It is not the case that if the light switch in my room is pressed in a certain direction, the light will go on. (r)

There is no difficulty in holding that p, itself a consistent statement, entails both q and r; for q and r are not contradictories. They are not contradictories because q is made true by the fact that the light will go on if the switch is pressed upward, while r is made true by the fact that the light will not go on (but will go off) if the switch is pressed downward. (Thus the antecedents of q and r would have to be symbolized using different sentence-letters.) Likewise, R and R_1 are not contradictories, because their antecedents refer to different anticipated passages of experience, i.e. to different anticipated sequences of ways of being appeared to.

The above objection, though mistaken, is instructive. For it provides an illustration of a point that should be kept in mind in connection with the view that statements referring to physical things are logically equivalent to conjunctions of statements describing ways of being appeared to. This view must not be taken to imply that we can actually provide specimen 'translations' of various thing-statements into logically equivalent conjunctions of appear-statements. We cannot do this, because our language simply does not contain a vocabulary suited for detailed, play-by-play descriptions of the ways we are appeared to. This is why, in order to describe certain kinaesthetic ways of being appeared to in R and R_1, we had to use the vague term 'certain' (a term which masked the fact that R and R_1 are not really contradictories and thereby made the objection seem plausible). When it comes to describing kinesthetic and tactual ways of being appeared to especially, our language can only classify these in a very general way; and the same thing is true to a lesser extent for gustatory, olfactory and visual ways of being appeared to.[46] As a result, it is not *in fact* possible to 'translate' thing-statements into logically equivalent conjunctions of appear-statements. But this does not mean that it is *in principle* impossible to do so. The situation may be compared to one in which we are translating, say, from French into English and we run into a French expression that has no counterpart in English.[47] In such a situation it is not in fact possible to translate the expression, but it is possible in principle. All that would be required is a certain enrichment of English. Likewise, the inadequacy of our language for describing ways of being appeared to does not show that it is in principle impossible to 'translate' thing-statements into logically equivalent conjunctions of appear-statements. And if it is in principle possible to do this — i.e. if statements about physical things *could*, given a suitable enrichment of our language, be reformulated as logically equivalent conjunctions of statements referring solely to the ways we are and would be appeared to — this would surely suffice to establish that our knowledge of physical things is exhaustively knowledge of the ways they do and would appear to us.

Our reply to Chisholm's argument suggests an answer to another well-known objection to phenomenalism. This is that since a physical thing can

be perceived under an infinite number of different observation conditions
(e.g. seen from an infinite number of points), a thing-statement would have to
entail an infinite number of appear-statements.[48] Keith Lehrer has correctly
pointed out, however, that the theoretical possibility of perceiving a thing
under an infinite number of different observation conditions does not imply
that there are perceptually discriminable differences corresponding to each of
those conditions; e.g. a thing would look the same to a perceiver from two
different points if these were sufficiently close together.[49] In any case, starting from complex thing-statements which *include* a specification of the
observation conditions cuts the ground from under the objection.

At this point it will be asked: what gives us the right to start from complex
thing-statements such as P_1? In other words, how does our phenomenalism
explain how one can *know* that there is a certain physical thing before one,
and that the present conditions of observation as well as one's own physiological state are of a certain kind? The answer we must defend is that one can
know this by knowing a set of appear-statements that constitutes a logically
sufficient condition for the complex thing-statement. More precisely, the set
of appear-statements constitutes a logically sufficient condition for a statement asserting *that some physical thing is perceived* under certain conditions
of observation and while one is in a certain physiological state, from which it
follows that the thing exists (and that the conditions of observation and one's
physiological state are of a certain kind). It is this entailment of a perceptual
claim or judgment by a set of appear-statements which is crucial for epistemological purposes. Notice that if such an entailment can be successfully defended, then the Justification Thesis of the Causal Theory of Perception is
vindicated, though not in the manner in which proponents of the Causal
Theory have traditionally tried to vindicate it. For the claim to perceive
some physical thing can then be justified by a *deductive* (rather than by some
form of inductive) argument showing that the thing is causally required to
account for certain ways in which one is appeared to. Our combined theory,
then, is intended to incorporate *both* parts of the Causal Theory in its general
formulation (i.e. both the Analytic Thesis and the Justification Thesis).[50]

Chisholm does not attack the epistemologically crucial entailment of
thing-statements by appear-statements; his argument is directed only against
the entailment of appear-statements by simple thing-statements. Nevertheless,
Chisholm's critique brings out the nature of the difficulty that must be overcome if our combined theory is to be successful. The difficulty is that for any
way of appearing W, there are many different combinations of physical
properties, conditions of observation, and physiological states that can cause

W. To take a simple example, one might be appeared to yellowly because (*a*) one is seeing a yellow object in normal light and one's color-vision is normal, (*b*) one is seeing a white object in yellow light and one's color vision is normal, (*c*) one is seeing a white object in normal light while suffering from jaundice. Other explanations are possible too; e.g. one is hallucinating a yellow object. The problem phenomenalism (combined with the causal theory) faces, therefore, is this: how could a perceiver ascertain, solely on the basis of the ways he is appeared to, what particular combination of causes is at work?

Our question can be put as follows. Suppose that a person verifies the appear-statement:

> I seem to see a yellow object (I am appeared to yellow-objectly). (S_1)

Obviously, the truth of S_1 alone does not guarantee that the person is really seeing a yellow object. For as we have just noted, S_1 might be made true e.g. by the fact that one is seeing a white object in yellow light, or seeing a white object while suffering from jaundice, or hallucinating a yellow object. What additional appear-statements, then, would have to be true in order to entail a complex thing-statement such as:

> I see a yellow object in normal light and my vision, coordination, and tactual sense-receptors are completely normal (P)

— a statement which entails the existence, among other things, of a yellow physical object? According to our phenomenalism, the additional appear-statements are statements predicting how the perceiver would be appeared to under certain conditions. Now in formulating these hypothetical appear-statements, there is a pitfall to be avoided. Suppose for example that we were to conjoin S_1 with:

> If I should carry the object into direct sunlight and look at it, I would be appeared to yellowly. (S_{2i})

This statement is completely useless for our purposes. For although its consequent refers solely to a way the perceiver is appeared to, its antecedent does not refer solely to ways the perceiver is appeared to. Instead, it refers to a certain physical setting, a bodily action and, indeed, to the very object whose existence is supposed to be entailed by the conjunction of appear-statements being formulated. So S_{2i} is not a statement which refers solely to ways of being appeared to, and is therefore useless for the purpose of indicating how such statements might entail thing-statements. The mistake of overtly or

covertly referring to physical things in what are supposed to be purely experiential statements (i.e. sense-datum statements or appear-statements) has
sometimes been made by phenomenalists. One good example of this mistake,
as Chisholm points out, occurs in J. S. Mill's attempt to express his belief
that Calcutta exists in terms of 'permanent possibilities of sensation'. Mill
says, in effect, that this belief can be formulated as:

> If I should be transported to the banks of the Hoogly River, I
> would have Calcutta-sensations.[51]

Here again, the antecedent illegitimately refers to certain physical circumstances. To see more clearly why this is illegitimate, bear in mind that the
fundamental claim of phenomenalism is that our knowledge of physical
things is *exhaustively* knowledge of ways in which we are or would be
appeared to. But if this is so, then knowledge of the physical setting, of one's
own bodily movements, etc. must itself be expressible exhaustively in terms
of ways of being appeared to. Accordingly, S_{2i} must be reformulated as:

> If I should seem to carry the object into direct sunlight and to
> look at it, I would be appeared to yellowly. (S_2)

Here the phrase ' should seem to' indicates that the antecedent, no less than
the consequent, does not imply the existence of any physical objects or
bodily actions; it describes only a certain passage of experience which might
occur even in a realistic dream or hallucination.

It is clear, however, that the conjunction of S_1 and S_2 does not entail P.
For it might be made true, for example, by the fact that one is seeing a white
object while suffering from jaundice. To eliminate this possibility, other
appear-statements would have to be verified. One such statement might be:

> If I should seem to look at my own skin, I would not be appeared
> to yellowly. (S_3)

But the conjunction of S_1 & S_2 & S_3 still does not entail P. For its truth is
compatible with, say, one's suffering from a visual hallucination in which one
seems to be looking at a yellow object and examining the color of one's own
skin in direct sunlight. To eliminate this possibility, still other appear-statements would have to be verified. One such statement might be:

> If I should seem to squeeze the yellow object tightly, I would feel
> some pressure or resistance (would be appeared to 'resistance-ly').
> (S_4)

It seems safe to assert that verifying a set of appear-statements of the kind exemplified by $S_1 - S_4$ is *necessary* in order to ascertain the causes of one's being appeared to in a given way. But it is also clear that verifying $S_1 - S_4$ is still not *sufficient* to ascertain the causes of one's seeming to see a yellow object; since the conjunction of S_1 & S_2 & S_3 & S_4 is compatible either with one's really seeing a yellow object or, say, with one's suffering from a rather elaborate hallucination involving the sense of touch as well as of sight. Could the procedure of verifying such a set of appear-statements, if pursued thoroughly enough, ever be sufficient to ascertain the causes of one's perceptual experience? Only if this question can be answered in the affirmative can we say that a thing-statement such as P is entailed by some conjunction of appear-statements such as S_1 & S_2 & S_3 & S_4 & ... & S_n.

At this point, however, it may seem that no matter which and how many additional appear-statements are added to the set $S_1 - S_4$, the truth of the resulting conjunction can be accounted for by postulating an ever more realistic, systematic, and comprehensive hallucination or dream. But it is not *self-evident* that no matter what further appear-statements were added to $S_1 - S_4$, it would remain logically possible that the conjunction of S_1 & S_2 & S_3 & S_4 & ... & S_n described only a hallucination or a dream: the point needs to be argued. In recent years, philosophers have indeed given arguments intended to show that no set of appear-statements, no matter how complex, entails any statement asserting or implying the existence of any physical thing. In the following section, I shall attempt to refute the two most persuasive of these arguments.

6. EPISTEMOLOGICAL PHENOMENALISM (II): THE ENTAILMENT OF THING-STATEMENTS BY APPEAR-STATEMENTS

Suppose that a person has verified a set of appear-statements S_1 & ... & S_n, and assume that this set provides evidence for a thing-statement P. Could this evidence be logically conclusive, i.e. could S_1 & ... & S_n entail P? One quite familiar argument for holding that this question must be answered in the negative goes as follows.[52] No matter how much sensory evidence there is for a given thing-statement, it is always logically possible that new sensory evidence will disconfirm the statement. In other words, no matter how elaborate the set S_1 & ... & S_n is, it remains logically possible that some appear-statement S_{n+1} will be verified that provides evidence against P. So the conjunction of S_1 & ... & S_n with S_{n+1} does not entail P. But it follows from a principle of logic that if S_1 & ... & S_n entails P, then the conjunction of S_1 & ... & S_n with any statement must entail P. Therefore, S_1 & ... & S_n does not entail P.

It is true that a thing-statement for which there is good sensory evidence can be disconfirmed by new sensory evidence. This is indeed the way in which we discover that some of our perceptual judgments were mistaken. However, it does not follow that *any* thing-statement, no matter how much sensory evidence one has for it, can be disconfirmed by further experience. On the contrary, this premiss of the argument is false, as may be seen by considering the following example.

I am now being appeared to in ways characteristic of typing at my desk on a sunny day while well-rested and suffering from no sensory disorders. The ways I am now being appeared to are sequent upon others, characteristic of walking into my study, sitting down on the chair before the desk, uncovering the typewriter, cleaning the type with a clay-like substance, inserting paper, adjusting the ribbon, typing for some time. These ways of being appeared to constitute a coherent experiential history leading up to my now being appeared to in ways characteristic of typing. This history stretches back further than the experiences I have just mentioned: these are in turn sequent upon experiences characteristic of rising from bed, getting dressed, having breakfast and so forth. The history becomes fuzzy only when I try to recall my earliest waking moments and, before that, my last waking moments; and there is a blank between the last and first waking moments that I do clearly remember, broken by some conscious episodes that I take to have been dreams. Beyond this the history picks up again, exhibiting the same sort of coherence.[53]

What the premiss under consideration asserts is that any thing-statement I accept on the basis of the experiences I have just described — e.g. that there is now a typewriter before me — could be disconfirmed by further experience. But is this true? Suppose, for example, that what I take to be my typewriter were suddenly to start appearing to me in ways characteristic of a porcupine. It would be absurd, in light of the experiences just described, for me then to suspect that I might have been mistaken all along about the existence of a typewriter in my study. Rather, I would think that I was *now* suffering from an illusion or a hallucination in which I seemed to perceive a porcupine. Suppose the porcupine appearances were to persist. Then I might surmise that someone had surreptitiously replaced my tyepwriter with a porcupine while my attention was momentarily distracted. Conceivably — if every other hypothesis seemed out of the question — I might come to think that my typewriter had miraculously changed into a porcupine. But one hypothesis which it would be absurd for me to entertain is that there had never existed a typewriter in my study. Nor would this hypothesis become any less absurd if the disappearance of the typewriter were accompanied by the disappearance of all the work I think I remember typing on it, or by still more radical eventualities such as the disappearance of what I take to be my study, or my seeming to wake up in totally new surroundings. If the course of my experience were to change in some such radical way — if there occurred, so to speak, a complete 'break' in my experience — this would not disconfirm all the thing-statements that I accept on the basis of the experiences I have had up until now. Rather, it would show that the course of (physical) events had changed in radical and unforseeable ways. Thus, given a sufficient accumulation of sensory evidence in favor of a thing-statement, it is simply not true that the statement could be disconfirmed by new sensory evidence — i.e. that thing-statements are, as Ayer puts it, 'eternally on probation'.[54] Therefore, the above argument against the entailment of thing-statements by appear-statements fails.

Nevertheless, the argument is instructive. For it shows that any set of appear-statements that entails a thing-statement must be extremely extended and complex. Thus, it shows again why a phenomenalist must not be expected to prove his case by providing specimen 'translations' of thing-statements into appear-statements: not only, as we have already seen, is our language unsuited for precise, detailed descriptions of all the ways we are appeared to, but any set of appear-statements that constituted a logically sufficient condition for a thing-statement would be so complex that it is not in fact possible to specify the entire set. The best we can do is to list some of the statements that would go into such a set, as we did at the end of the previous section. It will be enough if we can establish that such a set of appear-statements can in principle be expanded so as to entail a statement implying the existence of certain physical things.

There is an influential argument, however, which purports to show that it is not even in principle possible to specify a set of appear-statements that entails a thing-statement, i.e. that no set of appear-statements, no matter how extended and complex, can possibly entail any statement implying the existence of any physical thing. Suppose that there is a powerful deceiver who can cause us to have any sensory experiences whatever though we never perceive any physical things. This deceiver can cause us to be appeared to in exactly the same way as any set of observation conditions, physiological states, and stimulus-objects. He can duplicate not only the ways of appearing which initially lead a perceiver to believe that (say) he is seeing an ordinary sugar cube under normal conditions of observation and while suffering from no sensory disorders, but also all the further ways of appearing which might be thought to show that this is indeed what he is seeing. Thus, no matter how many tests one performs in order to ascertain that one is not hallucinating or dreaming or misperceiving something because of abnormal conditions of observation, these tests can never enable one to know what are the real causes of one's perceptual experiences.

This Cartesian 'deceiver hypothesis' (as we called it in Chapter Five) has been revived in recent discussions of perceptual knowledge, usually in the form of suggesting that any stretch of sensory experience produced by physical things stimulating our sense-receptors could be exactly duplicated by very advanced scientists directly stimulating our brains.[55] Many contemporary epistemologists would contend that the deceiver hypothesis shows that no set of statements about the ways we are appeared to can possibly entail any statement about physical things.[56] I shall now argue, however, that it fails to demonstrate this negative proposition.

It will be useful to focus on a very clear statement of the deceiver hypothesis by John L. Pollock:

Phenomenalism . . . [maintains] that statements about the ways things appear to us may entail statements about physical objects. This basic position can be elaborated in various ways . . . . We need not go into these elaborations, however, because the basic unelaborated position can be shown to be wrong by itself . . . . Given any statement about the ways things appear to a person and any statement about physical objects, we can imagine circumstances in which the former would be true and the latter false, thus demonstrating that the former does not entail the latter. One way of doing this is to suppose that we have a group of neurophysiologists who have arrived at a complete neurophysiological account of perception. To test their account, they wire a subject into a very complicated computer which directly stimulates his brain and they disconnect his sense organs from his brain. They could then arrange for things to appear any way at all to him. Given any statement P about the ways things appear to him and any statement Q about the physical world, they could make P true independently of the truth or falsity of Q, thus showing that P does not entail Q.[57]

As Pollock concedes in a footnote, this example does not really show that the neurophysiologists could make P true independently of the truth or falsity of *any* statement about the physical world, because statements about the computer (as well as the neurophysiologists, the subject's brain, etc.) must be true for the circumstances described in the example to obtain. This could be avoided by changing the example so as to involve a purely spiritual, authentically Cartesian genius deceiving a disembodied Cartesian mind. But it is not necessary to alter Pollock's example in order to preserve its force. For we may take the thing-statement Q, as suggested on pages 187–191 above, to be a statement asserting that some physical thing *is perceived* (under certain conditions of observation and while the perceiver is in a certain physiological state), from which it *follows* that the thing exists. We can then take the example as an attempt to show that any thing-statement in this narrower (but epistemologically prior) sense can be false while any appear-statement is true. For so long as all the subject's perceptual experiences are being produced by a computer directly stimulating his brain, he is hallucinating and so not perceiving any physical things. This is not altered by the fact that the computer, the neurophysiologists, etc. must exist to generate the hallucination, and would remain true even if the neurophysiologists made the subject hallucinate that his brain was wired into a computer operated by a team of neurophysiologists, i.e. even if the content of the hallucination were to correspond to reality.

A phenomenalist might object, however, that using the deceiver hypothesis as an argument against his position begs the question. For Pollock is asserting that his version of the deceiver hypothesis — i.e. the neurophysiologist example — shows how any appear-statement could be true while any thing-statement were false. But if, as phenomenalsim maintains, a sufficiently complex appear-statement P entails a thing-statement Q, then there cannot be an example showing how P could be true and Q false; anymore than there can be an example showing how 'John is a husband' could be true and 'John is married' false. However, Pollock could reply that it is the phenomenalist who is begging the question: since, as the neurophysiologist example shows, P could be true and Q false, it is no good insisting that P entails Q. In other words, a critic of phenomenalism would hold that the force of the neurophysiologist example places the burden of proof on the phenomenalist. After all, no phenomenalist has ever specified exactly a set of appear-statements which according to him entails a thing-statement; and, for the reasons that we have given, it does not seem that this can be done. Rather, phenomenalists have commonly rested their case on the plausibility of the idea that verifying a sufficiently complex set of appear-statements would conclusively establish a thing-statement: what else would? But a critic such as Pollock would claim that the neurophysiologist example shows that this idea is demonstrably false. For it shows that 'we can imagine circumstances' in which any stretch of a person's perceptual experience could be duplicated while he perceived no physical things, thereby 'demonstrating' that any appear-statement P, no matter how complex, could be true while any thing-statement Q were false and so that P does not entail Q.[58]

However, the neurophysiologist example does not really demonstrate this negative proposition. For in order to demonstrate that *any* statement *P* describing the ways a person is appeared to could be true while any thing-statement *Q* were false, the example must show how *any stretch of any person's* perceptual experiences could be duplicated without his perceiving any physical things. Otherwise, it remains possible that *some stretch of some person's* perceptual experience cannot be so duplicated, and so that some statement *P* describing the ways some person is appeared to does entail a thing-statement *Q*. But the example cannot possibly show that any stretch of any person's perceptual experience could be duplicated without his perceiving any physical things. For if it is true that any such stretch of experience can be so duplicated, then this must apply not only to the experimental subject's experience but also to the experience of the neurophysiologists. We must allow that each neurophysiologist's perpectual experiences (including among others those of wiring the subject into the computer, disconnecting his sense organs from his brain, etc.) could be perfectly duplicated though he had never perceived any physical things nor, *a fortiori*, performed any scientific experiments. It follows that the neurophysiologists would have no way of telling whether they were really performing the experiment Pollock describes or only hallucinating such an experiment. But this is not the point I wish to stress. Rather, the crucial point is that if any stretch of anyone's perceptual experience can be duplicated without his perceiving any physical things, then there *is* no way of telling whether the example describes (*a*) the neurophysiologists duplicating the subject's perceptual experiences by directly stimulating his brain, or (*b*) the neurophysiologists hallucinating that they are duplicating the subject's perceptual experiences by directly stimulating his brain. We may fail to see this because we are likely to read into Pollock's example a hypothetical observer (namely, ourselves) who can determine whether the neurophysiologists are really experimenting or only hallucinating the experiment, because this makes a difference to the experiences that *he* can obtain. But this assumes, contrary to what the example is supposed to show, that there is someone (i.e. the hypothetical observer) to whose experiences it *does* make a difference whether he ever perceives physical things or is perpetually hallucinating. If these alternatives need make no difference whatever either to the experiences obtainable by the experimental subject or those obtainable by the neurophysiologists or those obtainable by *anyone* else, then there is no basis for saying that the example describes (*a*) rather than (*b*). The upshot is that we cannot tell what the example describes if any stretch of anyone's perceptual experience can be duplicated without his perceiving any physical things. My reply to Pollock, then, is that if any such stretch of experience could be so duplicated — and so if any appear-statement P, no matter how complex, could be true while any thing-statement Q were false — then it would be impossible to describe the sort of example that he uses to show that this is so.

Let me state the reasons for this claim more fully, in the form of an argument. The first premiss is:

(1)   If it is possible to describe circumstances in which a person's perceptual experiences are duplicated by directly stimulating his brain, then there must be some way of telling, at least in principle, whether a given description applies to these circumstances.

This is an instance of a general principle: we can describe X only if there is in principle some way of telling whether a description applies to X. In saying that there must be some way of *telling* whether a description applies to X, I mean only that there must be some reasonable way of determining whether the description (correctly) applies to X. The intuitive idea here is that describing a thing requires more than merely uttering or writing down a suitable string of words: it requires that we be able to connect or match the thing with the description. But if there is no reasonable way of determining whether any description applies to a thing — i.e. if nothing whatever would constitute favorable evidence or tend to confirm that any description correctly applies to the thing — then we cannot relate or connect any description with the thing. This may be obscured by the fact that descriptive words like 'red', 'round', and 'loud' naturally call to mind, for those who understand them, the kind of non-linguistic evidence on the basis of which they are applied. It is difficult for us to think of such a word, or of any descriptive term or phrase that we are able to understand, wholly apart from the non-linguistic evidence that would justify its application. But suppose, counterfactually, that nothing whatever could tend to confirm that a thing was red or round or loud. Then we would have no conception of redness or roundness or loudness, and 'red', 'round', and 'loud' would not be genuine descriptive terms. This point can surely be generalized to other, less obviously observational terms.

It may be objected that premiss (1) implies a verifiability criterion of meaning, according to which a nonanalytic statement is meaningful only if it is in principle verifiable or confirmable by some sort of observation. There are well-known difficulties with such a criterion of meaning; e.g. that no one has succeeded in formulating it rigorously in a way that does not either rule out as meaningless certain scientific statements or countenance as meaningful allegedly meaningless metaphysical statements, that it rules out as meaningless all normative and evaluative statements (at least on the most plausible construals of such statements), and that it is self-defeating because, being it-self neither an analytic statement nor an empirical generalization, the verifi-ability criterion rules itself out as meaningless. This is not the place to launch into an extended discussion of verificationism.[59] Rather, to meet the objec-tion it will suffice to point out that premiss (1) does *not* commit us to any general critierion of meaning. For it implies only that a genuinely *descriptive* statement — one that succeeds in describing some actual or possible object or state of affairs — must be one such that something would tend to confirm it or would count as evidence in its favor. The premiss does not even imply that the evidence in question must consist of *observations* of some sort: it leaves the question of how we are to tell whether a given description correctly applies completely open. This is an extremely weak form of verificationism, if it can be called 'verificationism' at all. As such, premiss (1) should be con-sidered on its own merits, apart from the difficulties associated with the verifiability criterion of meaning. It will then be evident that the premiss imposes a very weak, but essential requirement for describing the neuro-physiologist example. Surely it is a minimal requirement for describing any-thing that there be, at least in principle, some way of telling whether a description applies to it.

The second premiss is:

(2)   If any set of ways of appearing answering to the description of any objective circumstances would also answer to the description of a hallucination of these circumstances, then there is no way of telling, even in principle, whether a given description applies to circumstances in which a person's perceptual experiences are duplicated by directly stimulating his brain.

This is an instance of the general principle that if any set of ways of appearing answering to the description of any objective circumstances would also answer to the description of a hallucination of these circumstances, then there is in principle no way of telling whether a given description applies to some particular objective circumstances X (since it could just as easily apply to an X-hallucination instead). This principle must be carefully distinguished from something that I am not saying. I am not saying that *some* ways of appearing answering to the description of any objective circumstances could not also answer to the description of a hallucination of these circumstances without making it impossible to tell whether a description applies to some particular objective circumstances X. A realistic hallucination of certain objective circumstances is precisely a situation in which we *are* appeared to in a number of ways that would *also* answer to the description of those circumstances; yet the existence of such hallucinations does not make it impossible for us ever to tell whether a given description correctly applies to some objective circumstances. What I am saying is that it is not the case that both (*a*) *any* set of ways of appearing (no matter how orderly, systematic, and prolonged) answering to the description of any objective circumstances (no matter how encompassing) would also answer to the description of a hallucination of these circumstances, and (*b*) there is, at least in principle, a way of telling whether a given description correctly applies to some particular objective circumstances X (rather than to an X-hallucination). In other words, it is not the case both that any stretch of perceptual experience could be hallucinatory, and that we can tell whether a description applies to X.

It might be objected that even if any set of ways of appearing answering to the description of any objective circumstances would also answer to the description of a hallucination of these circumstances, we still have a way of telling whether a description applies to some particular objective circumstances X rather than to a hallucination of X — namely, that we *intend* the description to apply to the former rather than the latter. But this suggestion will not hold up under scrutiny. Suppose I want to describe a cheetah but do not know how to distinguish cheetahs from tigers. All the ways of appearing known to me belonging to either animal belong to both, so that my familiarity with these animals' various ways of appearing does not enable me to tell cheetahs from tigers. It would be absurd to suggest that in order to gain this ability, all I have to do is intend to describe a cheetah rather than a tiger. Nor would it help to reply that in describing the type of objective circumstances envisioned by Pollock — i.e. circumstances in which a person's perceptual experiences are duplicated by directly stimulating his brain — we are only performing a thought-experiment which, as such, is whatever we imagine it to be. For this only means that the neurophysiologist example deals with purely imaginary circumstances, and that we are free to imagine whatever we like. But my inability to distinguish cheetahs from tigers would remain unaffected even if these were purely imaginary beasts, and I can exercise my freedom to imagine the one rather than the other only if I can tell the difference between them.

Another, more general objection that might be raised against premiss (2) goes as follows. The proposition that any set of ways of appearing answering to the description of any objective circumstances would also answer to the description of a hallucination of those circumstances does, to be sure, imply that we cannot have *logically conclusive* (i.e. deductive) sensory evidence that

a given description correctly applies to some particular objective circumstances X (in the case at hand, to circumstances in which a person's perceptual experiences are duplicated by directly stimulating his brain). It does not
follow, however, that there is not in principle some way of telling whether a
given description applies to X, in the sense of 'some way of telling' required
for premiss (2) to connect with premiss (1), where it means only 'some
reasonable way of determining' that the description correctly applies to X
(when it does). For even if we can never have logically conclusive sensory
evidence that a certian physical description does correctly apply to X (in the
form of a set of appear-statements which entails that the description so
applies), there are other reasonable ways of determining that the description
applies.

To refute this objection, we need to examine alternative possible ways of
determining whether a given description applies to X. Our examination of
these alternatives will be brief, for the argument of previous sections of this
book has put us in a position to see that the most plausible alternatives are
unsatisfactory.

It might be suggested that (i) we can have purely *inductive* sensory evidence
that a given description correctly applies to X, i.e. that some set of appear-
statements, though it does not entail that the description applies, renders this
more probable than not, thereby providing a reasonable way of determining
that the description applies. But in light of our critique of traditional attempts
to establish the Justification Thesis of the Causal Theory of Perception by
some form of inductive argument in Sections 4 and 5 of Chapter Five, it is
clear that this will not do. The fact that we are now construing sensory
evidence as consisting of statements about ways of being appeared to or
ways of sensing rather than statements about immediate objects of perception (sense-data) does not alter the logic of the issue. Any attempt to provide
a purely inductive justification of perceptual judgments solely from premisses about ways of appearing presupposes that both:

(a)   The only way in principle of determining whether any physical
        thing is perceived (and so of determining whether a given physical
        description correctly applies to some objective circumstances X)
        is by being appeared to in certain ways,

and

(b)   There is only a contingent connection between any set of ways
        of appearing, no matter how orderly, systematic, and prolonged,
        and the perception of any physical thing.

But holding that both (*a*) and (*b*) are true, as we saw at length with respect to their sense-datum analogues in Chapter Five, makes it impossible to establish any kind of inductive connection between ways of being appeared to and the perception of physical things. For establishing such a connection requires that there be some independent way, i.e. some way *other* than being appeared to in certain ways, of determining whether a physical thing is perceived. But the availability of another way of determining this is precisely what is denied by (*a*). Therefore, alternative (*i*) is unsatisfactory.

Alternatively, it might be suggested that (*ii*) the *simplest* overall account of the ways one is appeared to is one according to which a given physical description applies to *X*, and that this fact provides a reasonable way of determining that the description correctly applies to *X*. But this appeal to simplicity fares no better than the appeal to induction. For as we saw in connection with our critique of stage II of Russell's argument for the Justification Thesis in Section 5 of Chapter Five, once we concede that overall accounts of the ways we are appeared to other than that these are normally caused by physical objects stimulating our sense-receptors are logically possible (i.e. once we concede that any set of ways of appearing answering to the description of *any* objective circumstances, no matter how encompassing, would also answer to the description of a hallucination of those circumstances), we cannot deny that some of these overall accounts – e.g. that absolutely all the ways we are appeared to, including being appeared to as if *X* obtains, are produced by a fantastically complex computer directly stimulating our brains, or are the result of a preestablished harmony among the perceptions of a multitude of incorporeal monads, or are symbols in a Berkeleyan God's 'Divine Language' – are just as *simple* as an overall account according to which a given physical description correctly applies to *X*. Such rival accounts can be ruled out on grounds of parsimony only if one presupposes the reasonableness of an overall account into which they introduce unecessary complications, which would here beg the question.

Finally, it may be suggested that (*iii*) there is some set of 'rules of evidence' or epistemic principles of justification, such as those proposed by Chisholm, in virtue of which certain ways one is appeared to (in conjunction with ostensible memories of certain concurring facts) would render 'evident' or reasonable the proposition that a given description correctly applies to *X*. But as we saw in connection with our discussion of Critical Cognitivism in Section 4 of the present chapter, to the extent that the epistemological problems concerning perception that have led philosophers to try to show how perceptual judgments can be justified by reference to sense-data or to ways of appearing are genuine ones, Chisholmian principles do not help to resolve them (while if these problems were spurious, such principles would be otiose since perceptual judgments could be regarded as 'self-justifying').[60] For since these principles are not principles of deduction (else our sensory evidence that a certain physical description correctly applies to X *could* be logically conclusive as claimed by phenomenalism), and cannot be justified by induction (as is clear from the discussion of alternative (*i*) above), their status is problematic. So our puzzlement concerning how perception can yield knowledge of the physical world just gets transferred from the difficulties that arise when we reflect on such things as perception under abnormal conditions of observation, alternative possible causes of perceptual experience, and hallucinations to the principles themselves: *why* do they provide a *reasonable* way of determining that a given description correctly applies to X rather than to an X-hallucination, as opposed to expressing a mere prejudice in favor of the former alternative? Proponents of such principles would argue that unless the principles provide a reasonable way of determining whether a given description correctly applies to X, there is no reasonable way of determining this. But this does nothing to show that the principles *do* provide a reasonable way of determining whether the description applies. Yet, if we concede that (1) the Deceiver Hypothesis (either in Pollock's version or in some other version) is logically possible, and that (2) the Deceiver Hypothesis cannot be shown to be improbable relative to any set of appear-statements, then we cannot justifiably regard the Critical Cognitivist's principles as providing a *reasonable* way of determining that a given description really applies to X rather than to an X-hallucination, unless some justificatory argument can be given for them. But no such statement is forthcoming, and it is doubtful that one can be given; unless the Deceiver Hypothesis is not logically possible after all (in which case the Critical Cognitivist's principles may be useful heuristic rules of evidence, but are not *ultimate* principles of epistemic justification). Thus, alternative (*iii*) is unsatisfactory.

While I cannot claim that (*i*)–(*iii*) exhaust the logical possibilities, they certainly appear to be the most plausible alternatives: hence I now rest my case for premiss (2).

The third premiss of my argument is:

(3)   If any stretch of anyone's perceptual experience can be duplicated without his perceiving any physical things, then any set of ways of appearing answering to the description of any objective circumstances would also answer to the description of a hallucination of those circumstances.

This is simply the generalization of a point made earlier, viz. that if we suppose that any stretch of anyone's perceptual experience can be duplicated without his perceiving any physical things, then we must grant that the neurophysiologists' perceptual experiences could be exactly duplicated if they were entirely hallucinatory, that the perceptual experiences of an observer attempting to determine whether the neurophysiologists were really experimenting or only hallucinating the experiment could be exactly duplicated if they were entirely hallucinatory, etc.

The conclusion which follows from premisses (1)–(3) is:

(4)   If it is possible to describe circumstances in which a person's perceptual experiences are duplicated by directly stimulating his brain, then it is not the case that any stretch of anyone's perceptual experience can be duplicated without his perceiving any physical things.

In other words, if any stretch of anyone's perceptual experience could be duplicated without his perceiving any physical things, then we could not describe the sort of situation which is supposed to show that this is so. Therefore, the fact that we can describe a situation in which various perceptual experiences are duplicated by directly stimulating someone's brain (or in any other manner) cannot possibly support the proposition that any stretch of anyone's perceptual experience could be duplicated without his perceiving any physical things, nor its corollary that any appear-statement P, no matter how complex, could be true while any thing-statement Q were false. On the contrary, since it is true that

(5)   It is possible to describe circumstances in which a person's perceptual experiences are duplicated by directly stimulating his brain,

we can conclude by *modus ponens* from (4) and (5) that

(6)   It is not the case that any stretch of anyone's perceptual experience can be duplicated without his perceiving any physical things.

In order to forestall a possible misunderstanding, it should be noted that (5) does not mean that

(5a)   We can describe circumstances in which *any* sequence of experiences a person has had or might have by perceiving physical things is duplicated by directly stimulating his brain, but only that

(5b)   We can describe circumstances in which *some* sequences of
experiences a person has had or might have by perceiving physical
things are duplicated by directly stimulating his brain.

Thus, there is no difficulty in holding that (5) and (6) are both true; as there
might be if (5) were interpreted as (5a) rather than as (5b). For while it seems
difficult to resist the inference from (5a) to the *negation* of (6), the inference
from (5b) to the negation of (6) is not similarly compelling. On the contrary,
the point of my argument is precisely that just because we can describe a
situation in which various stretches of perceptual experience are duplicated
by directly stimulating someone's brain, it does not follow that we can
universally generalize from this to the conclusion that *any* stretch of *any*
person's perceptual experience can be duplicated without his perceiving any
physical things. For the truth of such a generalization would undercut our
ability to describe the sort of situation in question (or any other objective
circumstance).

Since we are taking (5) to mean (5b) rather than (5a), the antecedent of
premiss (1) should also be interpreted as meaning (5b). This does not mean
that we have failed to meet Pollock (who may well believe that (5a) is true)
on his own ground. For since (5b) is a necessary condition of (5a) (but not
conversely), in demonstrating that (5b) implies (6) we have also shown that
(5a) implies (6). That is to say, we have shown that statement (4) of our
argument is true whether its antecedent is interpreted as (5b) or as (5a). But
in demonstrating the truth of (6) we may argue from (5b) only; we need not
concede the truth of (5a) for any portion of our argument. Indeed, since (as
noted in the preceding paragraph) it seems plausible that (5a) implies the
negation of (6), yet our argument shows that (5a) implies (6), the argument
seems to show that (5a) implies a contradiction and is therefore false. And if
this is so, then Pollock's example does not even show that any stretch *of the
experimental subject's* perceptual experience could be duplicated without his
perceiving any physical things. It shows only that some stretches of his perceptual experience could be so duplicated.[61] But there must be perceptual
tests which would show him whether he was hallucinating. Only the subject's
practical circumstances — i.e. having his sensory experiences programmed by
the computer — would prevent him from carrying out these tests. But his
inability to carry them out would show him, just as effectively as a 'negative'
test result, that he was hallucinating.

It might be insisted, however, that (5a) is true, and that therefore our argument shows that (5a), appearances to the contrary notwithstanding, does not imply the negation of (6): We can indeed describe circumstances in which any stretch of a certain person's perceptual experience is duplicated by directly stimulating his brain; nevertheless it is not the case that any stretch of *any* person's perceptual experience can be duplicated without his perceiving any physical things. Our objector could then continue as follows: 'Your argument does, to be sure, show that not any stretch of anyone's perceptual experience could be duplicated without his perceiving any physical things. But it leaves open the possibility that any stretch of *some* person or persons' perceptual experience could be so duplicated. Therefore, there is an important sense in which it fails to refute the deceiver hypothesis. It does not show that any particular person is not the subject of an experiment such as the one Pollock describes, in which any stretch of the person's perceptual experience can be duplicated without his perceiving any physical things. Indeed, how do you know that you yourself are not the subject of such an experiment?'

I am inclined to reject this objection on the grounds that (5a) does imply the negation of (6) as well as (6), and so must be false. But it is not necessary to insist that this is so; a more direct reply to the objection is available. This is to point out that my argument can be formulated in the first-person singular, and can therefore be used by any particular person to show that he himself is not the subject of a Pollock-type experiment. The first-person formulation, which may here also serve to summarize the argument, goes as follows:

(1′)   If I can describe circumstances in which a person's perceptual experiences are duplicated by directly stimulating his brain, then I must have some way of telling, at least in principle, whether a given description applies to these circumstances.

(2′)   If any set of ways I am appeared to answering to the description of any objective circumstances would also answer to the description of a hallucination of those circumstances, then I have no way of telling, even in principle, whether a given description applies to circumstances in which a person's perceptual experiences are duplicated by directly stimulating his brain.

(3′)   If any stretch of my perceptual experience can be duplicated without my perceiving any physical things, then any set of ways I am appeared to answering to the description of any objective circumstances would also answer to the description of a hallucination of those circumstances.

∴ (4′)   If I can describe circumstances in which a person's perceptual experiences are duplicated by directly stimulating his brain, then it is not the case that any stretch of my perceptual experience can be duplicated without my perceiving any physical things.

(5′)   I can describe circumstances in which a person's perceptual experiences are duplicated by directly stimulating his brain.

∴ (6′)   It is not the case that any stretch of my perceptual experience can be duplicated without my perceiving any physical things.

The only premiss that calls for any additional comment is (1′). For it might be objected that (1′) is not as plausible as (1): can't I describe circumstances in which a person's perceptual experiences are duplicated by directly stimulating his brain even though *I* have in principle no way of telling whether a description applies to these circumstances, provided that someone else does? In reply, we may first note that it is obscure how I could have in principle no way of telling whether a description applies to *X* if another person does. There could of course be practical circumstances (e.g. inexperience, lack of conceptual sophistication, or lack of education) preventing me, but not other persons, from *in fact* having a way of telling whether the description applies. But it does not seem that I could have *in principle* no way of telling whether the description applies, while other beings endowed with the same kind of cognitive faculties as I do have such a way of telling.

Even waiving this point, however, the objection fails. For (1′), properly understood, is not any less plausible than (1). Admittedly, there is a sense in which I can 'describe' *X* even if I have in principle no way of telling whether any description applies to *X*. I can utter certain sounds or make certain marks which others could understand as a description of *X* (provided they had a way of telling whether a description applies to *X*). This sort of performance is like the 'describing' of a complex object by a trained parakeet: it is describing without any understanding of one's own utterances. And that is the only sense in which I can 'describe' *X* if I have in principle no way of telling whether a description applies to *X*, i.e. if nothing whatever would tend to confirm or count as evidence for me that any description correctly applies to *X*. But obviously one cannot draw any philosophical conclusions, such as the falsity of the view that complex appear-statements entail thing-statements, from one's ability to describe the neurophysiologist case in *this* sense.

I conclude that the neurophysiologist case, and deceiver hypotheses in general, provide no refutation of the thesis that sufficiently complex appear-statements entail statements asserting that certain physical things are perceived (under certain conditions of observation and while the perceiver is in a certain physiological state), from which it follows that those things exist. Indeed, it is a necessary condition of our being able to describe such cases (to the extent that we can describe them, as indicated by (5b) above) that this thesis be true. Thus the Deceiver Hypothesis provides no reason to think that phenomenalism, combined with the causal theory of perception, does not provide a satisfactory account of the justification of perceptual judgments. And since we have answered the other major objections to the phenomenalist element of our combined theory, we may conclude that the theory provides a unified and plausible account of perceptual knowledge.

NOTES

[1] A possible exception is C. I. Lewis, though what Lewis suggests is the compatibility of phenomenalism with *realism* rather than with a causal analysis of perceiving (the latter entails the former but not conversely). See Lewis's *An Analysis of Knowledge and Valuation* (Open Court, La Salle, Illinois, 1946), pp. 187n–188n, and his essay, 'Realism or Phenomenalism', *Philosophical Review* LXIV (1955), 233–247.

One philosopher who has explicitly suggested that phenomenalism may be compatible with a causal analysis of perceiving is H. P. Grice. Grice says: ". . . it is by no means clear that to accept a causal analysis of perceiving is to debar oneself from accepting Phenomenalism; there seems to be no patent absurdity in the idea that one could, as a first stage, offer a causal analysis of 'X perceives M', and then re-express the result in phenomenalist terms. If the CTP [i.e. the Causal Theory of Perception] is to be (as it is often regarded as being) a rival to Phenomenalism, the opposition may well have to spring from the second clause of the initial formulation of the theory". ('The causal Theory of Perception', p. 108, in G. J. Warnock, *The Philosophy of Perception*, Oxford University Press, 1967, pp. 85–112.)

Grice is here suggesting that the analytic thesis of the causal theory, which he calls the theory's 'first clause', is compatible with phenomenalism. So the traditional opposition between the two theories may have to be viewed as stemming only from the justification thesis of the theory, which Grice calls its 'second clause'. In concluding his essay, however, Grice suggests that *both* parts of the causal theory may be compatible with phenomenalism: "I have already suggested that the first clause neither obviously entails nor obviously conflicts with Phenomenalism; I suspect that the same may be true of the second clause". (p. 112) There is no inconsistency in Grice's remarks. For his first remark (the opposition between the two theories may stem from the second clause) can be taken as making the historical point that proponents of the causal theory have always characterized the argument described in the justification thesis as an inductive argument of some sort. In that case the justification thesis does conflict with the phenomenalist contention that the relation between sense-data statements and physical-thing statements is a deductive one or a conceptual one. However, in his second remark (the second clause may be compatible with phenomenalism), Grice may be suggesting that it is by no means an essential feature of the justification thesis that the argument it describes be an inductive one: the argument showing that the existence of a certain physical thing is causally required to account for one's sense-data *could* be a deductive one, even if historically it has been formulated as an inductive argument.

2 *Foundations of Empirical Knowledge*, pp. 220–221, 229, 231; *The Problem of Knowledge*, p. 118.

3 Another factor, no doubt, is the mistaken idea that the causal theory implies that physical things are unobservable or unperceivable in principle, i.e. that they are somehow concealed by the 'veil of perception'. This fallacious conception of the causal theory (see Chapter Five, Section 3), which seems to have a strong hold on even so sophisticated a sense-datum philosopher as Ayer (cf. the passages referred to in the preceding footnote), is bound to make the causal theory seem radically incompatible with phenomenalism, since on the latter theory physical things certainly are perceivable.

4 It might be thought that this should be expressed, rather, in some such way as 'I see an elongated, pointed, silver sense-datum'. But there seems to be no good reason to restrict ourselves to sensible-quality terms in describing sense-data. In either case, however, a question arises concerning 'conceptual parasitism': How can (*i*) 'I sense a sense-datum of kind *K*' be so understood that it does not presuppose (is not 'parasitic upon') knowledge about physical objects? It seems, for example, that (*i*) must not be taken to mean the same as (*ii*) 'I sense a sense-datum of the kind that physical objects of kind *K* would produce under normal conditions of observation'; unless 'physical object of kind *K*' can defensibly be taken to mean 'physical object that would produce sense-data of kind *K* under normal conditions of observation', in which case (*ii*) is an acceptable interpretation of (*i*) but we still face the problem of defining 'normal conditions of observation' without circularity. For important discussions of this difficult issue, see Roderick Firth, 'Sense-Experience', pp. 15–18 in *Handbook of Perception* (Academic Press, New York, 1974), pp. 1–18; and R. M. Chisholm, *Theory of Knowledge*, pp. 34–37 and especially *Perceiving: A Philosophical Study*, pp. 48–53 and 133–137. (Chisholm discusses the issue as it applies to the adverbial analysis of perceptual experience to be shortly presented.)

5 This idea seems to be the basis of Isaiah Berlin's objections to phenomenalism in his 'Empirical Propositions and Hypothetical Statements', *Mind* LIX (1950); reprinted in R. J. Swartz, *Perceiving, Sensing and Knowing*, pp. 364–393.

6 Thomas Reid, *Essays on the Intellectual Powers of Man*, Essay I, Chapter 1, Section 12; C. J. Ducasse, *Nature, Mind and Death* (Open Court, La Salle, Illinois, 1949), Chapter 13; R. M. Chisholm, *Perceiving: A Philosophical Study*, Chapter Eight; R. M. Chisholm, *Theory of Knowledge*, pp. 33–34 and 95–96. Unless otherwise noted, all page references to Chisholm's *Theory of Knowledge* in this chapter will be to the first (1966) edition.

7 *Theory of Knowledge*, p. 33.

8 *Theory of Knowledge*, po. 94–95.

9 *Theory of Knowledge*, p. 33.

10 *Theory of Knowledge*, pp. 34, 95–96; cf. *Perceiving: A Philosophical Study*, p. 116.

11 Cf. Roderick Firth, 'Sense Experience', p. 13, in *Handbook of Perception* (Academic Press, New York, 1974), pp. 1–18.

[12] Some of the puzzling questions about sense-data were considered in Chapter Two, Section 2 and others in Chapter Six, Section 2. For a brief but incisive discussion, see Chisholm, *Perceiving: A Philosophical Study*, pp. 117–120; for a fuller, systematic discussion, see J. W. Cornman, *Perception, Common Sense, and Science*, pp. 78–89.

[13] R. M. Chisholm, *Perceiving: A Philosophical Study*, p. 113.

[14] *Perceiving: A Philosophical Study*, p. 128.

[15] They are equally relational properties of the perceiver. Thus, S's being appeared to F-ly by x or x's appearing F-ly to S is a relational property of x and a relational property or relational state of S.

[16] R. M. Chisholm, *Perceiving: A Philosophical Study*, pp. 120–125 and *Theory of Knowledge*, p. 96.

[17] C. J. Ducasse, 'Moore's "The Refutation of Idealism",' pp. 233, 235, 239, in P. A. Schilpp (ed.), *The Philosophy of G. E. Moore*, Third Edition, Vol. 1 (Open Court, La Salle, Illinois, 1968), pp. 225–251.

[18] This does not mean, of course, that there is no possible way whatever to tell them apart; but rather that if they can be distinguished at all, this can be done only on the basis of their differing relations to other ways of being appeared to. It cannot be done by simple comparison of the ways of being appeared to in question, apart from their relations to other ways of being appeared to.

[19] Notice that, putting the matter in this way, we need no longer say, as on the linguistic version of the sense-datum theory, that in a perceptual experience we sense elements which are common to indistinguishable hallucinatory and non-hallucinatory experiences (cf. Chapter Six, Section 3). This categorical assertion, which suggests that there is after all some single type of object or entity which is sensed in both sorts of cases, is reducible to the disjunctive assertion that in a perceptual experience, either we are appeared to F-ly by a physical thing or we are appeared to F-ly but not by a physical thing. The only 'common element' that remains is the *way* we are appeared to, which is not a concrete entity or object but a universal that can characterize either a relational property of an object or a non-relational conscious state. (Whether such universals can in turn be reduced to resembling particulars need not be discussed here.)

[20] This distinction is explained very clearly by Roderick Firth in 'Sense Experience', pp. 5–6, in *Handbook of Perception* (Academic Press, New York, 1974), pp. 1–18. Firth calls the second type of judgments 'psychophysical perceptual judgments', because "they entail the existence of objects . . . that constitute part of the subject-matter of the physical sciences [and] also entail the existence of perceptual experiences . . . that constitute part of the subject-matter of psychology". (p. 5)

[21] Compare Chapter Five, Section 2, pp. 111–112.

[22] Roderick Firth, 'The Men Themselves; or the Role of Causation in Our Concept of Seeing', pp. 361–362, in H–N Castañeda (ed.), *Intentionality, Minds, and Perception* (Wayne State University Press, Detroit, 1967), pp. 357–382.

[23] This can be seen by simply substituting the analytic thesis into the proposition within single quotes. The substitution yields a tautology: 'knowledge of physical things acquired by its being the case that those things, by stimulating the perceiver's sense-receptors in a way to be indicated by examples, are part-causes of the ways the perceiver is appeared to, is knowledge of what are in fact certain causes of the ways the perceiver is appeared to'.

[24] One way of maintaining that the child is justified in his perceptual beliefs although

he cannot yet justify them is to adopt a 'principle of implicit reasons' such as the one proposed by J. L. Pollock. According to Pollock's principle, 'I perceive mother' could be the child's 'implicit reason' for his belief that she is present, because (*i*) it entails that she is present, (*ii*) the child's epistemologically relevant circumstances are such (we can suppose) that he *could* justifiably believe (if only he had the requisite conceptual sophistication) that he perceives his mother, and (*iii*) these circumstances are the psychological cause of his believing that his mother is present. See John L. Pollock, 'Perceptual Knowledge', pp. 305–306, *Philosophical Review* (Vol. LXXX, No. 3 [July 1971]), pp. 287–319; also *Knowledge and Justification* (Princeton University Press, Princeton, 1974), pp. 60–64.

[25] This analysis is a bit oversimplified, because the thing perceived is never the sole cause of the way it appears but only a part-cause. The implications of this point are discussed in the next section in connection with R. M. Chisholm's criticism of phenomenalism.

[26] This example is adapted from one suggested by Marshall Swain.

[27] Roderick M. Chisholm, *Perceiving: A Philosophical Study*, p. 77.

[28] *Perceiving*, pp. 159–160.

[29] *Perceiving*, p. 190.

[30] R. M. Chisholm, *Theory of Knowledge*, pp. 61–62.

[31] *Theory of Knowledge*, p. 47. Chisholm adds a qualification to this principle (in order to meet an objection raised by Herbert Heidelberger) in the second edition (1977) of *Theory of Knowledge*, pp. 74–78. Cf. also Chisholm's essay, 'On the Nature of Empirical Evidence', in R. M. Chisholm and R. J. Swartz (eds.), *Empirical Knowledge: Readings from Contemporary Sources* (Prentice-Hall, Englewood Cliffs, N. J., 1973), pp. 224–249. These works should be consulted for the most recent and precise formulation of Chisholm's epistemic principles, and for his attempt to define knowledge in such a way as to avoid the well-known Gettier counterexamples to the justified-true-belief analysis of knowledge. However, since the refinements presented in these works do not alter the general contours of Chisholm's position, I do not take account of them in the text, above.

[32] *Perceiving: A Philosophical Study*, pp. 109–112.

[33] Cf. *Perceiving*, Chapter Six; *Theory of Knowledge*, Chapter 4; 'On the Nature of Empirical Evidence', in Chisholm and Swartz (eds.), *Empirical Knowledge: Readings from Contemporary Sources*, p. 245.

[34] A. J. Ayer, *The Problem of Knowledge*, p. 7.

[35] Chisholm, *Theory of Knowledge*, pp. 24–25 and Chapters 2–4 *passim*.

[36] R. M. Chisholm, *Theory of Knowledge*, p. 2. This passage should be compared with the previous-quoted one from the Preface of Ayer's *The Problem of Knowledge*.

[37] *Theory of Knowledge*, p. 25n.

[38] *Perceiving: A Philosophical Study*, Appendix entitled 'Phenomenalism', pp. 189–197. Reprinted in Canfield and Donnell (eds.), *Readings in the Theory of Knowledge* (Appleton-Century-Crofts, New York, 1964), pp. 469–474 and (with minor modifications) in Engle and Taylor (eds.), *Berkeley's Principles of Human Knowledge* (Wadsworth Publishing Co., Belmont, 1968), pp. 83–88. See also R. M. Chisholm, 'The Problem of Empiricism', *Journal of Philosophy* XLV (1948), reprinted in R. J. Swartz (ed.), *Perceiving, Sensing, and Knowing* (University of California Press, Berkeley, 1977), pp. 347–354. For replies to Chisholm's argument different from the one to be proposed

here, see Roderick Firth, 'Radical Empiricism and Perceptual Relativity', *The Philosophical Review* 59 (1950), pp. 164–183, 319–331 and C. I. Lewis, 'Professor Chisholm and Empiricism', *The Journal of Philosophy* **XLV** (1948), reprinted in Swartz, *Perceiving, Sensing, and Knowing.*
[39] *Perceiving: A Philosophical Study*, p. 192.
[40] *Perceiving: A Philosophical Study*, p. 192.
[41] Cf. A. J. Ayer, *The Problem of Knowledge*, p. 120. For a fuller discussion of this point, see C. I. Lewis, *An Analysis of Knowledge and Valuation* (Open Court, La Salle, Illinois, 1946), pp. 213–217.
[42] The 'seem to' locution used here, as well as the particular form of both the thing-statement *P* and the appear-statement *R*, were originally suggested by C. I. Lewis in *An Analysis of Knowledge and Valuation*, Chapters VII and VIII. The 'seem to' locution is equivalent to our root 'appeared to *F*-ly' ('sensing *F*-ly') locution. Thus *R* could be reformulated, albeit awkwardly, as 'If I should be appeared to (sense) whitely, cubically and grittily and appeared to (sense) my-reaching, grasping and biting-ly, then I would be appeared to (sense) sweetly'.
[43] *Perceiving: A Philosophical Study*, p. 189.
[44] 'The Problem of Empiricism', p. 348n. Reprint in R. Swartz (ed.), *Perceiving, Sensing, and Knowing*, pp. 349–354. Originally published in *The Journal of Philosophy* **XLV** (1948).
[45] R. M. Chisholm, 'Theory of Knowledge', pp. 326–327 in Chisholm, Feigl, Frankena, Passmore, and Thompson, *Philosophy* (Prentice-Hall, Englewood Cliffs, New Jersey, 1964), pp. 239–344.
[46] Cf. A. J. Ayer, *The Foundations of Empirical Knowledge*, p. 238.
[47] This analogy is taken from James W. Cornman and Keith Lehrer, *Philosophical Problems and Arguments*, Second Edition (Macmillan, New York, 1974), p. 102.
[48] Paul Marhenke, 'Phenomenalism', p. 297, in Max Black (ed.), *Philosophical Analysis* (Cornell University Press, Ithaca, N. Y., 1950), pp. 299–322. Cf. also Ayer, *The Foundations of Empirical Knowledge*, pp. 240–241.
[49] Cornman and Lehrer, *Philosophical Problems and Arguments*, Second Edition, p. 107.
[50] See Note 1 of the present chapter and Chapter Five, Section 1.
[51] See Chapter Six, Section 2, page 140. Cf. Chisholm, *Perceiving: A Philosophical Study*, p. 194.
[52] Ayer endorsed this argument in *The Foundations of Empirical Knowledge*, p. 40 and pp. 239–240; and C. I. Lewis gives a very similar argument in *An Analysis of Knowledge and Valuation*, pp. 176–177 and Chapter VII, *passim*. In later writings, however, Ayer rejects the argument for the same reason that I shall give below. See his 'Phenomenalism', pp. 134–138, in *Philosophical Essays*, pp. 125–166, and *The Problem of Knowledge*, pp. 125–126.
[53] Obviously, I am here assuming the reliability of memory. I do not think that the epistemological questions that might be raised concerning memory are as perplexing as those concerning perception, but I cannot undertake to defend this claim in the present work. *If* it were necessary to treat memory in a manner strictly parallel to perception, then the foregoing description would have to be recast in terms of certain ways of being appeared to *seeming* to be sequent upon others, i.e. of an *ostensible* experiential history.

[54] A. J. Ayer, *Philosophical Essays*, p. 140.

[55] See for example John L. Pollock, *Knowledge and Justification* (Princeton University Press, Princeton, 1974), pp. 3–4, 10, 53–54; Gilbert Harman, *Thought* (Princeton University Press, Princeton, 1973), p. 5; James W. Cornman and Keith Lehrer, *Philosophical Problems and Arguments: An Introduction*, Second Edition (Macmillan, New York, 1974), pp. 81–112, 130–131, 134–135; Michael A. Slote, *Reason and Scepticism* (Humanities Press, New York, 1970), Chapters 1–3.

[56] A notable exception is O. K. Bouwsma, 'Descartes' Evil Genius', *The Philosophical Reivew* LVIII (1949), pp. 141–151; reprinted in Sesonske and Fleming (eds.), *Meta-Meditations: Studies in Descartes* (Wadsworth Publishing Company, Belmont, California, 1965), pp. 26–36 and in O. K. Bouwsma, *Philosophical Essays* (University of Nebraska Press, Lincoln, 1969), pp. 85–97. Bouwsma, however, does not explicitly link his rejection of the deceiver hypothesis with phenomenalism.

[57] John L. Pollock, *Knowledge and Justification*, pp. 53–54.

[58] A related line of argument implicit in the quotation from Pollock is the following. Let P be a complex thing-statement, and let Q be a thing-statement asserting that some physical thing is perceived (under certain conditions of observation and while the perceiver is in a certain physiological state). Then the critic of phenomenalism can argue: (1) For any P and any Q, there is a statement R such that R is compatible with P and R entails not-Q. But (2) P entails Q only if it is not the case that any R compatible with P entails not-Q. Therefore, P does not entail Q. (Compare Chisholm's argument against the entailment of appear-statements by thing-statements, discussed in the preceding section.) Pollock's candidate for R would be: 'The subject's perceptual experiences are all being produced by a computer directly stimulating his brain'. Since this statement ascribes to the subject a state of total hallucination, it entails that he is not perceiving any physical things (not-Q).

However, someone who holds that P entails Q can hardly be expected to grant that P is compatible with any R that entails not-Q. The phenomenalist could accordingly reply that premiss (1) of his opponent's argument begs the question by asserting that R is compatible with P; and that in fact any R that entails not-Q must be incompatible with P. It would then be open to the critic, of course, to try to show that R is compatible with P, no matter how complex the phenomenalist makes P. This would be the function of the neurophysiologist example. My reply to this, argued for in the text below, is that if R is compatible with P no matter how complex P is, then it is impossible to describe the circumstances that are supposed to show that this is so.

[59] For an excellent discussion of the attempts to formulate a satisfactory verifiability criterion of meaning, see Carl G. Hempel, 'The Empiricist Criterion of Meaning', in A. J. Ayer (ed.), *Logical Positivism* (Free Press, New York, 1959), pp. 108–129. See also the article entitled 'Verifiability Principle' in Paul Edwards (ed.), *The Encyclopedia of Philosophy* (Macmillan, New York, 1967), Volume Eight, pp. 240–247.

[60] Indeed, Chisholm's epistemology can plausibly be interpreted as holding that at least some perceptual judgments about physical objects are self-justifying. But if his epistemology is so interpreted, then the idea (prominent in Chisholm's work) that all such judgments are 'indirectly evident' ones must be justified by reference to 'directly evident' foundations loses its central place within his theory. It seems to me, though I shall not try to demonstrate this here, that Chisholm's position is ambiguous as to whether the 'rules of evidence' are (*a*) principles exhibiting how perceptual judgments are justified

by reference to directly evident foundations (as suggested especially by the 'Socratic' regress of justification Chisholm uses to make the distinction between the directly and the indirectly evident), or (b) principles to the effect that (at least some) perceptual judgments do not need to be justified by reference to any foundations (as suggested by the formulation of the principles themselves).

[61] This does not mean that the neurophysiologists could not have or test a complete neurophysiological account of perception, or that we are setting *a priori* limits for science. For it may well be that what cannot be duplicated by the computer is certain iterations of patterns of sensory experience, or certain patterns whose constituent elements can be duplicated.

BIBLIOGRAPHY

Armstrong, D. M., *Perception and the Physical World* (Humanities Press, New York, 1961).

Austin, J. L., *Sense and Sensibilia* (Oxford University Press, London, 1962).

Ayer, A. J., *Bertrand Russell* (Viking Press, New York, 1972).

Ayer, A. J., 'The Causal Theory of Perception', *Proceedings of the Aristotelian Society*, Supplementary Volume 51 (1977), 105–125.

Ayer, A. J., *The Foundations of Empirical Knowledge* (Macmillan, London, 1940).

Ayer, A. J., ed. *Logical Positivism* (Free Press, New York, 1959).

Ayer, A. J., 'Phenomenalism', in *Philosophical Essays* (Macmillan, New York, 1954 [1947], pp. 125–166.

Ayer, A. J., *The Problem of Knowledge* (Penguin Books, London, 1956).

Barnes, W. H. F., 'The Myth of Sense-Data', in R. J. Swartz (ed.), *Perceiving, Sensing, and Knowing* (University of California Press, Berkeley, 1976 [1944]), pp. 138–167.

Bennett, Jonathan, *Locke, Berkeley, Hume: Central Themes* (Clarendon Press, Oxford, 1971).

Berkeley, George, *Principles of Human Knowledge*, in C. M. Turbayne, (ed.), *Principles, Dialogues, and Philosophical Correspondence* (Bobbs-Merrill, Indiannapolis and New York, 1965 [1710]), pp. 2–101.

Berkeley, George, *Three Dialogues Between Hylas and Philonous*, in C. M. Turbayne (ed.), *Principles, Dialogues, and Philosophical Correspondence* (Bobbs-Merrill, Indiannapolis and New York, 1965 [1713]), pp. 103–211.

Berlin, Isaiah, 'Empirical Propositions and Hypothetical Statements', in R. J. Swartz (ed.), *Perceiving, Sensing, and Knowing* (University of California Press, Berkeley, 1976 [1950]), pp. 364–393.

Bouwsma, O. K., 'Descartes' Evil Genius', *Philosophical Review* 58 (1949), 141–151.

Bouwsma, O. K., 'Moore's Theory of Sense-Data', in G. J. Warnock (ed.), *The Philosophy of Perception* (Oxford University Press, London, 1967 [1942], pp. 8–24.

Brain, Russell, 'Hallucinations', Selection excerpted from *The Nature of Experience*, in R. J. Hirst (ed.), *Perception and the External World* (Macmillan, New York, 1965 [1959]), pp. 51–60.

Brain, Russell, *Mind, Perception and Science* (Blackwell, Oxford, 1951).

Chisholm, Roderick M., 'On the Nature of Empirical Evidence', in R. M. Chisholm and R. J. Swartz (eds.), *Empirical Knowledge: Readings from Contemporary Sources* (Prentice-Hall, Englewood Cliffs, N.J., 1973 [1970]), pp. 224–249.

Chisholm, Roderick M., *Perceiving: A Philosophical Study* (Cornell University Press, Ithaca, Press, 1957).

Chisholm, Roderick M., *Person and Object: A Metaphysical Study* (George Allen & Unwin, London 1976).

Chisholm, Roderick M., 'The Problem of Empiricism', in R. J. Swartz (ed.), *Perceiving,*

Sensing, and Knowing (University of California Press, Berkeley, 1976 [1948]), pp. 347–354.

Chisholm, Roderick M., 'Theory of Knowledge', in Chisholm, Feigl, Frankena, Passmore, Thompson, *Philosophy* (Prentice-Hall, Englewood Cliffs, N. J., 1964), pp. 233–344.

Chisholm, Roderick M., *Theory of Knowledge* (Prentice-Hall, Englewood Cliffs, N. J., 1966).

Chisholm, Roderick M., *Theory of Knowledge*, Second Edition (Englewood Cliffs, N. J., 1977).

Chisholm, Roderick M., and R. J. Swartz (eds.), *Empirical Knowledge: Readings from Contemporary Sources* (Prentice-Hall, Englewood Cliffs, N. J., 1973).

Cornman, James W., *Materialism and Sensations* (Yale University Press, New Haven and London, 1971).

Cornman, James W., *Perception, Common Sense, and Science* (Yale University Press, New Haven and London, 1975).

Cornman, James W., and K. Lehrer, *Philosophical Problems and Arguments: an Introduction*, Second Edition (Macmillan, New York, 1974).

Descartes, René, 'Meditations on First Philosophy', in *The Philosophical Works of Descartes*, Volume I, transl. by E. S. Haldane and G. T. R. Ross (Dover Publications, New York, 1955 [1641]), pp. 131–199.

Dicker, Georges, 'The Concept of Immediate Perception in Berkeley's Immaterialism', forthcoming in C. M. Turbayne (ed.), *Berkeley: Critical and Interpretative Essays* (University of Minnesota Press, Minneapolis).

Dicker, Georges, 'Is There A Problem About Perception and Knowledge?', *American Philosophical Quarterly* 15 (1978), 165–176.

Dicker, Georges, 'Primary and Secondary Qualities: A Proposed Modification of the Lockean Account', *The Southern Journal of Philosophy* 15 (1977), 457–471.

Dicker, Georges, 'Two Arguments from Perceptual Relativity in Berkeley's Dialogues Between Hylas and Philonous' (unpublished).

Dretske, Fred I., *Seeing and Knowing* (The University of Chicago Press, Chicago, 1969).

Ducasse, C. J., 'Moore's "The Refutation of Idealism" ', in P. A. Schilpp (ed.), *The Philosophy of G. E. Moore*, Third Edition (Open Court, La Salle, Illinois 1968 [1942]), pp. 225–251.

Ducasse, C. J., *Nature, Mind and Death* (Open Court, La Salle, Illinois, 1949).

Eccles, J., *The Brain and the Unity of Conscious Experience* (Cambridge University Press, Cambridge, 1965).

Firth, Roderick, 'The Men Themselves; Or the Role of Causation in our Concept of Seeing', in H. R. Casteñeda (ed.), *Intentionality, Minds, and Perception* (Wayne State University Press, Detroit, 1967), pp. 357–382.

Firth, Roderick, 'Radical Empiricism and Perceptual Relativity', *The Philosophical Review* 59 (1950), 164–183 and 319–333.

Firth, Roderick, 'Sense-Experience', in E. C. Carterette and M. P. Friedman (eds.), *Handbook of Perception, Volume I: Historical and Philosophical Roots of Perception* (Academic Press, New York, 1974), pp. 1–18.

Grice, H. P., 'The Causal Theory of Perception', in J. G. Warnock (ed.), *The Philosophy of Perception* (Oxford University Press, London 1967 [1961]), pp. 85–112. (Also in R. J. Swartz (ed.), *Perceiving, Sensing, and Knowing*, pp. 438–472.

Hamlyn, D. W., *Theory of Knowledge* (Doubleday & Company, Garden City, N.Y., 1970).

Harman, Gilbert, *Thought* (Princeton University Press, Princeton, 1973).

Hempel, C. G., 'The Empiricist Criterion of Meaning', in A. J. Ayer (ed.), *Logical Positivism* (Free Press, New York, 1959 [1950]), pp. 108–129.

Hirst, R. J. (ed.), *Perception and the External World* (Macmillan, New York, 1965).

Hirst, R. J., *The Problems of Perception* (George Allen & Unwin, London, 1959).

Hume, David, *A Treatise of Human Nature*, edited by L. A. Selby-Bigge (The Clarendon Press, Oxford, 1888 [1739]).

Hume, David, *An Inquiry Concerning Human Understanding*, in A. Flew (ed.), *Hume on Human Nature and Understanding* (Collier Books, New York, 1962 [1748]), pp. 21–163.

Lehrer, K. and Cornman, J., *Philosophical Problems and Arguments: An Introduction*, Second Edition (Macmillan, New York, 1974).

Leibniz, G. W., *Discourse on Metaphysics*, transl. by G. R. Montgomery (Open Court, La Salle, Illinois, 1902 [1686]).

Leibniz, G. W., *Monadology*, transl. by G. R. Montogmery (Open Court, La Salle, Ill., 1902, [1714]).

Lewis, C. I., *An Analysis of Knowledge and Valuation* (Open Court, La Salle, Illinois, 1946).

Lewis, C. I., *Mind and the World-Order* (Dover Publications, New York, 1956 [1929]).

Lewis, C. I., 'Professor Chisholm on Empiricism', in R. J. Swartz (ed.), *Perceiving, Sensing, and Knowing* (University of California Press, Berkeley, 1976 [1948]).

Lewis, C. I., 'Realism or Phenomenalism', *The Philosophical Review*, 64 (1955), 233–247.

Locke, John, *Essay Concerning Human Understanding*, ed. by A. D. Woozley (Meridian Books, Cleveland, 1969 [1689]).

Lovejoy, A. O., 'The Justification of Realism', Selection excerpted from *The Revolt Against Dualism*, in R. J. Hirst (ed.), *Perception and the External World* (Macmillan, New York, 1965 [1929]), pp. 224–234.

Mandelbaum, Maurice, *Philosophy, Science, and Sense Perception* (The Johns Hopkins Press, Baltimore, 1964).

Marhenke, Paul, 'Phenomenalism', in Max Black (ed.), *Philosophical Analysis* (Cornell University Press, Ithaca, 1950), pp. 299–322.

Mill, J. S., *An Examination of Sir William Hamilton's Philosophy*, Vol. I (William V. Spencer, Boston, 1865).

Moore, G. E., *Some Main Problems of Philosophy* (Collier Books, New York, 1966 [1953]).

Paul, G. A., 'Is There A Problem About Sense-Data?', in R. J. Swartz (ed.), *Perceiving, Sensing, and Knowing* (University of California Press, Berkeley, 1976 [1936]), pp. 271–287.

Pitcher, George, *A Theory of Perception* (Princeton University Press, Princeton, 1971).

Pollock, J. L., *Knowledge and Justification* (Princeton University Press, Princeton, 1974).

Pollock, J. L., 'Perceptual Knowledge', *The Philosophical Review* 80 (1971), 287–319.

Price, H. H., *Perception* (Methuen, London, 1932).

Reid, Thomas, *Essays on the Intellectual Powers of Man* (MIT Press, Cambridge, Mass., 1969 [1785]).

Russell, Bertrand, 'The Causal Theory of Perception', Selection excerpted from *The Analysis of Matter*, in R. J. Hirst (ed.), *Perception and the External World* (Macmillan, New York, 1965 [1927]), pp. 209–234.

Russell, Bertrand, 'The Relation of Sense-Data to Physics', in *Mysticism and Logic* (Doubleday, Garden City, New York, [1914]), pp. 140–173.

Ryle, Gilbert, *The Concept of Mind* (Barnes & Noble, New York, 1949).

Slote, Michael A., *Reason and Scepticism* (Humanities Press, New York, 1970).

Swartz, R. J. (ed.), *Perceiving, Sensing and Knowing: A Book of Readings from Twentieth-Century Sources in the Philosophy of Perception* (University of California Press, Berkeley, 1976 [1965]).

Unger, Peter, 'An Analysis of Factual Knowledge', *Journal of Philosophy* **65** (1968), 157–170.

Unger, Peter, *Ignorance: A Case for Scepticism* (Oxford University Press, London, 1975).

Warnock, J. G., *English Philosophy Since 1900*, Second Edition (Oxford University Press, New York, 1969).

Warnock, J. G. (ed.), *The Philosophy of Perception* (Oxford University Press, London, 1967).

BIBLIOGRAPHICAL NOTE

The following are useful bibliographies of works on perception:

(1) Edwards, P. and Pap, A. (eds.), *A Modern Introduction to Philosophy*, Third Edition, pp. 654–663 (Free Press, New York, 1973).

(2) Emmett, K. and Machamer, P., *Perception: An Annotated Bibliography* (Garland Publishing, Inc., New York & London, 1976).

(3) Swartz, R. J. (ed.), *Perceiving, Sensing, and Knowing*, pp. 527–539 (University of California Press, Berkeley, 1976).

INDEX OF NAMES

INDEX OF SUBJECTS

Ontological Phenomenalism (continued)
141; difficulties concerning public
observability of physical things in
129, 142–143; incompatible with
causal analysis of perceiving 8, 129–
133, 158, 175; its account of the
difference between 'appearance' and
'reality', contrasted with the Classical
Causal Theory's 125–128; its account of the difference between
'appearance' and 'reality' curiously
incomplete 133; its strengths and
weaknesses compared to the Classical
Causal Theory's 8, 80, 125–128,
143, 156; paradoxical character of
9, 141–142, 160; provides perceptual
criterion for distinguishing between
'appearance' and 'reality' 8, 127–128,
133, 143

Ordinary language: and hallucinations
69, 81–82; and sense-data 38

Ordinary-Language Philosophers 2–5, 49

'Other Minds', Russell's argument for
110–112

Perceiving, conception of, layman's
versus specialist's 86

'Perceptual acceptance' 57

'Perceptual assurance' 57

Perceptual judgments: combined theory's analysis of 174–175; distinction between those of the form
'this is (an) X' and 'I perceive X
(to be F)' 170–174; justification of,
Chapter Five, Section 4 and Section
5, passim, 182, Chapter Seven,
Section 6 passim

Perceptual knowledge: analysis of 14,
15–20, 22–26; self-reflective versus
non self-reflective 170–174

Perceptual verbs, two senses of 81–82

Permanent possibilities of sensation
9, 123, 138–142, 149, 192
See also possible sense-data

Permanently possible sense-data 138–
142. See also Permanent possibilities
of sensation; possible sense-data

Perspective, laws of 102, 112–115

Phenomenalism 6–9, 33, 79–80, 106,
117–118, 123, Chapter Six passim;
and scepticism 124–125; basic epistemological insight of 9, 168;
Chisholm's criticism of 151, 183–
187, 190–191; historical development of 143; in Ayer 8, 145–146,
148–149, 151, 154–155, 158, 195,
213 n. 52; in Berkeley 123, 134–
135, 138, 143; in Lewis 9, 213 n.
42, 213 n. 52; in Russell 137–138;
ontological and analytical versions of,
compared 8, 148–149, 151, 156;
plausibility of combining with Causal
Theory of Perception 156–158. See
also Analytical Phenomenalism; Epistemological Phenomenalism; Equivalence Thesis; Ontological Phenomenalism

Possible sense-data 123, 138–139, 148–
149, 160

Problem of perception and knowledge,
Introduction and Chapter One,
passim; arises antecedently to introduction of sense-data 3–6, 20–24,
26, 57–58, 75; commonly miscon-
ceived 3–6, 94; deepened by Arguments from Causation and Hallucination 28, 45, 57, 75; fundamentally
an antinomy 6, 24, 94; general contours of 3, 6, 24, 40, 94, 182;
regarded as pseudo-problem by
Ordinary-Language Philosophers 2–3;
treated cursorily by some epistemologists 1–2; two regresses involved in 3–4, 10 n.
See also regress(es)

Pre-established Harmony, Leibniz's theory of 115–117, 203

Reductionism: and Analytical Phenomenalism 160; and Epistemological
Phenomenalism 167–169; and Ontological Phenomenalism 129

Regress(es) 3–4, 10, 23–24, 26–27, 41,
44, 57–58, 63, 94, 98, 106, 109, 182

Representationalism 90–91

Rules of evidence, Chisholmian 2. See

PHILOSOPHICAL STUDIES SERIES
IN PHILOSOPHY

Editors:

WILFRID SELLARS, Univ. of Pittsburgh and KEITH LEHRER, Univ. of Arizona

Board of Consulting Editors:

Jonathan Bennett, Alan Gibbard, Robert Stalnaker, and Robert G. Turnbull